THE LOTUS SUTRA

BDK English Tripiṭaka Series

THE LOTUS SUTRA

Translated from the Chinese of Kumārajīva
(Taishō Volume 9, Number 262)

by

Tsugunari Kubo

and

Akira Yuyama

Revised Second Edition

Numata Center
for Buddhist Translation and Research
2007

Revised Second Edition, 2007
ISBN: 978-1-886439-39-9
Library of Congress Catalog Card Number: 2006939375

Published by
Numata Center for Buddhist Translation and Research
2620 Warring Street
Berkeley, California 94704

Printed in the United States of America

A Message on the Publication of the English Tripiṭaka

The Buddhist canon is said to contain eighty-four thousand different teachings. I believe that this is because the Buddha's basic approach was to prescribe a different treatment for every spiritual ailment, much as a doctor prescribes a different medicine for every medical ailment. Thus his teachings were always appropriate for the particular suffering individual and for the time at which the teaching was given, and over the ages not one of his prescriptions has failed to relieve the suffering to which it was addressed.

Ever since the Buddha's Great Demise over twenty-five hundred years ago, his message of wisdom and compassion has spread throughout the world. Yet no one has ever attempted to translate the entire Buddhist canon into English throughout the history of Japan. It is my greatest wish to see this done and to make the translations available to the many English-speaking people who have never had the opportunity to learn about the Buddha's teachings.

Of course, it would be impossible to translate all of the Buddha's eighty-four thousand teachings in a few years. I have, therefore, had one hundred thirty-nine of the scriptural texts in the prodigious Taishō edition of the Chinese Buddhist canon selected for inclusion in the First Series of this translation project.

It is in the nature of this undertaking that the results are bound to be criticized. Nonetheless, I am convinced that unless someone takes it upon himself or herself to initiate this project, it will never be done. At the same time, I hope that an improved, revised edition will appear in the future.

It is most gratifying that, thanks to the efforts of more than a hundred Buddhist scholars from the East and the West, this monumental project has finally gotten off the ground. May the rays of the Wisdom of the Compassionate One reach each and every person in the world.

NUMATA Yehan
Founder of the English
Tripiṭaka Project

August 7, 1991

Editorial Foreword

In January 1982, Dr. NUMATA Yehan, the founder of the Bukkyō Dendō Kyōkai (Society for the Promotion of Buddhism), decided to begin the monumental task of translating the complete Taishō edition of the Chinese Tripiṭaka (Buddhist canon) into the English language. Under his leadership, a special preparatory committee was organized in April 1982. By July of the same year, the Translation Committee of the English Tripiṭaka was officially convened.

The initial Committee consisted of the following members: (late) HANAYAMA Shōyū (Chairperson), (late) BANDŌ Shōjun, ISHIGAMI Zennō, (late) KAMATA Shigeo, KANAOKA Shūyū, MAYEDA Sengaku, NARA Yasuaki, (late) SAYEKI Shinkō, (late) SHIOIRI Ryōtatsu, TAMARU Noriyoshi, (late) TAMURA Kwansei, URYŪZU Ryūshin, and YUYAMA Akira. Assistant members of the Committee were as follows: KANAZAWA Atsushi, WATANABE Shōgo, Rolf Giebel of New Zealand, and Rudy Smet of Belgium.

After holding planning meetings on a monthly basis, the Committee selected one hundred thirty-nine texts for the First Series of translations, an estimated one hundred printed volumes in all. The texts selected are not necessarily limited to those originally written in India but also include works written or composed in China and Japan. While the publication of the First Series proceeds, the texts for the Second Series will be selected from among the remaining works; this process will continue until all the texts, in Japanese as well as in Chinese, have been published.

Frankly speaking, it will take perhaps one hundred years or more to accomplish the English translation of the complete Chinese and Japanese texts, for they consist of thousands of works. Nevertheless, as Dr. NUMATA wished, it is the sincere hope of the Committee that this project will continue unto completion, even after all its present members have passed away.

Dr. NUMATA passed away on May 5, 1994, at the age of ninety-seven, entrusting his son, Mr. NUMATA Toshihide, with the continuation and completion of the Translation Project. The Committee also lost its able and devoted Chairperson, Professor HANAYAMA Shōyū, on June 16, 1995, at the age of sixty-three. After these severe blows, the Committee elected me, then Vice President of Musashino Women's College, to be the Chair in October 1995. The Committee has renewed its determination to carry out the noble intention of Dr. NUMATA, under the leadership of Mr. NUMATA Toshihide.

The present members of the Committee are MAYEDA Sengaku (Chairperson), ISHIGAMI Zennō, ICHISHIMA Shōshin, KANAOKA Shūyū, NARA Yasuaki, TAMARU Noriyoshi, URYŪZU Ryūshin, YUYAMA Akira, Kenneth K. Tanaka, WATANABE Shōgo, and assistant member YONEZAWA Yoshiyasu.

The Numata Center for Buddhist Translation and Research was established in November 1984, in Berkeley, California, U.S.A., to assist in the publication of the BDK English Tripiṭaka First Series. The Publication Committee was organized at the Numata Center in December 1991. Since then the publication of all the volumes has been and will continue to be conducted under the supervision of this Committee in close cooperation with the Editorial Committee in Tokyo.

MAYEDA Sengaku
Chairperson
Editorial Committee of
the BDK English Tripiṭaka

Publisher's Foreword

On behalf of the members of the Publication Committee, I am happy to present this volume as the latest contribution to the BDK English Tripiṭaka Series. The Publication Committee members have worked to ensure that each volume in the series has gone through a rigorous succession of editorial and bookmaking efforts.

The initial translation and editing of the Buddhist scriptures found in this and other BDK English Tripiṭaka volumes are performed under the direction of the Editorial Committee in Tokyo, Japan, chaired by Professor Sengaku Mayeda, Professor Emeritus of Musashino University. Both the Editorial Committee in Tokyo and the Publication Committee, headquartered in Berkeley, California, are dedicated to the production of clear, readable English texts of the Buddhist canon. In doing so, the members of both committees and associated staff work to honor the deep faith, spirit, and concern of the late Reverend Dr. Yehan Numata, who founded the BDK English Tripiṭaka Series in order to disseminate Buddhist teachings throughout the world.

The long-term goal of our project is the translation and publication of the texts in the one hundred-volume Taishō edition of the Chinese Buddhist canon, along with a few influential extracanonical Japanese Buddhist texts. The list of texts selected for the First Series of this translation project may be found at the end of each volume in the series.

As recently appointed Chair of the Publication Committee, I am deeply honored to serve in the post formerly held by the late Dr. Philip B. Yampolsky, who was so good to me during his lifetime; the esteemed Dr. Kenneth K. Inada, who has had such a great impact on Buddhist studies in the United States; and the beloved late Dr. Francis H. Cook, a dear friend and colleague.

In conclusion, I wish to thank the members of the Publication Committee for the extraordinary efforts they have undertaken in the course of preparing this volume for publication: Senior Editor Marianne Dresser, Hudaya Kandahjaya, Eisho Nasu, Reverend Kiyoshi Yamashita, and Reverend Brian Nagata, President of the Numata Center for Buddhist Translation and Research.

John R. McRae
Chairperson
Publication Committee

Contents

Translators' Introduction

This translation was made from the Chinese version by Kumārajīva, the *Miaofalianhuajing,* in seven fascicles (Taishō Vol. 9, No. 262, 1c12–62b1). Originally from the royal family of Kucha in the present-day autonomous province of Xinqiang, China, Kumārajīva is generally believed to have translated the *Saddharmapuṇḍarīka-sūtra* (*Scripture of the White Lotus of the Marvelous Law*) into Chinese in 406 C.E.

In translating the Chinese text into English we used the Kasuga Edition of Kumārajīva's version of the *Lotus Sutra* as the basic text, rather than the Taishō Edition. With very few exceptions the readings in these two editions are almost exactly the same in meaning, and the differences are too slight to have any significant effect on the translation. We have tried to make our translation as readable as possible without straying from the original meaning.

The last line of the first verse in Chapter XXIII (Taishō Vol. 9, No. 262, 53b25), which we have translated as, "I have paid homage to the Bhagavat/In order to attain the utmost wisdom," has no corresponding reading in any extant Sanskrit manuscript, nor is it found in the Tibetan canon or the Chinese version translated from the Sanskrit by Dharmarakṣa in 267 C.E. (Taishō Vol. 9, No. 263). Furthermore, it is absent in a number of authoritative editions of the Buddhist canon in Chinese.

According to the late Professor Shōkō Kabutogi, the foremost specialist in various editions of Kumārajīva's version of the *Lotus Sutra,* the Kasuga Edition is superior to other editions. The most reliable edition, printed in 1263, is now kept at the Tōshōdaiji in Nara. We are pleased to say that this text was published in facsimile under the editorship of Dr. Kabutogi (Tokyo: The Reiyukai, 1979). Furthermore, at the advice of Dr. Kabutogi, the late Professor Yukio Sakamoto included this version of the text along with his three-volume Japanese translation in the pocketbook series published by Iwanami Shoten (Tokyo, 1962–67). In many cases, however, we have not necessarily followed the traditional Sino-Japanese interpretation.

In this connection we have consulted the Sanskrit and, on rare occasions, the Tibetan versions. Of the former, the so-called Central Asian recension, and in particular the Kashgar Manuscript, is of great importance. This manuscript was no doubt copied in the ancient oasis town of Khotan, but it is generally called the Kashgar Manuscript because the majority of the manuscript was obtained there in 1903 by N. F. Petrovsky, the Imperial Russian consul at the time. The manuscript unfortunately has not been kept intact. It is now scattered in a number of places throughout the world and some folios are missing or damaged. Nevertheless, the available portions have been almost completely reproduced in facsimile under the editorship of Professor Lokesh Chandra of the International Academy of Indian Culture in New Delhi (1976; reprinted by The Reiyukai in 1977). As the fruit of painstaking work, Professor Hirofumi Toda of Tokushima University published a romanization of this text (Tokushima, 1981).

It is interesting to note here that in a number of cases, particularly those of Chinese proper names, either in transliteration or translation, Kumārajīva's version agrees with the readings of the Central Asian Sanskrit recension rather than that in others, such as those found in Nepal or at the ancient site of Gilgit in the northwestern part of the Indian subcontinent and some of those found in Tibet. In such cases we have gladly adopted the version from the Central Asian recension, since some of the readings in Chinese were puzzling.

Within the Buddhist canon, the *Lotus Sutra* is one text which should be read as a whole. We recommend reading the text from the beginning and continuing chapter by chapter so that this magnificent drama can be fully grasped as it unfolds. In this sense, Chapter I can be seen as a dramatic prelude, while the well-known parables that emerge during the course of the sutra serve to clarify and enliven the entire narrative.

For the reader who wants a quick summary of the *Lotus Sutra,* we suggest the preface to Professor Leon Hurvitz's meticulous work, *The Scripture of the Lotus Blossom of the Fine Dharma* (New York: Columbia University Press, 1976).

Those who wish to conduct further research into the *Lotus Sutra* are advised to consult an indispensable bibliographical work by Professor Hajime Nakamura, *Indian Buddhism: A Survey with Bibliographical Notes* (Hirakata: Kansai University of Foreign Studies Publication, 1980), and an earlier work by Akira Yuyama, *A Bibliography of the Sanskrit Texts of the Saddharmapuṇḍarīkasūtra* (Canberra: Australian National University Press, 1970). The latter volume includes information on versions in other languages.

Acknowledgements

Our translation work on the first edition of this volume was first launched in the spring of 1980. Our hope was that the final result would be a text readily understandable to English readers. Since then the work has often been interrupted by other commitments. During these years we have been indebted to the assistance of a number of people. Among them, Dr. Gregory Shopen and Dr. Terry Abbott joined the first stage of our project and gave of their time selflessly. In the course of our revisions, Dr. James Hubbard spared no pains in going through the entire English text. We are grateful to him not only for his correction of our English but also for the suggestions stemming from his excellent knowledge of Buddhist Chinese.

In the very final stages, we decided to rapidly review the translation by once again comparing the Chinese with the Sanskrit versions. In this process we were assisted by Ms. Kiko Thiel and Dr. James Raeside, who helped us with nuances and shades of meaning in their native language. We must also thank Mr. S. Kawabata and Mr. T. Torii who was, throughout, unsparing in his efforts to guide the project to a conclusion. Last but not least, our heartfelt gratitude goes to the staff members of the International Institute for Buddhist Studies and the International Department of the Reiyukai for their untiring assistance.

We feel pleased and honored that our translation has been adopted in this series, and we believe this must indicate that the philosophy underlying our translation matches the goals of the Society for the Promotion of Buddhism (Bukkyō Dendō Kyōkai) and its English Tripiṭaka Series.

THE LOTUS SUTRA

Chapter I

Introduction

Thus have I heard. Once the Buddha was staying in the city of 1c
Rājagṛha, on the mountain called Gṛdhrakūṭa, together with a
great assembly of twelve thousand monks, all of whom were arhats
whose corruption was at an end, who were free from the confusion
of desire, who had achieved their own goals, shattered the bonds
of existence, and attained complete mental discipline. Their names
were Ājñātakauṇḍinya, Mahākāśyapa, Uruvilvakāśyapa, Gayākāśyapa, Nadīkāśyapa, Śāriputra, Mahāmaudgalyāyana, Mahākātyāyana, Aniruddha, Kapphiṇa, Gavāṃpati, Revata, Pilindavatsa,
Bakkula, Mahākauṣṭhila, Nanda, Sundarananda, Pūrṇamaitrāyaṇī-
putra, Subhūti, Ānanda, and Rāhula. All of them were great arhats,
known to the assembly. There were in addition two thousand others, both those who had more to learn and those who did not. The
nun Mahāprajāpatī was there, together with her six thousand
attendants; and also the nun Yaśodharā, Rāhula's mother, together 2a
with her attendants.

There were also eighty thousand bodhisattva *mahāsattva*s, all of whom were irreversible from highest, complete enlightenment (*anuttarā samyaksaṃbodhi*). They had obtained the *dhāraṇī*s, were established in eloquence, and had turned the irreversible wheel of the Dharma. Each had paid homage to countless hundreds of thousands of Buddhas, planted roots of merit in their presence, and had always been praised by those Buddhas. They had also cultivated compassion within themselves, skillfully caused others to enter the wisdom of a Buddha, obtained great wisdom, and reached the other shore. All of them were famous throughout countless worlds and had saved innumerable hundreds of thousands of sentient beings. They were Mañjuśrī, Avalokiteśvara, Mahāsthāmaprāpta, Nityodyukta, Anikṣiptadhura, Ratnapāni,

Bhaiṣajyarāja, Pradānaśūra, Ratnacandra, Candraprabha, Pūrṇacandra, Mahāvikramin, Anantavikramin, Trailokyavikrama, Bhadrapāla, Maitreya, Ratnākara, and Susāthavāha. There were altogether eighty thousand such bodhisattva *mahāsattvas*.

At that time Śakra, king of the *devas*, was also there, attended by twenty thousand *devaputras*. Candra, Samantagandha, and Ratnaprabha, and the great *devas* of the four quarters were there, together with a retinue of ten thousand *devaputras*. The *devaputras* Īśvara and Maheśvara were there, attended by thirty thousand *devaputras*. Brahma, the lord of the *sahā* world, as well as the great Brahma Śikhin and the great Brahma Jyotiṣprabha were there, together with a retinue of twelve thousand *devaputras*. The eight *nāga* kings—namely, Nanda, Upananda, Sāgara, Vāsukin, Takṣaka, Anavatapta, Manasvin, and Utpalaka—were also there, each of them surrounded by several hundreds of thousands of attendants.

There were four kings of the *kiṃnaras* whose names were Dharma, Sudharma, Mahādharma, and Dharmadhara, and each had several hundreds of thousands of attendants. The four kings of the *gandharvas* were there. They were Manojña, Manojñasvara, Madhura, and Madhurasvara, each of them also with several hundreds of thousands of attendants. There, too, were four kings of
2b the *asuras*, called Baḍin, Kharaskandha, Vemacitra, and Rahu, each with several hundreds of thousands of attendants. Mahātejas, Mahākāya, Mahāpūrṇa, and Maharddhiprāpta, the four kings of the *garuḍas*, were there together with several hundreds of thousands of attendants. Finally, King Ajātaśatru, Vaidehī's son, was also there with several hundreds of thousands of his attendants. Each of them, after having bowed at the Buddha's feet, withdrew and sat to one side.

At that time the Bhagavat was respectfully surrounded by the fourfold assembly (i.e., monks, nuns, laymen, laywomen), paid homage, honored, and praised. He then taught the bodhisattvas the Mahayana sutra called *Immeasurable Meanings* (*Mahānirdeśa*), the instruction for the bodhisattvas and the treasured lore of the

Buddhas. After having taught this sutra, the Buddha sat cross-legged, entered the *samādhi* called the "abode of immeasurable meanings" (*ananta-nirdeśa-pratiṣṭhāna*) and remained unmoving in both body and mind. *Māndārava* and great *māndārava* flowers, *mañjūṣaka* and great *mañjūṣaka* flowers then fell like rain from the sky, scattering upon the Buddha and all of his attendants; and the whole Buddha world quaked in six ways. At that time, that whole assembly of such humans and nonhumans as monks, nuns, laymen, and laywomen, the *deva*s, *nāga*s, *yakṣa*s, *gandharva*s, *asura*s, *garuḍa*s, *kiṃnara*s, *mahoraga*s, kings, and noble emperors, having experienced something unprecedented, were filled with joy, and with their palms pressed together they gazed attentively at the Buddha.

Then the Buddha emitted a ray of light from the tuft of white hair between his eyebrows. It illuminated all the eighteen thousand worlds in the east, down as far as the lowest hell, Avīci, and up as high as the Akaniṣṭha Heaven. All the sentient beings in those worlds living in the six transmigratory states became visible from this world. The Buddhas in those worlds were also seen, and the Dharma they were teaching could be heard. The monks, nuns, laymen, and laywomen and those who had practiced and achieved the path were also to be seen, while the bodhisattva *mahāsattva*s, of various background causes and conditions, endowed in various degrees with the willingness to understand and having various appearances, were also seen practicing the bodhisattva path. All of the Buddhas who had achieved *parinirvāṇa* were seen, as well as their relic stupas made of the seven precious treasures.

At that moment it occurred to Bodhisattva Maitreya: "The Bhagavat has now manifested the sign of great transcendent power. What could be the reason for this marvel? The Buddha, the Bhagavat, has now entered *samādhi*. Whom should I ask about this wonderful marvel? Who would be able to answer my question?"

Then he thought further: "This Mañjuśrī, Prince of the Dharma, has closely attended and paid homage to innumerable Buddhas of the past. He must certainly have seen such a marvelous sign before. I should ask him now."

2c At the same time it occurred to the monks, nuns, laymen, and laywomen, *devas*, *nāgas*, *yakṣas*, and others: "Now whom should we ask about the illumination and marvelous sign of this Buddha?"

Then Bodhisattva Maitreya, wanting to clear up his own confusion, and knowing the minds of the fourfold assembly of monks, nuns, laymen, and laywomen and of the *nāgas*, *yakṣas*, and other beings in that gathering, asked Mañjuśrī: "What is the reason for this marvelous sign, this great ray of light that illuminates the eighteen thousand worlds in the east and renders visible the adornments of all the Buddha worlds?"

Thereupon Bodhisattva Maitreya, wanting to elaborate the meaning of this further, spoke to Mañjuśrī in verse:

"O Mañjuśrī!
Why has the Leader
Emitted this great ray of light far and wide
From the tuft of white hair
Between his eyebrows,
Raining down *māndārava* and *mañjūṣaka* flowers,
And gladdening the people
With the fragrant winds of sandalwood?
For this reason
The earth is completely adorned,
And this world quakes in six ways.
And the fourfold assembly
Is completely enraptured,
Delighted in body and mind at the experience of
Such an unprecedented marvel.
From the depths of the Avīci Hell
Up to the summit of existence,
The ray of light from between his eyebrows
Illuminates the eighteen thousand worlds,
Which shimmer like gold,
And, throughout all these worlds,
The births and deaths of the living beings

Of the six transmigratory states of existence,
And the good and bad deeds,
Through which they have received
Good and bad consequences,
Are all to be seen from here.
The Buddhas, the Sage Lord (Narendrasiṃhā),
Who teach the subtle and supreme sutra
Are also seen.
Uttering soft sounds
With their pure voices,
They teach innumerable myriads
Of *koṭi*s of bodhisattvas.
With their voices, deep and enticing
Like the sounds of Brahma
They make the people eager to hear them.
In each world they teach the True Dharma;
They illuminate the Buddha-Dharma
And enlighten sentient beings
By means of various explanations
And innumerable illustrations.
To those who are suffering
And are cast down by old age, illness, and death 3a
They teach nirvana
To extinguish their sufferings.
To those who have merit,
Have paid homage to the Buddhas
And seek the excellent Dharma,
They teach the ideal of the *pratyekabuddha*.
To those heirs of the Buddhas
Who have practiced in various ways
And are seeking the utmost wisdom,
They teach the pure path.
O Mañjuśrī!
Abiding here, I see and hear
Thousands of *koṭi*s of things in this way.

There are many such things.
I shall now explain them in brief.
In these worlds I see bodhisattvas,
Equal in number to the sands of the Ganges River,
Seeking the path of the Buddhas
According to their various situations.
Some undertake the practice of giving gifts,
Joyfully giving gold, silver, coral, pearls,
Jewels, conch shells, agates, diamonds,
Servants, carts, and ornamented litters—
They give these things joyfully,
Transferring the merit
To the path of the Buddhas,
Wishing to obtain this vehicle
Which is the highest in the three worlds,
And praised by all the Buddhas.
Other bodhisattvas give gifts
Such as ornamented carts yoked with four horses
And furnished with railings,
Canopies, and decorated eaves.
Moreover, I see bodhisattvas
Who, seeking for the highest path,
Give gifts such as their bodies, flesh, hands,
And feet, as well as their wives and children.
Moreover, I see bodhisattvas
Who are joyfully giving their heads, eyes, and bodies,
While searching for the wisdom of the Buddhas.
O Mañjuśrī!
I see kings making pilgrimages to the Buddhas,
Asking about the highest path,
Abandoning their prosperous lands,
Palaces, subjects and harems,
Shaving their heads and beards,
And wearing the robes of the Dharma.
I see some bodhisattvas becoming monks,

Dwelling apart in tranquility,
Reciting the sutras with contentment.
I also see bodhisattvas
Persistent and courageous,
Going into remote mountains
And contemplating the Buddha path.
I see some abandoning worldly desires,
Dwelling always in lonely places,
Practicing profound meditations
And obtaining the five transcendent powers.
I see bodhisattvas
Meditating with palms pressed together,
Praising the Kings of the Dharma
With thousands of myriads of verses.
I also see bodhisattvas,
Profound in wisdom and firm in resolution,
Asking the Buddhas questions,
Listening carefully and retaining everything.
Furthermore, I see heirs of the Buddhas,
Endowed with concentration and wisdom,
Teaching the Dharma by innumerable illustrations
For the benefit of living beings,
Leading and inspiring the bodhisattvas
By joyously teaching the Dharma,
Destroying Māra and his minions
And beating the drums of the Dharma.
I also see bodhisattvas
Who are tranquil and silent in ease,
And never exult
Even in the homage paid by *deva*s and *nāga*s.
I see bodhisattvas
Dwelling in forests, radiating light,
Alleviating the suffering of beings in the hells 3b
And causing them to enter the Buddha path.
I also see heirs of the Buddhas

Who have never fallen asleep,
And are constantly wandering in forests
In search of the Buddha path.
I see some who are pure like jewels,
Endowed with integrity
And faultless in behavior,
In search of the Buddha path.
Furthermore, I see heirs of the Buddhas
In search of the Buddha path,
Who have the power of perseverance
And patiently endure
Those of excessive pride
Who abuse them verbally and physically.
I see bodhisattvas
Who have been searching for the Buddha path
For thousands of myriads of *koṭi*s of years,
And who have renounced idlers and foolish companions
And approached the wise.
Having singlemindedly rid themselves of inner confusion
They are meditating in mountain forests.
I also see bodhisattvas seeking
For the highest path,
Who are giving food and drink,
And a hundred kinds of medicine
To the Buddha and the sangha.
They give superb garments and clothing
Worth thousands of myriads,
And priceless robes
To the Buddha and the sangha.
They give thousands of myriads of *koṭi*s
Of treasured monasteries made of sandalwood,
And various kinds of excellent bedding
To the Buddha and the sangha.
They give clean garden groves
Full of flowers and fruits,

Fountains and bathing pools
To the Buddha and the sangha.
Thus they give such various excellent things,
With joy and vigor,
Seeking the supreme path.
There are also bodhisattvas
Who are teaching innumerable sentient beings
The Dharma of tranquility
In various ways.
Furthermore, I see bodhisattvas
Who have perceived the essential character
Of all *dharma*s (phenomena) to be without duality,
Just like empty space.
I also see heirs of the Buddhas
Who are seeking the highest path
Through this subtle wisdom,
Their minds free of attachment.
O Mañjuśrī!
There are bodhisattvas
Who pay homage to the relics (*śarīra*s) of the Buddhas
After their *parinirvāṇa*s.
I also see heirs of the Buddhas
Who have built stupas
As numerous as the sands of the Ganges River,
With which to decorate the Buddha worlds.
These jeweled stupas are magnificent—
Five thousand *yojana*s in height and
Two thousand *yojana*s in both length and width.
On each of these stupas
Are one thousand banners, flags, and canopies,
And jeweled bells ringing harmoniously.
And *deva*s, *nāga*s, humans, and nonhumans
Constantly give offerings of
Perfume, flowers, and music to them.
O Mañjuśrī!

The heirs of the Buddhas
Have decorated the stupas
In order to pay homage to the relics.
These worlds have been spontaneously
Made as extraordinarily beautiful
As the king of the heavenly trees
When his flowers bloom.
Because the Buddha has emitted this ray of light,
I and those with me in the assembly can see
3c These worlds of marvelous and varied beauty.
The wisdom and transcendent powers
Of all the Buddhas are extraordinary;
By emitting a single ray of light
He has illuminated innumerable lands.
Seeing this, we attain
That which we have not met with before.
O Mañjuśrī, Heir of the Buddhas!
We entreat you to rid us of our confusion!
The fourfold assembly is joyfully
Looking up at you and me.
Why did the Bhagavat emit this ray of light?
O Heir of the Buddhas, now answer!
Resolve our confusion and gladden us!
Why is he emitting this ray of light?
Will the Buddha teach us the True Dharma
That he obtained while he sat
On the terrace of enlightenment (*bodhimaṇḍa*)?
Will he predict enlightenment to us?
It is not for a trifling reason
That all the Buddha lands, ornamented
With various jewels,
And all the Buddhas have been made visible.
O Mañjuśrī!
You should know that the fourfold assembly,
*Nāga*s, and *deva*s,

Look forward to hearing
What you shall reveal."

Thereupon Mañjuśrī spoke to Bodhisattva Mahāsattva Maitreya and the other worthy beings: "O sons of a virtuous family! I am very sure that the Buddha, the Bhagavat, will now teach the great Dharma, rain down the great Dharma, blow the conch of the great Dharma, beat the drum of the great Dharma, and reveal the meaning of the great Dharma.

"O sons of a virtuous family! I have seen Buddhas in the past who have shown this marvel and have taught the great Dharma immediately after emitting a ray of light. Therefore, you should know that in the very same way the Buddha has now emitted this light and has shown this marvel in order to cause all sentient beings to hear and understand the Dharma which in all the worlds is difficult to understand.

"O sons of a virtuous family! In the past, more than innumerable, unthinkable, incalculable *kalpa*s ago, there was a Buddha called Candrasūryapradīpa, a Tathāgata, Arhat, Completely Enlightened, Perfect in Knowledge and Conduct, Well-Departed, Knower of the World, Unsurpassed, Tamer of Humans, Teacher of Devas and Humans, Buddha, Bhagavat. He taught the True Dharma that was good in the beginning, good in the middle, and good in the end. It was profound in meaning, elegant in speech, and endowed with the character of the pure path of discipline and integrity.

"To those seeking for the *śrāvaka* vehicle he taught the Dharma with respect to the Four Noble Truths, causing them to overcome birth, old age, sickness, and death and to attain nirvana. He taught the Dharma with respect to dependent origination to the *pratyekabuddha*s; and to the bodhisattvas he taught the Dharma with respect to the six perfections (*pāramitā*s), causing them to attain highest, complete enlightenment and perfect all-knowledge (*sarvajñātā*).

"Then there was another Buddha named Candrasūryapradīpa, and after him another Buddha also named Candrasūryapradīpa.

And so in this way twenty thousand Buddhas all had the same name Candrasūryapradīpa. They also had the same family name Bharadvāja.

"O Maitreya! You should know that these Buddhas, beginning from the first up to the last, all had the same name Candrasūrya-
4a pradīpa, endowed with the ten epithets. The Dharma that they taught was good in the beginning, the middle, and the end.

"The last Buddha fathered eight princes before he renounced household life. The first was called Mati, the second Sumati, the third Anantamati, the fourth Ratimati, the fifth was called Viśeṣamati, the sixth Vimatisamudghātin, the seventh Ghoṣamati, and the eighth was called Dharmamati. These eight princes were endowed with dignity and power, and each of them ruled over four great continents. Having heard that their father had renounced household life and obtained highest, complete enlightenment, all of them abandoned their kingdoms and also renounced household life. Each caused the spirit of the Mahayana to arise within him, practiced the pure path of discipline and integrity, and became an expounder of the Dharma. They all planted roots of good merit under many thousands of myriads of Buddhas.

"At that time, the Buddha Candrasūryapradīpa taught the Mahayana sutra called *Immeasurable Meanings,* the instruction for the bodhisattvas and treasured lore of the Buddhas. Having taught this sutra, he sat down cross-legged, undisturbed in body and mind among the great assembly and entered the *samādhi* called the 'abode of immeasurable meanings.'

"Then *māndārava* and great *māndārava* flowers, *mañjūṣaka* and great *mañjūṣaka* flowers fell like rain from the sky, scattering over the Buddha and all of his attendants. And the whole Buddha world quaked in six ways. At that time all in that assembly of humans and nonhumans—monks, nuns, laymen, laywomen, *deva*s, *nāga*s, *yakṣa*s, *gandharva*s, *asura*s, *garuḍa*s, *kiṃnara*s, *mahoraga*s, kings, and noble emperors—having experienced such an unprecedented marvel, were filled with joy and pressing their palms together they gazed attentively at the Buddha.

"Then the Buddha emitted a ray of light from the tuft of white hair between his eyebrows which completely illuminated all the eighteen thousand worlds in the east, in the same way that all of these Buddha worlds are visible now.

"O Maitreya! You should know that at that time there were twenty *koṭis* of bodhisattvas in the assembly who wanted to hear the Dharma. All of these bodhisattvas, having seen all the Buddha worlds completely illuminated by this ray of light, were struck with wonder and wanted to know why it was emitted.

"A bodhisattva named Varaprabha was there with his eight hundred disciples. At that time the Buddha Candrasūryapradīpa, having emerged from *samādhi,* remained sitting for sixty intermediate *kalpas* and revealed to Bodhisattva Varaprabha the Mahayana sutra called *Saddharmapuṇḍarīka,* the *White Lotus of the Marvelous Law* (hereafter *Lotus Sutra*), which was the instruction for bodhisattvas and the treasured lore of the Buddhas. The assembly also sat there undisturbed in body and mind listening to the Buddha's exposition for sixty intermediate *kalpas* as if only a single mealtime had passed; during that time not a single person among them experienced fatigue of body or mind.

"Having taught this sutra for sixty intermediate *kalpas*, the Buddha Candrasūryapradīpa made this proclamation to the assembly of Brahmas, *māras*, *śrāmaṇas*, brahmans, *devas*, humans, and 4b
asuras, saying:

> On this day during the middle watch of the night, the Tathāgata will enter nirvana without residue.

"Then the Buddha Candrasūryapradīpa gave this prediction to a bodhisattva called Śrīgarbha. Addressing the monks, he said:

> This Bodhisattva Śrīgarbha will become the next Buddha after me. He will be called Vimalāṅganetra, a Tathāgata, Arhat, Completely Enlightened.

"The Buddha, after having made this prediction, entered nirvana without residue during the middle of the night. After the

Buddha passed into extinction, Bodhisattva Varaprabha, having preserved the *Lotus Sutra,* taught it to humans for the full period of eighty intermediate *kalpa*s.

"This Bodhisattva Varaprabha was made the teacher for the Buddha Candrasūryapradīpa's eight princes. Varaprabha led and inspired them and caused them to be firm in highest, complete enlightenment.

"After paying homage to innumerable hundreds of thousands of myriads of *koṭi*s of Buddhas, all these princes attained the path of the Buddhas. The last of these to become enlightened was named Dīpaṃkara.

"Among the eight hundred disciples of Bodhisattva Varaprabha there was a man named Yaśaskāma who was attached to profit. Even though he had repeatedly recited the sutras he never became versed in them and forgot the greater part. That is why he was called Yaśaskāma, 'Fame Seeker.' But because he had also planted various roots of good merit, he was able to meet innumerable hundreds of thousands of myriads of *koṭi*s of Buddhas whom he rendered homage to, honored, revered, and praised.

"O Maitreya! You should know that Bodhisattva Varaprabha at that time was none other than myself, and Bodhisattva Yaśaskāma was none other than you. The marvel we see here is exactly the same as the previous one. Therefore I am certain that today the Tathāgata will teach the Mahayana sutra called the *Lotus Sutra,* the instruction for bodhisattvas and treasured lore of the Buddhas."

Thereupon Mañjuśrī, wanting to explain the meaning of this further, spoke to the great assembly in verse:

I remember that in the past,
Innumerable incalculable *kalpa*s ago,
There was a Buddha, the Best of Humans,
Called Candrasūryapradīpa.
This Bhagavat taught the Dharma,
Leading and inspiring innumerable sentient beings

And incalculable numbers of bodhisattvas,
To attain the wisdom of the Buddhas.
Before renouncing household life
The Buddha fathered eight princes.
Having seen the Great Sage
Renounce household life,
They also followed him
And practiced the pure path of discipline and integrity.
At that time the Buddha taught
And extensively illuminated the Mahayana sutra
Called *Immeasurable Meanings*
To the great assembly.
After having taught this sutra,
The Buddha sat down cross-legged
On the seat of Dharma and entered the *samādhi* 4c
Called the "abode of immeasurable meanings."
The heavenly *māndārava* flowers
Fell down like rain;
The heavenly drums resounded spontaneously.
All the *deva*s, *nāga*s, and *yakṣa*s
Paid homage to the Best of Humans.
All of the Buddha worlds suddenly quaked greatly.
And the Buddha emitted a ray of light
From the tuft between his eyebrows
And manifested various marvels.
This ray of light illuminated
The eighteen thousand Buddha worlds in the east
And revealed the conditions
Resulting from the karma of each sentient being.
Through this light of the Buddha
All the Buddha worlds appeared
As if they were decorated with various jewels
Such as lapis lazuli or crystal.
All the *deva*s, humans, *nāga*s,
*Yakṣa*s, *gandharva*s, and *kiṃnara*s

Were each seen paying homage to the Buddhas.
All the Tathāgatas, who had spontaneously attained
The path of the Buddhas,
Looked majestic and very beautiful
With bodies like golden mountains.
Each Bhagavat appeared like a golden image
In the midst of lapis lazuli,
Expounding the meaning
Of the profound Dharma to the great assembly.
There were innumerable *śrāvaka*s
In each of the Buddha worlds,
And they saw all the great assemblies
Because of the light of the Buddha.
There were also monks
Living in mountain forests,
Who, through persistence, possessed purity of conduct,
Which they protected like a precious jewel.
There were bodhisattvas,
As numerous as the sands of the Ganges River,
Practicing by giving (*dāna*), perseverance (*kṣānti*), and so on (i.e., the six perfections),
Who also became visible through the light of the Buddha.
There were bodhisattvas, who,
Having entered deep *samādhi,*
Were tranquil and undisturbed in body and mind,
And who were seen seeking for the highest path.
There were also bodhisattvas,
Who, knowing the tranquil character of the Dharma,
Were seen teaching the Dharma
And seeking the path of the Buddhas
In each of the Buddha worlds.
At that time the fourfold assembly,
Having seen the Buddha Candrasūryapradīpa
Manifest these great transcendent powers,
Became delighted, and asked each other

What the reason for this could be.
The Noble One, revered by *deva*s and humans,
Then emerged from *samādhi* and
Praised Bodhisattva Varaprabha, saying: 5a

> You are the Eye of the World.
> You are believed in by all and
> Possess the treasure house of the Dharma.
> You are the only one who can understand
> The Dharma that I have taught!

The Bhagavat praised Varaprabha, delighting him,
And taught this *Lotus Sutra*
For the full period of sixty intermediate *kalpa*s
Without rising from his seat.
This expounder of the Dharma, Varaprabha,
Firmly and completely
Preserved this most excellent Dharma
That was taught by the Buddha.
After having taught this *Lotus Sutra*
And having then gladdened the assembly
On that very day,
The Buddha told the assembly of *deva*s and humans:

> I have already taught you the meaning
> Of the essential character of all *dharma*s.
> Today I will enter nirvana
> In the middle of the night.
> Exert yourselves attentively
> And rid yourselves of negligence!
> The Buddhas are extremely hard to meet
> And can be encountered only once
> In *koṭi*s of *kalpa*s!

All the sons of the Bhagavat,
On hearing that the Buddha was to enter nirvana,
Became sad, thinking:

Why will the Buddha enter nirvana so soon?

The Noble Lord, the King of the Dharma,
Consoled the innumerable beings saying:

Do not fear after I enter nirvana!
This Bodhisattva Śrīgarbha has fully realized
The true character of freedom from corruption
And after me he will become
A Buddha named Vimalāṅganetra.
And then he will bring
Innumerable sentient beings to the path.

And that night the Buddha entered nirvana,
Like a fire that goes out when the wood is exhausted.
His relics were distributed
And innumerable stupas were built.
There were monks and nuns,
As numerous as the sands of the Ganges River,
Who increased their efforts
And sought for the highest path.
This expounder of the Dharma, Varaprabha,
Possessed of the treasure house of the Buddha,
Extensively proclaimed the *Lotus Sutra*
For eighty intermediate *kalpa*s.
All of the eight princes
Led and inspired by Varaprabha,
Became firmly established
In the highest path,
And met innumerable Buddhas.
After having paid homage to the Buddhas
And following them in their practice of the great path,
5b They all in turn received their predictions,
Becoming Buddhas in succession.
The last Buddha, the Highest of Devas,
Was called Dīpaṃkara,

And, as the leader of all the sages,
Had brought innumerable sentient beings to the path.
This expounder of the Dharma, Varaprabha,
Had one disciple who was lazy
And attached to fame and fortune.
This disciple ceaselessly sought these things
And amused himself from house to house.
He abandoned recitation of the sutras,
And, forgetting them,
Never became versed in them.
For this very reason he was named Yaśaskāma.
But since he had also performed many good deeds,
He was able to meet innumerable Buddhas.
He paid homage to all these Buddhas
And having practiced the great path after them,
Acquired all the six perfections and
Now meets the Lion of the Śākyas.
He shall subsequently become a Buddha called Maitreya
Who will extensively bring
Innumerable sentient beings to the path.
After the *parinirvāṇa* of that
Buddha Candrasūryapradīpa,
The lazy one was none other than you;
And the expounder of the Dharma, Varaprabha,
Was no one but myself.
When I saw the Buddha Dīpaṃkara
He also revealed this marvel of light.
That is why I know that this Buddha
Will now teach the *Lotus Sutra*.
This sign is just like the previous marvel.
It is the skillful means of all the Buddhas.
The Buddha has now emitted this ray of light
In order to reveal
The essential character of *dharma*s.
Now it should be clear to everyone.

Wait attentively with palms pressed together!
Having rained the Dharma,
The Buddha will satisfy those seeking the path.
If there is anyone seeking the three vehicles
Who still has any doubts,
The Buddha will completely remove them,
Extinguishing them with none left over.

Chapter II

Skillful Means

At that time the Bhagavat arose tranquilly with insight out of *samādhi* and addressed Śāriputra: "Profound and immeasurable is the wisdom of the Buddhas. The gate to their wisdom is hard to enter and difficult to understand. None of the *śrāvaka*s and *pratyekabuddha*s may be capable of understanding it. Why is this? The Buddhas have closely attended innumerable hundreds of thousands of myriads of *koṭi*s of other Buddhas. They have exhaustively carried out practices with courage and persistence under uncountable numbers of Buddhas, their names becoming universally renowned. They have perfected this profound and unprecedented Dharma, and their intention in adapting their explanations to what is appropriate is difficult to understand. 5c

"O Śāriputra! After attaining Buddhahood I expounded the teaching extensively with various explanations and illustrations, and with skillful means (*upāya*) led sentient beings to rid themselves of their attachments. Why is this? Because all the Tathāgatas have attained perfect mastery of skillful means, wisdom, and insight.

"O Śāriputra! The wisdom and insight of the Tathāgatas is extensive, profound, immeasurable, and unhindered. They are possessed of power, fearlessness, meditation, liberation, and *samādhi* that is profound and endless. They have completely attained this unprecedented Dharma.

"O Śāriputra! The Tathāgatas can, through various methods, skillfully illuminate the Dharma with gentle speech and gladden the hearts of the assemblies.

"O Śāriputra! To put it briefly, the Buddhas have attained this immeasurable, limitless, and unprecedented Dharma. Enough, O Śāriputra, I will speak no further. Why is this? Because the Dharma that the Buddhas have attained is foremost, unique, and difficult to understand. No one but the Buddhas can completely know the real aspects of all *dharmas*—that is to say their character, nature, substance, potential, function, cause, condition, result, effect, and essential unity."

Thereupon the Bhagavat spoke these verses to explain this meaning again:

> The Heroes of the World are inconceivable,
> Neither *devas*, humans, nor any other sentient beings
> Are able to comprehend them.
> No one is able to discern the power, fearlessness,
> Liberation, *samādhi,* and
> Other attributes of the Buddhas.
> Formerly, under innumerable Buddhas,
> They have fully accomplished their practices
> And the Dharma, which is profound and excellent,
> Hard to perceive and difficult to understand.
> Having pursued these practices
> For innumerable *koṭis* of *kalpas*,
> I attained the result on the terrace of enlightenment
> And understood completely.
> I and the Buddhas of the ten directions
> Know such matters,
> Such as the great results and rewards,
> And the meaning of various aspects and characteristics.
> It is impossible to explain this Dharma;
> The powers of speech fail.
> No other sentient being is able to understand it,
> Except for those bodhisattvas
> Who, in their belief, are willing to understand.
> Even the multitude of the Buddha's disciples,
> Who have formerly paid homage to all the Buddhas,
> Who have put an end to all their corruption
> And are bearing their last bodies,

Are not able to understand it. 6a
Even if this whole world
Were filled with those such as Śāriputra,
And they tried together to comprehend it,
They still would not be able to understand completely
The wisdom of the Buddhas.
Again, even if the worlds of the ten directions
Were filled with such disciples
As Śāriputra,
And they tried together to comprehend it,
They still would not be able to completely understand.
And even if the worlds of the ten directions
Were filled with *pratyekabuddha*s,
As numerous as bamboo trees in a grove,
Who had keen wisdom
And were bearing their last bodies,
Free from corruption,
Even if they tried together singlemindedly,
For innumerable *kalpa*s,
To comprehend the wisdom of the Buddhas,
Still they would not understand it in the least.
Even if the worlds of the ten directions
Were packed as thick as stalks of rice,
Flax, bamboo, and reeds
With bodhisattvas, recent aspirants to enlightenment,
Who had paid homage to innumerable Buddhas—
Though they fully understood the meaning
And could expound the Dharma,
Even with this subtle wisdom,
If they tried together singlemindedly to comprehend,
For as many *kalpa*s as the sands of the Ganges River,
They still would not be able to know
The wisdom of the Buddhas.
Even if bodhisattvas,
As numerous as the sands of the Ganges River,

Who had reached the stage of nonretrogression,
Tried together singlemindedly to comprehend it,
Still they would not be able to know.

The Buddha, still speaking to Śāriputra, said:

I have already attained the profound and subtle Dharma
That is incorruptible
And beyond all comprehension.
Only I and the Buddhas of the ten directions know this.
O Śāriputra! You should know that the words
Of the Buddhas are never inconsistent.
You should trust fully in the Dharma
That the Buddha expounds;
The Dharma of the Bhagavat
Has been in existence for a long time.
I will now definitely expound the truth.
I address myself to the *śrāvaka*s
And those seeking the *pratyekabuddha* vehicle.
It was I who caused them to become free
From the bondage of suffering, and to attain nirvana.
I have revealed the teaching of the three vehicles
With the power of the skillful means of the Buddhas
So as to free the sentient beings
From their various human attachments.

At that time it occurred to the great assembly of twelve hundred *śrāvaka*s, arhats free from corruption, beginning with Ājñāta-
6b kauṇḍinya, and the other monks, nuns, laymen, and laywomen
who had set out to become *śrāvaka*s and *pratyekabuddha*s: “Why
has the Bhagavat just now so earnestly praised skillful means? For
what reason has he declared that the Dharma that the Buddhas
have attained is very profound and difficult to understand? Why
has he said that their intention in adapting their teaching to what
is appropriate is so difficult to comprehend that all the *śrāvaka*s
and *pratyekabuddha*s are not able to understand it?

"As long as the Buddha taught the meaning of the single liberation we thought we had attained that Dharma and achieved nirvana. But now we do not understand what he means."

At that time Śāriputra, aware of the confusion of the fourfold assemblies and himself also feeling confused, addressed the Buddha saying: "O Bhagavat! For what reason and on what grounds have you so earnestly praised the unique skillful means of the Buddhas and the profound and subtle Dharma that is difficult to understand? Never before have I heard such a thing from the Buddha. Now Bhagavat, I entreat you to explain this because the fourfold assemblies are confused. O Bhagavat! Why have you so earnestly praised the Dharma that is profound, subtle, and difficult to understand?"

Thereupon Śāriputra, wanting to further explain what he meant, spoke these verses:

> O Great Seer, Sun of Wisdom!
> Now, after a long time,
> You have taught this Dharma, saying,
>
> > I have attained the inconceivable Dharma,
> > That is to say, power, fearlessness,
> > *Samādhi*, meditation, and liberation.
> > No one has ever questioned the Dharma
> > That I attained on the terrace of enlightenment.
> > No one has ever questioned my intentions,
> > So difficult to conceive.
>
> Without being asked
> You explained it by yourself
> And praised the path you have practiced, saying,
>
> > The wisdom the Buddhas have attained
> > Is extremely subtle!
>
> The arhats free from corruption
> And those seeking nirvana
> Have all fallen into confusion.

Why has the Buddha said this?
Those seeking to become *pratyekabuddha*s,
Monks, nuns, *deva*s, *nāga*s,
*Yakṣa*s, *gandharva*s, and the others
Glanced at each other in confusion
And looking toward the Best of Humans asked:

O Buddha! We entreat you to explain why this is so!

The Buddha has said that I am the foremost
Among the *śrāvaka*s, yet now I am confused
About my own knowledge and unable to understand.
Is it the ultimate Dharma?
Is it a path to be practiced?
6c The sons born from the mouths of the Buddhas
Stand waiting with palms pressed together,
Looking at the Buddha.
I entreat you to proclaim the truth,
Speaking in the finest voice!
The *deva*s, *nāga*s, and others,
As numerous as the sands of the Ganges River,
As many as eighty thousand bodhisattvas
Who are seeking Buddhahood, and noble emperors
Who have come from myriads of *koṭi*s of countries,
Are all standing respectfully with palms pressed together
Asking how to accomplish the path.

Then the Buddha addressed Śāriputra, saying: "Enough, enough! Speak no more! If I explained this matter, the *deva*s and humans in all the worlds would be astounded."

Then Śāriputra again addressed the Buddha: "O Bhagavat! Please explain it! I entreat you to explain it, because in this assembly there are innumerable hundreds of thousands of myriads of *koṭi*s of incalculable sentient beings, sharp in faculties and possessed of wisdom, who have previously encountered the Buddhas. When they hear the teaching of the Buddha they will trust, believe, and accept it."

Thereupon Śāriputra spoke in verse to explain this again:

O King of the Dharma, the Best of Humans!
I entreat you to explain it.
Please explain it without hesitation!
In this assembly there are innumerable sentient beings
Who will trust and accept it.

Then the Buddha again tried to dissuade Śāriputra, saying: "If I explain it, the *deva*s, humans, and *asura*s in all the worlds will be astounded, and arrogant monks will certainly go to their downfall."

At that time the Bhagavat again spoke in verse:

Enough, enough! Speak no more!
The Dharma that I have attained
Is excellent and incomprehensible.
Though the arrogant hear it,
They will never accept it.

And again Śāriputra addressed the Buddha, saying: "O Bhagavat! Please explain it! Please explain it! In this assembly there are people like me and others, numbering into the hundreds of thousands of myriads of *koṭi*s of beings, who have been led and inspired by the Buddhas in their former existences. Such people will certainly trust, believe, and accept it. And they will benefit, profit, and receive solace from it for a very long time."

Thereupon Śāriputra spoke these verses to elaborate on what he meant:

O Best of Humans!
Please teach the ultimate Dharma!
I am the eldest son of the Buddha.
Please illuminate and explain it!
Innumerable beings in this assembly
Will certainly trust and accept this Dharma,
Because the Buddha in former existences

Led and inspired such people.
7a All of them will attentively listen and accept,
Their palms pressed together,
To the words of the Buddha.
I entreat you to illuminate and explain it
For the assembly of twelve hundred people like me,
And the others seeking Buddhahood.
When they hear this Dharma
They will bring forth great joy.

Then the Bhagavat spoke to Śāriputra, saying: "You have now persistently asked me three times. How could I possibly not explain it to you? Therefore listen carefully and pay close attention! I will now illuminate and explain it."

When he said this, five thousand monks, nuns, laymen, and laywomen in the assembly immediately got up from their seats, bowed to the Buddha, and left. What was the reason for this? Because the roots of error among this group had been deeply planted and they were arrogant, thinking they had attained what they had not attained and had realized what they had not realized. Because of such defects they did not stay. And the Bhagavat remained silent and did not stop them.

Then the Buddha addressed Śāriputra: "My assembly here is free of useless twigs and leaves; only the pure essence remains.

"O Śāriputra! Let the arrogant ones go! Listen carefully and I will explain it to you."

Then Śāriputra replied: "Indeed, O Bhagavat, I greatly desire to hear it."

Then the Buddha addressed Śāriputra: "Only very rarely do the Buddha Tathāgatas teach such a True Dharma as this, as rarely as the *uḍumbara* flower blooms.

"O Śāriputra! Trust and accept what the Buddha teaches! My words are never false.

"O Śāriputra! The real intention of all the Buddhas in adapting their explanations to what is appropriate is difficult to understand.

Why is this? Because I have expounded the teachings with innumerable skillful means and various kinds of explanations and illustrations. Yet this Dharma is beyond reason and discernment. Only the Buddhas can understand it. Why is this? Because the Buddha Bhagavats appear in this world for one great purpose alone. O Śāriputra! Now I will explain why I said that the Buddha Bhagavats appear in this world for only one great purpose.

"The Buddha Bhagavat appear in this world to cause sentient beings to aspire toward purity and the wisdom and insight of the Buddhas. They appear in this world to manifest the wisdom and insight of the Buddhas to sentient beings. They appear in this world to cause sentient beings to attain the wisdom and insight of a Buddha's enlightenment. They appear in this world in order to cause sentient beings to enter the path of the wisdom and insight of a Buddha.

"O Śāriputra! For this one great reason alone the Buddhas have appeared in this world."

The Buddha addressed Śāriputra, saying: "The Buddha Tathāgatas lead and inspire only bodhisattvas. All the acts of a Buddha 7b
are always for one purpose. The Buddhas manifest their wisdom and insight solely to inspire sentient beings to enlightenment.

"O Śāriputra! A Tathāgata teaches sentient beings the Dharma only through the single Buddha vehicle. There is no other, neither a second nor a third.

"O Śāriputra! The true nature of all the Buddhas of the ten directions is exactly like this.

"O Śāriputra! All the Buddhas of the past expounded the teachings for the sake of sentient beings, using incalculable and innumerable skillful means and various explanations and illustrations. These teachings were all for the sake of the single Buddha vehicle. All these sentient beings, hearing the Dharma from the Buddhas, finally attained omniscience.

"O Śāriputra! All the future Buddhas who will appear in the world will expound the teachings for the sake of sentient beings, using incalculable and innumerable skillful means and various explanations and illustrations. These teachings will all be for the single Buddha vehicle. All sentient beings who hear this Dharma from these Buddhas will ultimately attain omniscience.

"O Śāriputra! All the Buddha Bhagavats of the present, in immeasurable hundreds of thousands of myriads of *koṭi*s of Buddha worlds of the ten directions, teach the Dharma to sentient beings using incalculable and innumerable skillful means with various explanations and illustrations to benefit many of them and cause them to feel at peace. These Dharmas are all of the single Buddha vehicle. All the sentient beings who hear the Dharma from these Buddhas will ultimately attain omniscience.

"O Śāriputra! These Buddhas lead and inspire only bodhisattvas, because they want to teach sentient beings with the wisdom and insight of the Buddha, to enlighten sentient beings with the wisdom and insight of the Buddha, and to cause sentient beings to enter the path of the wisdom and insight of the Buddha.

"O Śāriputra! I too am now like this. Having understood the various desires and deep-rooted inclinations of sentient beings, I teach the Dharma according to their capacities through the power of skillful means, using various explanations and illustrations.

"O Śāriputra! I do this in order to cause them to attain the omniscience of the single Buddha vehicle.

"O Śāriputra! Since there is no second vehicle in the worlds of the ten directions, how could there be a third!

"O Śāriputra! The Buddhas appear in the troubled world of the five defilements, which are the defilement of the *kalpa*, the defilement through desire's confusion, the defilement of sentient beings, the defilement of views, and the defilement of lifespan. Therefore, O Śāriputra, in the period of the decadent *kalpa*, because sentient beings are filthy, greedy, jealous, and develop roots of error, all the Buddhas illuminate the three [vehicles] with the power of skillful means in order to teach the single Buddha vehicle.

"O Śāriputra! If any of my disciples declare that they are arhats or *pratyekabuddha*s, and do not listen or comprehend that all the

Buddha Tathāgatas teach only the bodhisattvas, they are not disciples of the Buddhas, nor are they arhats or *pratyekabuddhas*.

"Again, O Śāriputra! If there are any monks or nuns who would 7c
declare that they have attained arhatship, that they are bearing their last bodies and are destined for complete nirvana, and yet who have not sought highest, complete enlightenment, they should be considered arrogant people.

"Why is this? Because there is no case in which a monk who has actually achieved arhatship does not believe in this Dharma, except after the Buddha has entered *parinirvāṇa* and there is no Buddha present.

"What is the reason for this? Because after the *parinirvāṇa* of the Buddha it is hard to find people who preserve, recite, and understand the meaning of the sutras like this. But if they should meet other Buddhas they will immediately understand this teaching.

"O Śāriputra! You should wholeheartedly accept and preserve the words of the Buddha. The words of the Buddha Tathāgatas are never false. There are no other vehicles, only the single Buddha vehicle."

Thereupon the Bhagavat, wanting to elaborate the meaning of this further, uttered these verses:

In the fourfold assembly there were five thousand
Monks and nuns who were excessively proud,
Laymen who were arrogant,
And laywomen who were unaccepting.
They did not see their own defects,
Being faulty in self-discipline,
And clung to their shortcomings;
These of little wisdom have already left.
Through the virtuous dignity of the Buddha
The dregs of the assembly have departed.
Having little virtue,
These people were incapable of accepting this Dharma.
Free of useless twigs and leaves,

Only the pure essence of this assembly remains.
O Śāriputra, listen carefully!
All the Buddhas teach the Dharma
That they have attained
Through the immeasurable power of skillful means,
For the sake of sentient beings.
Completely knowing their intentions,
Their various ways of practice,
Their wishes and capacities,
And the good and bad karma
Of their previous lives,
The Buddha gladdens all sentient beings
With the power of words and skillful means,
Using examples and illustrations.
The Buddha teaches by means of sutras, verses,
Stories of his past deeds, and of past events,
Miraculous tales, explanatory tales,
Allegories, poems, and exegeses.
8a The Buddha teaches nirvana
To those with dull faculties,
Who are satisfied with lowly aspirations
And attached to birth and death,
Who have not practiced the profound path
In the presence of innumerable Buddhas
And are confused by suffering.
Having devised this skillful means
I enable them to enter the wisdom of the Buddhas.
But I have never said
That all of you would attain
The path of the Buddhas.
I have never said this
Because the occasion never arose.
Now is precisely the right time for me
To teach definitively the Mahayana.
I apply these nine kinds of teachings

According to the capacities of sentient beings.
I teach these sutras
Because they are the basis for entering the Mahayana.
I teach the Mahayana sutras
To those heirs of the Buddhas
Who are pure in mind, mild, and receptive,
Have keen faculties,
And who have practiced the profound path
Under immeasurable Buddhas.
I predict that such people
Will attain the path of the Buddhas
In their future lives,
Because they keep the Buddhas in mind
With profound thoughts
And practice pure conduct.
Hearing that they shall attain Buddhahood
They will be filled with great joy;
Because a Buddha knows their intentions
He teaches the Mahayana.
Those *śrāvaka*s or bodhisattvas,
Who have heard even a single verse
Of the Dharma that I have taught,
Will all become Buddhas.
There can be no doubt about it.
In the Buddha worlds of the ten directions
There is only the Dharma of the single vehicle.
Apart from the skillful means of the Buddhas,
There is neither a second nor a third [vehicle].
A Buddha merely uses provisional words
In order to lead sentient beings.
All the Buddhas appear in the world
To teach the wisdom of the Buddhas.
Only this one thing is real,
The other two are not true.
In the end,

A Buddha does not save sentient beings
Through an inferior vehicle.
The Buddhas themselves
Abide in the Mahayana;
The Dharma that they have attained,
Is adorned with meditation, wisdom, and power;
And through these they save the sentient beings.
I would be ungenerous
If I were to lead and inspire even a single person
Through an inferior vehicle,
Having attained the highest path,
The universal Dharma of the Mahayana.
This is simply not possible.
If anyone takes refuge in the Buddha,
The Tathāgata will not deceive him.
A Tathāgata has neither stinginess nor jealousy
And has detached himself
From the evils of the phenomenal world.
8b That is why the Buddhas of the ten directions
Are the only ones who have no fear.
Having a body adorned with the marks of a Buddha,
Emitting a ray of light that illuminates the worlds
And revered by immeasurable sentient beings,
I teach the signs of the true aspects
Of the phenomenal world.
O Śāriputra! You should now know
That originally I made a vow
To make all sentient beings my equal
Without any difference.
Now I have already fulfilled this vow
That I made in the past.
I will lead and inspire all sentient beings
And cause them to enter the path of the Buddhas.
If I met sentient beings
And taught them till the end the path of the Buddhas,

Those with little understanding
Would be confused and perplexed
And would not accept the teaching.
I know that these sentient beings
Have never cultivated the roots of good merit.
They are attached to the desires of the five senses,
Disordered by delusion and passion,
And have fallen into the three troubled states of being
Because of these desires.
They are wandering through
The six transmigratory states,
Tormented by every kind of suffering.
They are continually being born as tiny embryos
In one world after another.
These people of few qualities and little merit
Are afflicted by various sufferings.
They enter into the jungle of sixty-two false views
Such as "This exists" or "This does not exist."
They are so firmly and deeply attached to false teachings
That they cannot get rid of them.
They are arrogant, proud, deceitful, and dishonest.
They have heard neither the names
Nor the True Dharma of the Buddhas
For thousands of myriads of *koṭi*s of *kalpa*s.
Such people are difficult to save.
That is why, O Śāriputra, I devised the method of teaching
The way to extinguish all suffering through nirvana.
Even though I taught nirvana,
It is not the true extinction.
Every existing thing from the very beginning
Has always had the mark of quiescence.
The heirs of the Buddhas who practice this path
Will thereafter become Buddhas in the future.
With the power of skillful means
I have presented the teachings of the three vehicles.

Yet all of the Bhagavats
Teach the path of the single vehicle.
This great assembly
Should now rid itself of confusion.
8c The words of the Buddhas are not inconsistent.
There is only the single vehicle;
There is no other.
In the past innumerable *kalpa*s
There appeared immeasurable and incalculable Buddhas,
Hundreds of thousands of myriads of *koṭi*s in number,
Who have attained *parinirvāṇa*.
All the Bhagavats
Taught the characteristics of all *dharma*s
With the power of innumerable skillful means,
Using various examples and illustrations.
All these Bhagavats
Taught the Dharma of the single vehicle,
Led and inspired immeasurable sentient beings,
And enabled them to enter the path of the Buddhas.
Understanding the deepest desires of the entire world
Of the *deva*s, humans, and other beings,
The Great Sage Lord has illuminated
The highest meaning
With diverse skillful means.
All those sentient beings
Who encountered and heard the teaching
Of the Buddhas of the past,
And who accumulated various merits
Through acts of giving (*dāna*), integrity (*śīla*), perseverance (*kṣānti*),
Diligence (*vīrya*), meditation (*dhyāna*), and wisdom (*prajñā*) (i.e., the six perfections)
Have certainly attained the path of the Buddhas.
And after the *parinirvāṇa* of the Buddhas,
Those sentient beings with well-governed minds

Have certainly attained the path of the Buddhas.
After the Buddhas attained *parinirvāṇa*,
All those who paid homage to the relics,
Who made myriads of *koṭi*s of stupas
Extensively and beautifully adorned with gold, silver,
Crystal, mother of pearl, agate, ruby,
Lapis lazuli, and pearl;
Those who made rock stupas,
Stupas out of sandal, aloe, deodar, and other woods,
As well as brick, tile, mud, and other materials;
All those who made Buddha stupas
Out of piles of earth in desolate places;
And even children in play
Who made Buddha stupas out of heaps of sand—
All such people have certainly attained
The path of the Buddhas.
And all those who made images of the Buddhas
Carved with their extraordinary marks
Have certainly attained the path of the Buddhas.
All those who made Buddha images
Out of the seven treasures,
Decorated with brass, copper, pewter, lead,
Tin, iron, wood, mud, glue, lacquer, and cloth,
Have certainly attained the path of the Buddhas. 9a
All those who made or had others make Buddha images
Painted with the one hundred embellishing
Marks of merit,
Have certainly attained the path of the Buddhas.
This even includes children in play
Who have drawn a Buddha image
With a blade of grass or a twig,
Brush or fingernail.
Such people, having gradually accumulated merit
And perfected great compassion,
Have certainly attained the path of the Buddhas.

Leading and inspiring the bodhisattvas,
They save countless sentient beings.
All those who paid homage to stupas,
Sculpted or painted images,
Honoring them with flowers, perfumes,
Banners, and canopies;
Those who paid homage with all kinds of sweet music—
With drums, horns, conches, pipes, flutes, lutes, harps,
Mandolins, gongs, and cymbals;
Those who joyfully praised the qualities of the Buddhas
With various songs or
Even with a single low-pitched sound,
Have certainly attained the path of the Buddhas.
Those who, even with distracted minds
Have offered a single flower to a painted image
Will in time see innumerable Buddhas.
Or those who have done obeisance to images,
Or merely pressed their palms together,
Or raised a single hand, or nodded their heads,
Will in due time see immeasurable Buddhas.
They will attain the highest path
And extensively save innumerable sentient beings.
They will enter nirvana without residue
Just as a fire goes out after its wood is exhausted.
Those who, even with distracted minds,
Entered a stupa compound
And chanted but once, "Homage to the Buddha!"
Have certainly attained the path of the Buddhas.
Anyone who heard this teaching,
Either in the presence of a past Buddha
Or after their *parinirvāṇa*,
Has certainly attained the path of the Buddhas.
The future Bhagavats, Tathāgatas,
Immeasurable in number,
Will teach the Dharma with skillful means.

All the Tathāgatas 9b
Will save sentient beings
With immeasurable skillful means,
Causing them to enter the wisdom of the Buddhas
That is free from corruption.
Of those hearing this Dharma
There will be no one
Who will not become a Buddha.
The original vow of the Buddhas
Was to cause all sentient beings to universally
Attain the very same Buddha path
That I have practiced.
Even though the Buddhas of the future
Will teach hundreds of thousands of *koṭi*s
Of innumerable paths to the Dharma,
Their teachings will actually be
For the sake of the single vehicle.
All the Buddhas, the Best of Humans,
Know that all *dharma*s are ever without substance
And that the Buddha-seeds germinate
Through dependent origination.
That is why they will teach the single vehicle.
Having realized on the terrace of enlightenment
That the state of the Dharma
Is permanent and unchangeable in this world,
The Leaders will teach with skillful means.
The present Buddhas of the ten directions,
As numerous as the sands of the Ganges River,
Revered by *deva*s and humans,
Appear in the world and teach this Dharma
To make sentient beings feel at peace.
They know the utmost tranquility,
And although they teach various paths
With the power of skillful means,
Their teachings are actually for the Buddha vehicle.

Knowing the character of sentient beings—
Their deep intentions, past acts,
Wishes, persistence, and strength,
Their keen or dull faculties—
The Buddhas teach with skillful means
Using various explanations, illustrations, and words,
In accordance with the capacities of sentient beings.
Now I too reveal the path of the Buddhas
Through various paths to the Dharma
To make sentient beings feel at peace.
Through the power of my wisdom
I know the dispositions and desires of sentient beings,
And explain various teachings with skillful means,
Enabling them all to obtain joy.
O Śāriputra!
You should know that through the Buddha-eye
I see beings wandering in the six states of existence
Who are poor, deprived of merit and wisdom,
Who are entering into the bitter path of birth and death,
And are suffering repeatedly and without end.
They are deeply attached to the desires of the five senses,
Just as yaks are attached to their tails.
Obstructed by greed, they are blind and cannot see.
9c They do not seek the Buddha who has great power,
Nor the Dharma that cuts off suffering.
Deeply immersed in false views,
They try to eliminate suffering through suffering.
I feel great compassion
For such sentient beings.
Sitting on the terrace of enlightenment for the first time,
Looking at the *bodhi* tree
And walking about,
During those twenty-one days
I was thinking thus:

The wisdom I have attained
Is subtle and supreme.
But the faculties of sentient beings are dull.
They are attached to pleasures and blinded by delusion.
How can I save such beings?

Then Brahma and his *devaputra*s, Śakra,
The world-protectors of the four quarters,
Maheśvara and the other *deva*s,
Together with a retinue of hundreds
Of thousands of myriads of attendants,
Paid their respects with palms pressed together
And begged me to turn the wheel of the Dharma.
Then I thought:

If I only praise the Buddha vehicles,
Those beings who are submerged in suffering
Will not believe this Dharma.
Because they reject and do not believe the Dharma,
They will fall into the three troubled states of being.
I would rather not teach the Dharma
And instead immediately enter nirvana.

Then I thought of the power of skillful means
Practiced by past Buddhas.
This path that I have attained
Should now also be taught as the three vehicles.
When I thought this,
The Buddhas of the ten directions appeared
And with beautiful voices praised me saying:

O Śākyamuni! Splendid!
O Supreme Leader,
You have attained the highest Dharma,
And yet still use the power of skillful means,
Following all the other Buddhas.

We too have attained the best and utmost Dharma
And with discretion have explained the three vehicles
For the sake of sentient beings.
Those with little wisdom
Seek inferior teachings
And do not believe that they will become Buddhas.
That is why we use skillful means
And with discretion teach of various results.
Although we teach the three vehicles
It is just for the instruction of the bodhisattvas!

O Śāriputra!
You should know
That when I heard this profound
And beautiful roar of the Noble Lions,
I chanted with joy, "Homage to the Buddhas!"
10a And I thought:

Since I have been born in this defiled world
I will follow the other Buddhas
And expound what they have expounded.

After contemplating this
I set out for Vārāṇasī.
All *dharma*s have the tranquil character
Of the Dharma:
This could not be expressed in words,
So I taught the five monks
Through the power of skillful means.
This I named: "Turning the Wheel of the Dharma,"
And immediately the word nirvana appeared in it
And the different designations for Arhat (Buddha),
Dharma, and Sangha.
From a great many *kalpa*s ago
I have always taught like this:
I have praised and illuminated
The teaching of nirvana,

Saying that it ends the sufferings
Of birth and death.
O Śāriputra!
You should know that I see
Immeasurable thousands of myriads of *koṭi*s
Of the Buddha's heirs,
Who, having set out for the Buddha path,
And heard the Dharma explained with skillful means,
Have respectfully come before the Buddha.
Then I thought:

> The reason why the Tathāgatas appear is
> To explain the wisdom of the Buddhas.
> Now is precisely the right time for this!

O Śāriputra!
You should know that
Those who have dull faculties and little wisdom,
And those who are attached to mere signs and
Are arrogant cannot accept this teaching.
Now I am happy and fearless.
Having openly set aside skillful means,
I will teach only the highest path
To all the bodhisattvas.
Having heard this teaching
The bodhisattvas and twelve hundred arhats,
Freeing themselves from the web of doubt,
Will all become Buddhas.
Just as the Buddhas in the three periods
Of the past, present, and future,
Teach the true nature of the Dharma,
Now I too will expound the Dharma
That is beyond conception.
All the Buddhas
Appear in worlds far away
And are difficult to meet.

Even if they appear in this world
It is difficult to hear their teaching.
Even in immeasurable, innumerable *kalpa*s
It is difficult to hear this Dharma,
And those who are able to hear this Dharma
Are also hard to find.
They are just like the *uḍumbara* flower
Which appears only once in a very long while
And, beloved by all,
Is considered a wonder among *deva*s and humans.
10b Those who, hearing this teaching,
Happily praise the Buddhas
By uttering even a single word
Have already paid homage to all Buddhas
Of the three periods.
Such people are even more extraordinary
Than the *uḍumbara* flower.
All of you, have no doubts!
I, the King of the Dharma,
Now proclaim to the great assembly:

> I lead and inspire the bodhisattvas
> Only with the path of the single vehicle;
> I am here without disciples.

O Śāriputra and all of you!
The *śrāvaka*s and bodhisattvas should know
That this True Dharma is the hidden essence
Of all the Buddhas.
In the troubled worlds of the five kinds of defilement,
Sentient beings are only attached to various desires,
And ultimately do not seek the path of the Buddhas.
In the future the impure will hear
The Buddha teach the single vehicle,
But they will be confused and will not accept it.
They will reject the Dharma

And fall into the troubled states of being.
To those who are modest and pure,
And seek the path of the Buddhas,
I will praise extensively
The path of the single vehicle.
O Śāriputra!
You should know that the Dharma
Of all the Buddhas is like this.
They teach the Dharma
With myriads of *koṭis* of skillful means,
According to the capacities of sentient beings;
The inexperienced cannot understand this.
You have come to know with certainty the skillful means
Of the Buddhas, the Teachers of the World,
That are expounded in accordance
With people's capacities.
All of you, have no further doubts!
Let great joy arise in your hearts
And know that you will all become Buddhas!

Chapter III

A Parable

Thereupon Śāriputra stood up ecstatic and joyful, pressed his palms together and, gazing at the Buddha, the Bhagavat, said: "Now, hearing the words of this Dharma from the Bhagavat, my heart 10c
is full of joy for I have experienced something unprecedented. What is the reason for this? In the past when I heard this Dharma from the Buddha and saw the bodhisattvas receive their predictions, I was not included. I grieved because I thought I had been deprived of the immeasurable wisdom and insight of the Tathāgata.

"O Bhagavat! While I was dwelling alone under forest trees, whether sitting or walking, I was constantly thinking this: 'Since we have also realized the true nature of the Dharma, why has the Tathāgata tried to save us with the teachings of the inferior vehicle?'

"The fault is ours, not the Bhagavat's. Why is this? If we had waited for your explanation about the way to achieve highest, complete enlightenment, we certainly would have been able to save ourselves by means of the Mahayana. However, we did not understand that you were teaching with skillful means, according to what is appropriate to us. When we first heard the Buddha's teaching, we immediately accepted, contemplated, and understood it.

"O Bhagavat! Since long ago I have reproached myself incessantly day and night. But now from the Buddha we have heard the unprecedented Dharma that we have never heard before, and it has removed all our doubts.

"I have obtained peace and tranquility in body and mind. Today I have finally realized that I am truly the heir of the Buddha, born from the mouth of the Buddha, incarnated from the Dharma, and that I have inherited a part of the Buddha-Dharma."

Then Śāriputra, wanting to elaborate this meaning, spoke again in verse:

When I heard the words of this Dharma,
Experiencing something unprecedented,
My heart overflowed with joy,
And I was rid of all my doubts.
From long ago, ever since I heard
The teaching of the Buddha,
I have not lost the Mahayana.
The words of the Buddhas are extremely rare
And are capable of ridding sentient beings
Of their suffering.
Although I had already attained
Freedom from corruption,
By hearing the Buddha's voice,
I have also been rid of my anxiety.
Whether I was dwelling
In mountain valleys or under forest trees,
Whether I was sitting or walking,
Grieving and blaming myself deeply,
I thought incessantly:

How have I deceived myself!

I am also the heir of the Buddhas,
Having entered the same incorruptible Dharma.
Nevertheless, in the future,
I shall not be able to explain the highest path.
The golden color, the thirty-two marks,
The ten powers, and the liberations
Are all in the same Dharma;
And yet I have not attained any of these.
Moreover, such qualities as
The eighty excellent and eighteen special characteristics
Are completely lost to me.
11a When I was wandering alone,
I saw the Buddha in the great assembly
Filling the ten directions with his fame

And greatly benefiting sentient beings.
I then thought:

> I have lost all these benefits
> Because I have been deceiving myself.

I thought about this constantly day and night
And wanted to ask the Bhagavat:

> Have I or have I not lost these?

I always saw the Bhagavat
Praising the bodhisattvas.
That is why I pondered over such matters
As these both day and night.
Now I have heard the words of the Buddha,
Explaining to sentient beings
The incorruptible Dharma,
Which is difficult to comprehend,
And making them enter
The terrace of enlightenment.
Formerly, I was attached to false views
And was a teacher of brahmans.
The Bhagavat, knowing my mind,
Removed the false views and taught nirvana.
I got rid of false views completely
And attained the teaching of emptiness.
At that time I considered myself
To have attained nirvana.
But now I have become aware
That this was not the real nirvana.
When I become a Buddha
I shall be endowed with the thirty-two marks,
And be honored by *devas*, humans, *yakṣas*, and *nāgas*.
Only then can it be said that I have
Permanently attained nirvana without residue.
Before the great assembly

The Buddha has proclaimed
That I will become a Buddha.
After hearing these words of the Dharma,
I was immediately rid of all my doubts.
When I first heard this teaching of the Buddha's,
I was greatly startled and thought:

> I wonder if Māra, acting like the Buddha,
> Is confusing me!

But the Buddha, who teaches skillfully
By means of various explanations and illustrations,
Has made my mind tranquil like the ocean.
While listening to him
I was freed from the web of my doubts.
The Buddha has said that immeasurable Buddhas
Who have attained *parinirvāṇa* in the past,
Established in the use of skillful means,
Have also taught this Dharma.
Immeasurable Buddhas in the present and future
Will also teach this Dharma
With various skillful means.
The present Bhagavat,
From the time he was born
And renounced household life
Until he obtained the path
And turned the wheel of the Dharma,
Has also taught through skillful means.
11b The Bhagavat teaches the real path,
But the Wicked One does not.
Therefore I know definitely
That it was not Māra acting like the Buddha.
Because I fell into a web of doubt,
I thought that Māra was impersonating the Buddha.
When I heard the voice of the Buddha,
Profound and very subtle,

Fluently explaining the pure Dharma,
I became full of great joy.
My doubts are completely and forever exhausted,
And I have achieved the true wisdom.
I will definitely become a Buddha,
Honored by *deva*s and humans.
I will turn the wheel of the highest Dharma
And lead and inspire the bodhisattvas.

At that time the Buddha said to Śāriputra: "I will now reveal to you before the great assembly of *deva*s, humans, *śrāmaṇa*s, and brahmans that in the past, in the presence of two hundred thousand *koṭi*s of Buddhas, I led and inspired you constantly for the sake of the highest path. You have followed my instructions for a long time. Because I led you with skillful means, you were born in my Dharma.

"O Śāriputra! In the past I inspired you to seek the Buddha path. Yet just now you had completely forgotten this and considered yourself to have attained nirvana. Now, because I want you to remember the path that you practiced according to your original vow in the past, I will teach the *śrāvaka*s the Mahayana sutra called the *Lotus Sutra,* the instruction for the bodhisattvas and treasured lore of the Buddhas.'

"O Śāriputra! In the future after immeasurable, limitless, and inconceivable *kalpa*s, you will have paid homage to thousands of myriads of *koṭi*s of Buddhas, preserved the True Dharma, and mastered the path practiced by the bodhisattvas. You will become a Buddha called Padmaprabha, a Tathāgata, Arhat, Completely Enlightened, Perfect in Knowledge and Conduct, Well-Departed, Knower of the World, Unsurpassed, Tamer of Humans, Teacher of Devas and Humans, Buddha, Bhagavat.

"Your land will be called Viraja. Its earth will be level and pure, ornamented, peaceful, and rich. The *deva*s and humans will prosper. The earth will be made of lapis lazuli with a well-planned network of roads like a chessboard bordered with golden cords.

Rows of seven-jeweled trees, which are always full of flowers and fruits, will line the borders of these roads. The Tathāgata Padmaprabha will also lead and inspire sentient beings by means of the three vehicles.

"O Śāriputra! When that Buddha appears, even though his will not be a troubled world, he will teach the three vehicles because of his original vow. This *kalpa* will be called Mahāratnapratimaṇḍita, meaning 'Adorned with Great Jewels.' Why will it be called Mahāratnapratimaṇḍita? Because in that world the bodhisattvas will be like great jewels. The number of these bodhisattvas will be immeasurable, limitless, inconceivable, and beyond all comparison, known only by those with the power of the Buddha's wisdom.

"When they want to walk they will step on jeweled flowers.
11c And these bodhisattvas will not be those who are just setting out. Over a long time they will have planted roots of good merit and practiced the pure path of discipline and integrity in the presence of immeasurable hundreds of thousands of myriads of *koṭi*s of Buddhas. They will always be praised by the Buddhas and continually practice the Buddha wisdom. They will be endowed with transcendent powers and know well all the teachings of the Dharma. They will be honest, without falsity, and firm in recollection. That world will be filled with bodhisattvas like these.

"O Śāriputra! The lifespan of this Buddha Padmaprabha will be twelve intermediate *kalpa*s, not including the period after he becomes a prince and before he becomes a Buddha; and the lifespan of the people in that world will be eight intermediate *kalpa*s.

"After these twelve intermediate *kalpa*s have passed, the Tathāgata Padmaprabha will predict Bodhisattva Dhṛtiparipūrṇa's attainment of highest, complete enlightenment and will address the monks, saying:

> This Bodhisattva Dhṛtiparipūrṇa will become the next Buddha after me. His name will be Padmavṛṣabhavikrama, a Tathāgata, Arhat, Completely Enlightened. His Buddha world will also be like this one.

"O Śāriputra! After the *parinirvāṇa* of the Buddha Padmaprabha the True Dharma will remain in the world for thirty-two intermediate *kalpa*s and the Semblance Dharma will also remain in the world for thirty-two intermediate *kalpa*s."

Then the Bhagavat, wanting to elaborate on the meaning of this again, spoke these verses:

O Śāriputra! In the future
You will become a Buddha of universal wisdom
Named Padmaprabha,
Who will save innumerable sentient beings.
Having paid homage to innumerable Buddhas,
Perfected the bodhisattva practice,
And the qualities, including the ten powers,
You will attain the highest path.
After immeasurable *kalpa*s have passed,
The *kalpa* will be called Prabhūtaratna,
And the world will be called Viraja,
Pure and without dirt.
The earth will be made of lapis lazuli
And the roads, bordered with golden cords,
Will be lined with variegated trees of the seven treasures
Which are always full of flowers and fruits.
The bodhisattvas in that world
Will be always firm in recollection.
All of them will be completely endowed
With transcendent powers and the perfections
And will have properly practiced the bodhisattva path
In the presence of innumerable Buddhas.
Such *mahasattva*s as these
Will be led and inspired by the Buddha Padmaprabha.
When this Buddha becomes a prince
He will abdicate his kingship
And give up his worldly fame.
Bearing his last body,

He will renounce household life
And attain the path of the Buddha.
This Buddha Padmaprabha will live in the world
For twelve intermediate *kalpa*s.
And the lifespan of the people in this world
Will be eight intermediate *kalpa*s.
After the *parinirvāṇa* of this Buddha,
The True Dharma will last in the world
12a For thirty-two intermediate *kalpa*s,
During which time many sentient beings
Will be saved.
After the extinction of the True Dharma,
The Semblance Dharma will last
For thirty-two intermediate *kalpa*s.
The relics of the Buddha
Will be distributed widely
And *deva*s and humans will pay them homage.
All that the Buddha Padmaprabha does
Will be exactly like this.
That very Best of Humans,
Who will be foremost and without comparison,
Is none other than you.
You should be delighted to hear this!

At that time the fourfold assembly of monks, nuns, laymen, and laywomen and the great assembly of *deva*s, *nāga*s, *yakṣa*s, *gandharva*s, *asura*s, *garuḍa*s, *kiṃnara*s, and *mahoraga*s saw Śāriputra receive his prediction of highest, complete enlightenment in the presence of the Buddha. They rejoiced greatly and became immeasurably happy. All of them removed their outer garments and proffered them to the Buddha as offerings.

Śakra, the lord of *deva*s, and Brahma, together with innumerable *devaputra*s also made offerings to the Buddha of their heavenly beautiful garments, heavenly *māndārava* flowers, and great *māndārava* flowers. Their heavenly garments floated and fluttered in the air, while in the sky the *devas* played hundreds of thousands of myriads of kinds of music together at one time. They rained down various heavenly flowers and said: "In the past the Buddha turned the wheel of the Dharma for the first time in Vārāṇasī. Now he has turned the wheel of the utmost and greatest Dharma again."

Thereupon the *devaputras* spoke these verses in order to explain this again:

> In the past you turned the wheel of the Dharma
> Of the Four [Noble] Truths in Vārāṇasī;
> And you illuminated and explained the Dharma
> Of the origination and extinction of the five aggregates.
> You have now again turned the wheel
> Of the subtlest, utmost, and greatest Dharma.
> This Dharma is extremely profound;
> Only a few will be able to believe it.
> Since long ago we have frequently heard
> The teaching of the Bhagavat,
> Yet we have never before heard
> Such a profound and supreme teaching.
> When the Bhagavat taught this Dharma
> We were all delighted.
> And now Śāriputra, possessed of great wisdom,
> Has received his prediction from the Bhagavat.
> In the same way, we too,
> Shall certainly become Buddhas.
> We shall become peerless,
> Unrivaled in all the world.
> The path of the Buddha,
> Which is difficult to understand,
> Is taught with skillful means
> According to what is appropriate for sentient beings.
> May the merits of our beneficial acts,
> Whether of the past or the present,

12b And those acquired in meeting the Buddha,
Be completely transferred to the Buddha path.

At that time Śāriputra said this to the Buddha: "O Bhagavat! I now have no further doubts. I have received the prediction of the highest supreme enlightenment in the presence of the Buddha.

"When all those twelve hundred who have attained complete mental discipline were still under training in the past, the Buddha constantly led and inspired them, saying: 'My teaching overcomes birth, old age, illness, and death and it leads to nirvana.' Both those who were still in training and those who were not thought that they were free from false views about the self, existence and nonexistence, and declared that they had attained nirvana. Yet now, in the presence of the Bhagavat, they have heard what they have never heard before and have fallen into doubt.

"Splendid, O Bhagavat! I entreat you to explain to the fourfold assembly the reason why, and free them from their doubts!"

Then the Buddha said to Śāriputra: "Did I not previously tell you that all the Buddha Bhagavats explain the Dharma with various explanations and illustrations using skillful means, all for the sake of highest, complete enlightenment!? All of these teachings are for leading and inspiring the bodhisattvas.

"Moreover, Śāriputra, I will now clarify what I mean with illustrations. Those with wisdom will be able to understand through these illustrations.

"O Śāriputra! Suppose there were an aged and extremely affluent man, either in a town, city, or country, who has immeasurable wealth, abundant estates, mansions, and servants. He has a spacious house, yet it only has a single entrance. Suppose many people live there, as many as one, two, or even five hundred people. The buildings are in poor repair, the fences and walls are crumbling, the pillar bases are rotten, and the beams and framework are dangerously tilted.

"Suddenly and unexpectedly, fires break out everywhere, setting the house swiftly aflame. The children of this man, ten, twenty, or thirty in number are in the house.

"The affluent man, seeing the fire breaking out everywhere, becomes alarmed and terrified. He thinks:

> I am capable of escaping through the burning entrance in safety, but my children are absorbed in play within the burning house and are not aware [of the fire], do not know, are not alarmed or terrified, and the fire is approaching them! They are not troubled about their suffering nor do they intend to leave the house.

"O Śāriputra, this affluent man thought:

> Since I am still physically strong I could take the children out of the house in the folds of my garment or on top of a desk.

"He further thought:

> There is only one entrance to this house and it is very narrow. The children, who are immature and still unaware, are attached to their place of play. They may fall into danger and be burned by the fire. I should now tell them of the danger; this house is already burning! They must escape as quickly as they can to avoid being burned by the fire!

"After considering this he urged the children according to his thought:

> Children! Run out immediately!

"Although their father in his concern has given them the proper 12c
advice, the children are immersed in their play and do not accept it; they are neither alarmed nor afraid and have no intention of leaving [the burning house]. Moreover, they do not even know what a fire is, the condition of the house, or what they may lose. They merely run about, back and forth, looking at their father.

"Thereupon the affluent man thought:

> This house is already engulfed in flames. If my children and I do not get out, we shall perish in the fire. I will now use skillful means to help my children escape from this disaster.

"Since the father already knew that his children were attached to various rare toys and unusual things that each of them liked, he said to them:

> The toys you are fond of are rare and hard to obtain. If you do not take them you will certainly regret it later. Right now, outside the house, there are three kinds of carts. One is yoked to a sheep, one to a deer, and one to an ox. Go play with them. Children! Run out of this burning house immediately and I will give you whatever you want!

"The children, hearing what their father had said about the rare toys, became excited and, in their eagerness to get to them they pushed each other out of the way in a mad rush out of the burning house.

"Then the affluent man saw that his children had got out safely and were sitting unharmed in an open area at a crossroad. He was relieved, happy, and joyful. The children said to their father:

> Father, please give us the toys you promised: those [three] carts, one yoked to a sheep, one to a deer, and one to an ox!

"O Śāriputra, the affluent man then gave each child the same kind of large cart. These carts were tall and spacious, adorned with various jewels, and encircled with railings full of hanging bells. On the tops of the carts were canopies also decorated with various kinds of jewels. These carts were draped with jeweled cords and hung with flower garlands. They were thickly piled with fabrics, and red pillows had been placed about. These carts were each yoked to an ox with a spotlessly white hide. These oxen had beautiful bodies with powerful muscles, even gaits, and were as swift as the wind; and there were many attendants guarding them. Why did the affluent man give these carts? Because the man had great and immeasurable wealth and his abundant storehouses were full. He thus thought further:

> Since my treasure has no limit, I should not give my children inferior carts. These are my children and I love them all

> equally. I have an immeasurable number of large carts such as these, decorated with the seven treasures. I should equally distribute them to each child without discrimination. Why is this? Even if I gave carts like these to everyone in the country, their number would not be exhausted. Why should I not give them to my own children?

"At that time, the children each climbed into a great cart and had an unprecedented experience, one beyond their original expectations. 13a

"O Śāriputra! What do you think about this? This affluent man gave to his children equally a large cart decorated with precious treasures. Has he deceived them or not?"

Śāriputra replied: "No Bhagavat! The affluent man only tried to help his children escape from the disastrous fire. He saved their lives and did not deceive them. This is by no means a deception. Why? Because by saving their lives they obtained marvelous toys. Moreover, they were saved from the burning house by skillful means.

"O Bhagavat! If this affluent man had not given them even the smallest cart, it still would not have been a deception. Why is this? Because this affluent man thought before:

> I will help my children escape with skillful means.

"This is why it was not a deception. How much more so, since the affluent man, knowing that he had immeasurable wealth and wanting to benefit them equally, gave each of his children a large [ox]cart."

The Buddha said to Śāriputra: "Splendid, splendid! It is exactly as you have said. O Śāriputra, the Tathāgata is also just like this. That is to say, as the father of the entire world, he permanently dispels fear, distress, anxiety, ignorance, and blindness. He has attained immeasurable wisdom, insight, power, and fearlessness, as well as great transcendent powers and the power of wisdom. He has attained the perfection of skillful means and of wisdom. With his great mercy and compassion he incessantly and indefatigably seeks the welfare of all beings and benefits them all.

"The Tathāgata appears in the triple world, which is like a decaying old house on fire, to rescue sentient beings from the fire of birth, old age, illness, and death, anxiety, sorrow, suffering, distress, delusion, blindness, and the three poisons of greed, hatred, and ignorance. Thus he leads and inspires sentient beings and causes them to attain highest, complete enlightenment.

"The Tathāgatas see all sentient beings burning in the fire of birth, old age, illness, and death, anxiety, sorrow, suffering, and distress. Because of the desires of the five senses and the desire for monetary profit they also experience various kinds of suffering. Because of their attachment and pursuits they experience various kinds of suffering in the present; and in the future they will suffer in the states of existence of hell, animals, and hungry ghosts (*pretas*). If they are born in the heavens or in the human world they will experience a variety of sorrows such as suffering from poverty and destitution, separation from loved ones, or suffering from encounters with those they dislike.

"Although sentient beings are immersed in such sorrows, they rejoice and play. They are not aware, shocked, startled, or disgusted nor do they seek release. Running around in the burning house of the triple world, they experience great suffering and yet they do not realize it.

"O Śāriputra! Seeing these things the Buddha thought:

> Since I am the father of sentient beings I must rid them of their immeasurable suffering and distress. I will cause them to rejoice through the immeasurable and limitless pleasure of the Buddha wisdom.

"O Śāriputra! The Tathāgata further thought:

> If I proclaim the Tathāgata's wisdom, insight, power, and
> 13b fearlessness to sentient beings with my transcendent powers and the power of my wisdom alone, without using skillful means, it will be impossible to save them. Why is this? Because these sentient beings have not escaped from birth, old age,

illness, and death; anxiety, sorrow, suffering, and distress; and are being burned in the blazing house of the triple world. How would they be able to understand the Buddha's wisdom?

"O Śāriputra! Although that affluent man had physical strength he did not use it. He only earnestly employed skillful means to save his children from the disaster of the burning house, and later he gave each of them a large cart decorated with precious treasures. The Tathāgata is exactly like this.

"Although the Tathāgata has power and fearlessness he does not use them, but rescues sentient beings from the burning house of the triple world only through wisdom and skillful means, teaching the three vehicles to the *śrāvaka*s, *pratyekabuddha*s, and the Buddhas, saying:

> Do not take pleasure in living in this burning house of the triple world. And do not thirst after inferior objects, sounds, smells, flavors, and tangibles. If you are attached to these objects and have desires, then you will be burned. Leave the triple world in haste and you will obtain the three vehicles—the vehicles for the *śrāvaka*s, *pratyekabuddha*s, and Buddhas. I definitely guarantee this to you. In the end it will come true. You should be diligent and persistent!

"The Tathāgata attracts sentient beings through this skillful means, saying further:

> You should know that the Noble Ones praise the teachings of these three vehicles that are self-directed, unrestricted, and independent. When they ride in them, sentient beings will enjoy faculties free from corruption and also powers, paths to enlightenment, meditation, liberation, and concentration. And they themselves will attain immeasurable ease and pleasure.

"O Śāriputra! Those beings, wise by nature, who accept the Dharma from the Buddha Bhagavat, who are diligent, persistent, and wish to escape from the triple world quickly, and who are seeking nirvana, are all practicing the *śrāvaka* vehicle. They are like those children who left the burning house seeking the cart yoked to a sheep.

"Those beings who accept the Dharma of the Buddha Bhagavat, who are diligent and persevere in seeking the wisdom of the Self-generated One and enjoy tranquility for themselves, who profoundly know the causes of and reasons for existence, are all practicing the *pratyekabuddha* vehicle. They are just like those children who left the burning house seeking the cart yoked to a deer.

"Those beings who accept the Dharma of the Buddha Bhagavat, who are diligent and persevere in seeking the wisdom of the Omniscient One, the wisdom of the Buddha, the wisdom of the Self-generated One, the wisdom acquired without a teacher, the wisdom and insight, powers, and fearlessness of the Tathāgata; who are compassionate, put immeasurable sentient beings at ease, benefit *deva*s and humans, and save all beings, are all practicing the Mahayana. Bodhisattvas are called *mahāsattva*s (great beings) because they seek this vehicle. They are just like those children who left the burning house seeking the cart yoked to an ox.

13c "O Śāriputra! That affluent man saw his children leave the burning house safely and arrive at a safe place. Knowing that he had immeasurable wealth, he gave a large cart equally to each child. The Tathāgata is exactly like this. As the father of all sentient beings he sees that immeasurable thousands of *koṭi*s of sentient beings escape from the dangers, sufferings, and fears of the triple world through the gates of the Buddha's teaching and attain the pleasure of nirvana.

"Then the Tathāgata thought:

> Because I possess the treasure house of the Dharma of all the Buddhas, which contains immeasurable limitless wisdom, power, and fearlessness, and because all sentient beings are my children, I will give them equally the Mahayana. I will not allow anyone to attain nirvana merely for himself but will cause everyone to attain it through the Tathāgata's nirvana.

I will give sentient beings who have escaped from the triple world all the toys of the Buddha's meditations and liberations, which are of one character and one kind, are praised by the Noble Ones, and which produce pure and supreme pleasure.

"O Śāriputra! At first that affluent man attracted his children with three kinds of carts, then later gave them only the safest and best large [ox]cart, adorned with jewels. Moreover, that affluent man was never accused of telling a lie. The Tathāgata is exactly like this. He tells no lies.

"In the beginning the Tathāgata teaches the three vehicles in order to lead sentient beings. And later he saves them through only the Mahayana. Why is this? Because the Tathāgata possesses the treasure house of the Dharma, which contains immeasurable wisdom, power, and fearlessness. And although he is able to give the teaching of the Mahayana to all sentient beings, not all of them can accept it.

"O Śāriputra! You should know that the Buddhas, with the power of skillful means, teach the single Buddha vehicle, dividing and teaching it as three."

Then the Buddha, wanting to elaborate on the meaning of this again, spoke these verses:

Suppose there were an affluent man
Who had a large house,
And this house was very old,
On the verge of collapsing.
The halls were extremely dangerous,
The pillar bases rotten and disintegrating,
The beams and framework dangerously tilted,
And the stairways were falling apart.
The fences and walls were cracked,
The plaster was peeling off,
The thatched roof was falling down,
The rafters and eaves were coming apart,

The partitions were everywhere askew,
And the whole place was covered with filth.
Five hundred people lived there,
And moving around helter-skelter were
Kites, owls, hawks, eagles, crows, magpies,
Doves, pigeons, lizards, snakes, vipers,
Scorpions, centipedes, millipedes,
Newts, myriapods, ferrets, badgers, mice,
Rats, and other harmful creatures.
It was filled with stench,
And there were places overflowing with excrement.
All kinds of bugs
Had gathered there.
There were foxes, wolves, and vermin
Devouring, trampling, and gnawing on corpses,
Scattering bones and flesh about;
And a pack of dogs,
14a Forcing each other out of the way,
Rushed to the spot—
Frightened and exhausted from hunger,
They were searching everywhere for food,
Fighting among themselves, snatching at food,
Biting, snarling, and barking at each other.
This house was terrifying,
Corrupted to this grotesque condition:
Ogres of the mountains and valleys,
*Yakṣa*s, and demons were everywhere
Devouring human flesh.
There were various poisonous insects,
All kinds of harmful birds of prey,
And beasts who were producing, rearing,
And protecting their offspring.
*Yakṣa*s were scrabbling and fighting to devour them.
And after sating themselves,
Evil thoughts would arise in them.

The sound of their fighting
Was terrifying.
The *kumbhāṇḍa* demons were crouching on the ground,
Sometimes rising up a foot or two.
Roaming about, pleasing themselves as they liked,
They would catch two legs of a dog,
Beat it until it could not bark
And grabbing the dog's neck with their legs,
Terrify it for their own amusement.
There were also other demons living there
With large bodies, naked, dark, and gaunt.
They were screaming horrifying howls,
Crying out while searching for food.
Other demons were there,
Some with needlelike throats,
While others had necks
Like a cow's head;
Some had those of human flesh-eaters or dog-devourers.
Their hair was disheveled like rank weeds
And they were destructive and malicious.
Driven by hunger and thirst,
They were crying and scurrying about.
*Yakṣa*s, hungry ghosts,
And various malicious birds and beasts
Were peering out of the windows
And running frantically in all directions,
Driven by hunger.
In this house, with its immeasurable terrors,
There were many such horrendous things as these.
Now suppose this old and decaying house
Belonged to a man,
And this man came out from it a short distance.
Soon after, the house suddenly
Burst into flames behind him.
The fire instantly spread in all directions.

The frame, beams, rafters, and pillars exploded,
And shaking, split and crashed,
While the fences and walls collapsed.
All the demons screamed out loudly.
The hawks, eagles, other birds,
And *kumbhāṇḍa* demons, panicked and terrified,
Could not get out.
Malicious beasts and poisonous insects
Concealed themselves in holes.
There were also *piśāca* demons dwelling there
Who, because of little merit,
Were chased by the flames.
They were tearing at each other,
Drinking blood and eating flesh.
A horde of vermin had already died off,
And the large malicious beasts
Raced to devour them,
While the smoke of the stench flowed
And filled everywhere.
As the centipedes, millipedes,
And poisonous snakes rushed,
14b Burning, out of their holes
The *kumbhāṇḍa* demons devoured them
One after another.
The hungry ghosts, with their hair on fire,
Ravenous, thirsty, and suffering from the heat,
Frantically scurried about.
In this way, the house was extremely terrifying
With poison and fire,
And disasters more than one.
Then the householder, who was standing
Outside the entrance of the house,
Heard someone say:

> Just a moment ago,
> In the midst of their play,

Your children entered this house.
Being young and ignorant,
They are attached to playing games.

Hearing this, the affluent man was startled
And went into the burning house
To save them from the disaster of the fire.
As he thought fit, he warned the children
And explained the various dangers:

There are malicious demons, poisonous insects,
And the fire is raging everywhere.
There are endless horrors,
One right after another.
There are poisonous snakes, lizards, vipers,
Yakṣas, *kumbhāṇḍa* demons, vermin,
Foxes, dogs, hawks, eagles, kites,
Owls, and centipedes, all acutely suffering
From hunger and thirst
And all extremely terrifying.
These horrors are difficult to deal with,
How much more so the conflagration!

But the children, being ignorant,
Would not listen to their father's warning.
Still attached to their games,
They kept right on playing.
Thereupon the affluent man thought:

My children by doing this
Increase my distress!
There is nothing to enjoy now in this house.
Nevertheless, my children who are absorbed in play
Will not accept my instructions
And so will be hurt by the fire.

Then he immediately thought

That he should advise his children
Using various skillful means, and said:

> I have a variety of unusual toys
> Such as fine carts adorned with beautiful treasures,
> Yoked to sheep, deer, and oxen.
> They are just outside the gate.
> O children! Come out of the house!
> I had these carts made for you.
> Play with them as you like!

Hearing about these carts,
The children immediately started
To push each other out of the way
To get out of the house.
Arriving at an open area,
They escaped from the disaster.
The affluent man, seeing that his children
Had escaped from the burning house
And were standing at the crossroads,
Sat down on his lion seat.
Then he joyously said:

> Now I am happy!
> It is extremely difficult to raise these children.
> Foolish and ignorant,
> They entered a dangerous house
> Full of various poisonous insects,
> Terrifying ogres from mountains and valleys,
> And a raging fire that broke out in all directions.
> 14c In spite of this,
> These children were attached to playing their games.
> But by causing them to escape from the disaster,
> I have saved them.
> Therefore, my people, I now feel at ease.

Thereupon the children,

Seeing their father sitting in peace,
Approached him saying:

> Please, father,
> Give us the three kinds of carts
> Adorned with treasures
> That you just promised us,
> When you said that if we, your children, came out
> You would give us three kinds of carts
> Just as we like.
> Now is the right time.
> Give them to us right away!

This affluent man,
Who was extremely wealthy,
Had an abundance of treasures.
He had a number of great carts made,
Adorned with various precious things
Like gold, silver, lapis lazuli,
Mother-of-pearl, and agate.
They were beautifully decorated,
Encircled with railings,
And were covered with hanging bells
Attached to golden cords.
Over them was hung a net of pearls
With golden flower tassels
Hanging down everywhere.
They were all completely
Decorated in a variety of colors.
The bedding was made of soft silk
That was covered with
An extremely fine carpet of spotless white
Which cost thousands of *koṭi*s.
There were large white oxen,
Healthy and powerful with beautiful bodies,
Yoked to the jeweled carts,

And they were guarded by many attendants.
When they were given these fine carts,
The children were joyful and excited.
They got on the carts
And drove delightedly all about.
Amusing themselves in play,
They mastered them without difficulties.

The Buddha said to Śāriputra:

I am also like this.
I am the father of the world,
The best of the sages.
All sentient beings are my children.
They are deeply attached to worldly pleasures
And have no wisdom.
There is no peace in the triple world,
Just like in the burning house,
Which is full of various suffering
And which is extremely terrifying.
There are always the sufferings
Of birth, old age, illness, and death.
Such fires as these burn endlessly.
The Tathāgata, who has already left
The burning house of the triple world,
Lives in tranquility
And dwells at ease in the forest.
Now this triple world is my property
And the sentient beings in it are my children.
There are now many dangers here
And I am the only one who can protect them.
Although I give them advice,
They do not accept it,
Because they are tainted with desires
And have deep attachments.
15a On this occasion

I teach the three vehicles
Using skillful means.
Realizing the sufferings of the triple world,
I reveal and explain it
To cause sentient beings to
Escape from the mundane path.
If these children are resolute,
They are endowed with the three knowledges
And six transcendent powers.
Or they can become *pratyekabuddha*s or
Bodhisattvas who have reached
The stage of nonretrogression.
O Śāriputra!
I explain the single Buddha vehicle
To sentient beings, using this illustration.
If you are able to accept what I say,
You will all attain the Buddha path.
This vehicle is subtle, pure, and peerless.
There is nothing superior to it
In all the worlds.
This is what the Buddha enjoys.
All the sentient beings should praise,
Honor, and revere it.
There are immeasurable thousands of *koṭi*s
Of powers, liberations, meditations,
Wisdoms, and other attributes of the Buddha.
I cause my children to obtain such a vehicle
And let them play continuously,
Day and night, for *kalpa*s.
I cause the bodhisattvas as well as the *śrāvaka*s
To board this jeweled vehicle,
And lead them directly
To the terrace of enlightenment.
For this reason,
There is no other vehicle but

The skillful means of the Buddhas,
Even if one seeks in all the ten directions.
I tell you, O Śāriputra:
All of you are my children,
And I am thus your father.
Since you were burned by the fire
Of various sufferings for many *kalpa*s,
I saved you all
By leading you out of the triple world.
Although I have previously told you
About your *parinirvāṇa,*
You have only extinguished birth and death
And have not actually attained nirvana.
You should now seek only
The wisdom of the Buddha.
If there are any bodhisattvas in this assembly,
They should listen singlemindedly
To the real teaching of all the Buddhas.
Those sentient beings
Whom the Buddha Bhagavats
Lead and inspire with skillful means
Are all bodhisattvas.
Because people have little knowledge
And are deeply attached to pleasures,
I teach them the truth of suffering (i.e., the First Noble
  Truth).
And those sentient beings rejoice,
Having attained
Such an unprecedented experience.
The truth of suffering taught by the Buddha
Is nothing but the truth.
To those who do not know the origin of suffering
  (i.e., the Second Noble Truth),
Who are deeply attached to its causes
And unable to abandon them even for a while,

I teach the truth about the path to its cessation
Using skillful means.
All the causes of suffering
Originate from excessive craving.
When this craving is extinguished,
The source is removed.
The cessation of suffering
Is called the Third [Noble] Truth.
One practices the path leading to its cessation (i.e., the Fourth Noble Truth] 15b
In order to attain the truth of cessation.
Removing the bonds of sufferings is called liberation.
In what sense have these people attained liberation?
They have merely removed false views
And called that liberation.
But actually, they have not yet completely attained it.
The Buddha has explained that these people
Have not actually attained nirvana:
I do not intend to lead them to nirvana
Because they have not yet attained the highest path.
I am the Lord of the Dharma
And have mastered the Dharma.
I appear in the world
To cause sentient beings to be at peace.
O, you, Śāriputra!
Teach this my Dharma sign
To benefit the world!
Wherever you may go,
Never propagate it recklessly.
You should know that those who hear,
Rejoice, and fully accept it
Have reached the stage of nonretrogression.
Those who accept the teaching of this sutra
Have formerly seen the Buddhas in the past,
Honored, and paid homage to them,

And also heard this teaching.
Those who are able to accept what you teach,
Will see me, you, the monks and the bodhisattvas.
This very *Lotus Sutra* shall be taught
Only to the profoundly wise.
Those of superficial awareness who hear it
Will become confused and will not comprehend it.
This sutra is beyond the comprehension
Of all the *śrāvaka*s and *pratyekabuddha*s.
O, you, Śāriputra!
Even you understood this sutra only through faith;
It is no wonder that the other disciples cannot.
They accept this sutra
Because they believe the Buddha's teaching,
But it is beyond their intellectual comprehension.
O Śāriputra!
Never teach this sutra
To those who are arrogant and lazy,
Or to those who hold
False views about the self.
Never teach it to those people
Of superficial awareness,
Who are deeply attached
To the desires of the five senses,
Since even if they heard it,
They would not understand.
Those people who will not accept
And who disparage this sutra,
Will consequently destroy the seed of the Buddha
In the entire world.
Now listen to what I teach
About the results of the errors of those people
Who frown upon and have doubts about this sutra.
Listen also to what I teach
Concerning the results of the errors of those people,

Who, whether at the time
Of the Buddha's presence in this world
Or after his *parinirvāṇa,* disparage this sutra,
And despise, hate, and hold grudges
Against the people who recite, copy, and preserve it.
When such people die,
They will go to the Avīci Hell,
And after spending a *kalpa* there,
Will be born in the same way
Again and again for innumerable *kalpas*. 15c
After coming out of this hell,
They will be reborn as animals.
If born as dogs or vermin,
Their bodies will be emaciated, dark-spotted,
Devoid of hair, with scabies and leprosy.
Tormented, hated, and despised by people,
They will constantly suffer from hunger and thirst.
With withered bones and flesh,
They will be in anguish while living
And covered with stones after death.
Because they destroyed
The seed of the Buddha,
They will suffer the consequences
Of their errors.
If they are born as camels or mules,
They will always have heavy burdens to carry.
They will be whipped repeatedly
And think of nothing but water and grass.
It is because they disparaged this sutra
That they suffer the consequences of their errors in this way.
If they are born as vermin and enter a village,
Children will beat them because they have scabies,
Leprosy, and perhaps a missing eye.
At times they will be tortured even to death.
After dying,

They will be reborn as giant snakes
With great bodies as long as five hundred *yojana*s.
Deaf, dumb, legless, slithering on their bellies,
Eaten at by small insects,
They will suffer day and night without respite.
They suffer the consequences of their errors in this way,
Because they disparaged this sutra.
If they are born as humans,
They will have dull faculties
And be runts who twitch and are crippled,
Blind, deaf, and humpbacked.
No matter what they may say
People will not believe them.
Their breath will always be foul.
They will be snatched at by demons.
Being poor and degraded and enslaved by others,
They will be emaciated from many illnesses
And will have nowhere to turn.
When they approach others,
They will be disdained.
Even if they manage to get something
They will immediately lose it.
Even if they study medicine
And cure themselves according to the correct method,
They will suffer from other illnesses again
And may even die.
When they get sick
No one will tend to them;
And even if they take the proper medicine
Their pain will increase.
Every hand will be turned against them,
Threatening them, pilfering and stealing from them.
They will fall helplessly into this plight
Because of their transgressions.
Such erring people will never see

The Buddha, the king of seers,
Preaching the Dharma and leading and inspiring people.
Such people will always be born
Into difficult circumstances.
Crazed, unheeding, and unthinking,
They will never hear the teaching.
They will be born deaf and dumb,
With defective faculties
For as many immeasurable *kalpa*s
As the sands of the Ganges River.
Though they will always find themselves in hell,
They will feel as if they were playing 16a
In a pleasure garden.
Although they are in other troubled states of being,
They will feel as if they were in their own home.
They will live among camels, mules, boars, and dogs.
These are the results of their error
In disparaging this sutra.
If they are born as human beings,
They will be deaf, blind, mute,
Impoverished, and decrepit.
Such will be their adornments.
They will have dropsy, gonorrhea,
Scabies, leprosy, and tumors.
Such diseases as these will be their clothing.
Their bodies will always be foul, filthy, and impure.
Their deep attachment to false views
About the self will cause
Their anger and passion to increase.
Their sexual desires will be insatiable,
With either birds or beasts as their objects.
These are the results of their
Errors in disparaging this sutra.

The Buddha said to Śāriputra:

If one were to explain
The consequences of the errors
Of those who disparage this sutra,
It would take more than a *kalpa*.
For that reason I am now telling you
Never to expound this sutra
To those who have little wisdom.
You should teach it
Only to those people of sharp faculties
Who are wise, learned, and understanding,
Who have good memories and erudition,
And are seeking the Buddha path.
You should teach it to those who have seen
Hundreds of thousands of *koṭi*s of Buddhas,
Who have planted good roots, and are resolute.
Teach it to those who strive,
Always practice compassion,
And give unsparingly of their bodies and lives.
You should teach it to those who are respectful
And devoid of hypocrisy,
Who are living alone
In mountains and valleys away from fools.
O Śāriputra!
You should teach it
To those who have left their bad companions
And made friends with virtuous people.
Teach it to the heirs of the Buddha
Who have good conduct, are as pure as jewels,
And who are seeking the Mahayana sutras.
You should teach it
To those who are free of anger,
Honest, flexible, always sympathetic to everyone,
And who honor all the Buddhas.
Teach it to the heirs of the Buddha
In the great assembly,

Who have pure thoughts
And who teach the Dharma without doubts,
Using various reasonings,
Illustrations, and explanations.
You should teach it to those monks
Who, always and everywhere in search of the Dharma,
Seek the Omniscient One,
To whom they joyfully press their palms together,
Touch their heads, and preserve
Only the Mahayana sutras with pleasure,
Who never preserve even a single verse
Of any other sutra.
Teach it to those who seek this sutra 16b
As intently as they seek for the relics of the Buddha,
Who after obtaining it will accept it
Respectfully, with bowed heads;
And will not seek any other sutra
And will never think about heretical scriptures.
O Śāriputra! I say to you:
I have described the characteristics of those
Who seek the Buddha path,
Though a *kalpa* would not suffice to do so in full.
You should teach the *Lotus Sutra*
To those who are able to accept it.

Chapter IV

Willing Acceptance

At that time the noble Subhūti, Mahākātyāyana, Mahākāśyapa, and Mahāmaudgalyāyana, having heard the unprecedented teaching from the Buddha and the Bhagavat's prediction of Śāriputra's highest, complete enlightenment, were filled with wonder and ecstatic joy. They immediately rose from their seats, straightened their garments, leaving their right shoulders bared, and touched their right knees to the ground. With rapt attention and with palms pressed together they bowed in veneration and, gazing at the Bhagavat's face, said to the Buddha: "We are the seniors of the sangha, old and feeble. We considered ourselves to have attained nirvana and to be incapable of further seeking highest, complete enlightenment, so we did not do so.

"It has been a long time since the Bhagavat taught the Dharma in the past. Now we sit with weary bodies and only contemplate emptiness, signlessness, and wishlessness. Neither the bodhisattva teaching, nor the carefree sporting with transcendent powers, nor the pure Buddha worlds, nor helping sentient beings attain enlightenment produced any eager desire in us.

"Why is this? Because the Bhagavat caused us to leave the triple world and to attain nirvana. But now we are old and feeble. We did not take even a single thought of pleasure in the Buddha's inspiration of the bodhisattvas to highest, complete enlightenment. And now in the presence of the Buddha we have heard the *śrāvakas* receive their prediction of highest, complete enlightenment and we are very joyful to have obtained such an unprecedented experience. We never considered that we would suddenly be able to hear this marvelous teaching; and we are overjoyed that we have attained such great benefits—an immeasurable treasure which we attained, though unsought and unawaited.

"O Bhagavat! We now wish to give an illustration to clarify what we mean: Suppose there were a man who, when he was still a child, left his father and ran away. Living in another region for a long time he passed the age of ten, twenty, even fifty years. The older he got the more impoverished he became. He went searching everywhere for food and clothing, and while he was wandering about he started back by chance in the direction of his native country. From the first the father had looked for his son but in vain; in the meantime he had stayed in the city and become extremely wealthy, and now possessed uncountable treasures.

16c "[The father's] storehouses were all filled to overflowing with gold, silver, lapis lazuli, coral, amber, crystal, and other such things. He had many servants, subordinates, and clerks as well as innumerable elephants, horses, carriages, cows, and sheep. He profited through lending and his trade with other countries was also great.

"Then the impoverished son, after wandering through many villages, from one country and city to another, finally reached the city where his father lived. Although the father had constantly thought about the son from whom he had been separated for over fifty years, he nevertheless had spoken to no one about it. He brooded and grieved in his heart, thinking to himself:

> I have become old and feeble; and although I have many treasures, and storehouses filled with gold, silver, and precious jewels, I have no son. When I die my treasures will be scattered and lost for lack of someone to whom to entrust them.

"It was for this reason that he was always thinking anxiously about his son. He also thought:

> If I could get my son back and leave my fortune to him I would be relieved and happy, and without further worry.

"O Bhagavat! At that time the impoverished son, who had been wandering about, taking odd jobs, by chance finally reached his father's house. Standing at the side of the gate he saw his father in the distance sitting on the lion seat with his feet propped up on a jeweled stool, respectfully surrounded by many brahmans, *kṣatriyas*, and householders. His body was adorned with pearl necklaces worth thousands of myriads. He was attended on both sides by clerks and servants holding whisker fans. Above was a jeweled canopy with various hanging flowered banners. Perfume was sprinkled on the ground, which was strewn with a variety of beautiful flowers. There were rows of precious objects, and people were coming and going, buying and selling. With various trappings such as these, the father appeared very majestic indeed.

"The impoverished son, seeing his father wielding such great power, became terrified and regretted that he had ever come to that place. He thought to himself:

> He must be a king or of a similar rank. This is not a place where I can obtain things as a hired worker. It would certainly be better for me to go to a poor village, a place where I can use my ability and easily obtain clothing and food. If I stay here for very long I will be seized and put to forced labor.

"Thinking this way, he quickly fled. At that time the wealthy man, sitting on the lion seat, realized that he had seen his son and became extremely happy. He then thought:

> Now there is someone to whom I can leave my fortune and treasures. I have been constantly thinking about my son but had no way to meet him, and now suddenly he has come. This is exactly what I wanted. Although I am old I still yearn for him.

"The man immediately dispatched his attendants to chase his son and bring him back. Then the attendants quickly ran and overtook him. The impoverished son was frightened and cried out in fear:

> I did nothing wrong! Why are you seizing me?

"The attendants grabbed him more firmly and forced him to return. Then the impoverished son thought:

> They have seized me even though I have done nothing wrong. I shall certainly be killed.

17a "He was so terrified that he collapsed unconscious on the ground. His father, seeing this from a distance, told the attendants:

> I don't need him. Don't force him to come! Pour cold water on his face and bring him to consciousness. Don't say anything more to him.

"What was the reason for this? The father knew that his son was of lowly aspiration, and that his own wealth and position would cause him problems. Although the father knew without doubt that the man was his son, he used skillful means and did not say to others, 'This is my son.'

"The attendant then said to the son:

> You are free to go wherever you wish.

"Then the impoverished son, happy because he had never felt such relief, stood up and went to a poor village to seek for food and clothing.

"At that time, wanting to get his son back, the wealthy man employed skillful means and secretly dispatched two attendants of wretched and humble appearance. He said to them:

> Approach the impoverished fellow and gently tell him that there is a place for him to work where he will be paid double. If he gives his assent then bring him back to work. If he asks you what kind of work there is for him to do, tell him that he will be employed to sweep dung and that both of you will work with him.

"Then the two attendants immediately went in search of the impoverished son. When they found him they told him this. At that time he took his pay and immediately went to work sweeping dung.

"The father, seeing his son, felt pity and wondered what to do. Then one day while looking through the window he saw his son in the distance appearing emaciated and wretched, soiled with dung and dirt. The father took off his necklaces, fine garments, and ornaments and put on torn, filthy clothes. Covering himself with dirt and taking a dung sweeper in his right hand, he made himself look fearsome. He said to his workers: 'Work hard and don't be lazy!'

"Through this kind of skillful means he was able to approach his son. He spoke to him further saying:

> You! I want you to always work here. Don't go anywhere else and I will pay you more. There will be no difficulty in getting the things you need, like utensils, rice, noodles, salt, and vinegar. I also have an old servant. If you need him I'll give him to you. Be at ease! I am just like your father, so don't worry about anything! Why am I doing this? Because I am old and you are still young. Whenever you work you are never lazy or sullen and never complain. I never see in you the bad qualities the other workers have. From now on you will be just like my own son.

"Then the wealthy man immediately addressed him as his child. At that time, even though the impoverished son rejoiced at being treated this way, he nevertheless still considered himself a humble employee. For this reason his father let him continue to sweep dung for twenty years. At the end of this period of time each had come to trust the other. Yet even though the son had free access to his father's house, he still lived in the same place as before.

"O Bhagavat! One day the wealthy man became ill and knew
he was going to die before long. He said to the impoverished son: 17b

> This is what I have been thinking and I want you to understand my intentions: I now have plenty of gold, silver, and precious treasures filling my storehouses. Get to know exactly how much is being taken in and out of them. Why do I want you to do this? Because you and I are one and the same. Take good care of our fortune and don't let it be lost!

"Then the impoverished son obeyed his instructions. Although he learned everything about the gold, silver, precious treasure, and the storehouses, he never wanted to take even the least amount. Nevertheless he still lived in the same place as before and was still not able to get rid of his feeling of inferiority.

"After a short time had passed the father knew that his son's mind had become composed, that his will had increased, and that he was ashamed of his former feelings. When the father was just on the verge of death he ordered his son to meet the king, ministers, *kṣatriyas*, householders, and relatives, who had already assembled there. The father then declared:

> This is my son, my own progeny. When we were in a certain city he left me and fled. He wandered around for more than fifty years undergoing hardships. His original name is Such-and-such, and my name is Such-and-such. Long ago when I was in that city I worried and searched for him. At last and unexpectedly I met up with him. This is my true son and I am, in truth, his father. All of the fortune I now possess belongs to my son. He already knows about our finances.

"O Bhagavat! At that time the impoverished son, hearing what his father said, became extremely happy at having obtained such an unprecedented experience. Then he thought:

> I never even considered receiving this; nevertheless, this treasure house has come into my possession, though unsought and unawaited.

"O Bhagavat! This very wealthy man is the Tathāgata, and all of us are the heirs of the Buddha. The Tathāgata has always said that we are his children. Because of the triple sufferings, O Bhagavat, we experienced pain, were confused, ignorant and attached to inferior teachings in life after life. Today the Bhagavat has made us think about getting rid of the dung of fallacies regarding the reality of the world and that, in this respect, we diligently strove to attain the nirvana only as one seeking a salary for a single day's labor. We had already attained it and were extremely happy and satisfied with it. We said to ourselves:

> Because we have made diligent efforts to comprehend the Buddha's teaching we have attained a great deal.

"But the Bhagavat had formerly perceived that we were attached to desires and content with lowly aspirations. While letting us be so he did not explain that we were to have a portion of the treasure house of the Tathāgata's wisdom and insight. Through the power of skillful means the Bhagavat has taught the wisdom of the Tathāgatas. Although we had attained nirvana from the Buddha as our salary for one day's labor, we thought we had attained much and did not seek the Mahayana.

"Furthermore, we have manifested and explained the wisdom of the Tathāgata for the bodhisattvas; but we ourselves had no aspirations regarding it.

"Why is this? The Buddha, knowing that we were content with 17c
lowly aspirations, taught us according to what is appropriate through the power of skillful means. But we did not know that we really were the heirs of the Buddha.

"Now we fully know that the Bhagavat is unstinting in regard to the wisdom of the Buddhas. What is the reason for this? We have actually been the heirs of the Buddha from long ago, even though we only yearned for the inferior teaching. If we had yearned for the superior teaching, then the Buddha would have taught the teachings of the Mahayana to us. Yet, in this sutra he has taught only the single vehicle.

"Now, in the past the Buddha reviled the *śrāvaka*s—those who yearned for the inferior teaching—in the presence of the bodhisattvas, but actually the Buddha inspired them also with the Mahayana. That is why we say that though we originally had no desire to seek the great treasure of the King of the Dharma it has now come to us unsought and unawaited. We have all attained what we should attain as the heirs of the Buddha."

Thereupon Mahākāśyapa, wanting to elaborate on the meaning of this further, spoke these verses:

Today we have heard the Buddha's words,
And we are joyful and ecstatic
At having attained such an unprecedented experience.
The Buddha has said
That the *śrāvaka*s will be able to become Buddhas.
The most magnificent jewels
Have been obtained without being sought or awaited.
Suppose there were a young and inexperienced child
Who left his father
And ran away to a distant country.
He wandered around for more than fifty years.
And his worried father looked for him everywhere.
The father, exhausted from searching for him,
Remained in a city
Where he had a house built
And enjoyed the desires of the five senses.
His family built up a vast wealth of much gold, silver,
Mother-of-pearl, agate, pearls, lapis lazuli,
Elephants, horses, cows, sheep, floats, carriages,
Peasants, servants, and other employees.
He earned interest through loans and deposits
And had buyers and sellers
Throughout all the other regions.
He was surrounded by thousands of
Myriads of *koṭi*s of people,
Who held him in awe;
Always loved by the king,
And deeply respected by the subjects
And powerful families.
There were many people
Coming and going on different business.
He was thus extremely wealthy

And very powerful.
And yet as he grew older,
He increasingly worried about his son.
Day and night he thought:

> Soon I will die.
> My foolish son has abandoned me
> For over fifty years.
> What should I do with the
> Various goods in my treasure houses?

At that time the impoverished son
Was going from town to town,
From one country to another,
Seeking food and clothing.
Sometimes he obtained them,
And sometimes he did not.
He was emaciated from hunger, 18a
And his body was covered with scabies.
Through his wanderings,
He gradually reached the city
Where his father lived,
And, after having been employed
At one place after another,
Finally ended up at his father's home.
At that time the wealthy man
Was sitting within the gate
On a lion seat, sheltered by
A huge jewel-covered canopy.
He was surrounded by his attendants
And guarded by his men.
Some were counting gold, silver, and jewels;
And some were settling the finances,
While others were keeping the accounts.
The impoverished son saw his father,
Who was extremely wealthy and dignified.

He wondered if this man were a king
Or someone of equal rank.
He became intimidated
And wondered why he had gone there.
He thought to himself:

> If I stay here for long
> I will be harassed and coerced into working.

Thinking this, he ran away
In search of a poor village
Where he could find employment.
At that time the wealthy man,
Who was sitting on the lion seat,
Saw his son in the distance.
Though he recognized him he told no one,
But sent his attendants
To pursue him and bring him back.
The impoverished son was terrified,
Cried out, and collapsed on the ground
In confusion, thinking:

> Since this man has seized me
> I shall certainly be killed.
> In vain did I come here
> In search of food and clothing.

The wealthy man knew that his son's thoughts
Were humble and foolish,
And that he would not believe what he said,
Nor believe that he was his father.
Then using skillful means,
He dispatched other men
With squint eyes, of small stature
And little dignity, saying to them:

> Tell him:

We will employ you
To sweep dung, at double your wages.

When he heard this
The impoverished son was overjoyed
And returned to sweep dung and clean houses.
The wealthy man
Constantly watched his son
Through the window and thought
That his son was foolish
And willingly did menial things.
Then the wealthy man
Put on torn and filthy clothes,
And, holding a dung sweeper,
Went out to his son.
He approached his son
Through this skillful means
And said to him:

Work hard!
I have already increased your wages
And given you more balm for your feet,
Given you sufficient food
And warm, thick mats.

He further advised him, saying sternly:

You should work diligently.

Then he gently added:

I will treat you like my son.

The wealthy man, being wise,
Gradually gave him freedom of the house;
And, after twenty years had passed,
Let him become involved
In the family business.

He showed him the gold,
Silver, pearls, and crystal,
And made him learn about
All aspects of the finances.
Yet the impoverished son still lived
In a thatched hut outside the gate,
18b And considered himself poor, thinking
That these things were not his own.
The father knew that his son
Was gradually becoming more noble;
And, wanting to give him his fortune,
He assembled the king, ministers,
*Kṣatriya*s, householders, and relatives.
He informed this great assembly, saying:

> This is my son.
> He left me and stayed away
> For fifty years.
> Twenty years have already passed
> Since I saw my son return here.
> Long ago I lost my son in a certain city
> And, after wandering around in search of him,
> I ended up staying here.
> I entrust to him all the houses and men
> That I possess.
> They are all at his disposal.

The son thought:

> Long ago I was poor and of lowly aspiration.
> Now at my father's place
> I have obtained an immense fortune
> Of such things as precious jewels and houses.
> I am overjoyed at having obtained
> Such an unprecedented experience!

The Buddha is also like this.

He knew that we yearned for the inferior teaching,
So he never taught us
That we should become Buddhas.
Yet he did tell us that we had attained
The stage of noncorruption,
That we had achieved the inferior vehicle,
And that we were the disciples of the *śrāvaka* vehicle.
The Buddha told us to teach that
Those who practiced the highest path
Would be able to become Buddhas.
Accepting the Buddha's teaching,
We explained the highest path
For the great bodhisattvas,
Using various explanations and illustrations,
And many figures of speech.
The heirs of the Buddha
Heard the teachings from us,
Contemplated day and night,
And practiced diligently.
The Buddhas instantly made their predictions saying:

> You will all be able to become Buddhas in the future.

We have explained the essence
Of the treasured teaching of the Buddhas
Only for the sake of the bodhisattvas,
But did not expound it for ourselves.
Just as the impoverished son
Who, after approaching his father,
Learned of various things
Yet did not want them,
So, although we explained the treasure house
Of the teaching of the Buddhas,
We never aspired to it.
We thought that we had ourselves attained nirvana
And considered this enough.

We understood only this
And did not think there was anything else.
Even if we heard
About the pure Buddha lands
And leading and inspiring sentient beings,
We never rejoiced in it.
Why is this?
Because although we thought thus:

> Every existence is quiescent,
> Neither produced nor extinguished,
> Neither large nor small,
> Incorrupted and unconditioned,

We felt no eagerness.
For days and nights we neither craved for
18c Nor were attached to the wisdom of the Buddhas,
Neither did we aspire to it.
Furthermore, we ourselves thought,
With regard to the Dharma itself,
That this was the ultimate goal.
After practicing the teaching
Of emptiness day and night,
We were able to shake off
The suffering of the triple world,
And, bearing our last bodies,
Abided in the nirvana with residue.
We were led and inspired by the Buddhas
So that our attainment of the path was not in vain;
And we have already been able
To pass on the benefits
We received from the Buddha.
Although we have expounded
The teaching of the bodhisattvas
To the heirs of the Buddha
To seek the Buddha path,

We never longed for this teaching.
Because he knew our minds
The Leader turned away from us.
At first he did not arouse our zeal
With the explanation that there exists
Real profit in the teaching.
Just as the wealthy man,
Who, knowing that his son was of lowly aspiration,
Broadened his son's mind using
The power of skillful means,
And only then entrusted his entire fortune to him.
The Buddha is also exactly like this.
He has manifested marvelous things
But perceiving that we were content
With lowly aspirations.
He brought control to our minds using
The power of skillful means,
And only then taught us the great wisdom.
Thus today we have obtained
An unprecedented experience.
The fact that we have now spontaneously obtained
What we had not longed for
Is just like the impoverished son
Who obtained innumerable jewels.
O Bhagavat!
We have now obtained the path and its fruit
And have obtained pure sight
Into the incorruptible Dharma.
For a long while we have maintained
The pure conduct of the Buddha;
Today for the first time
We have obtained the results.
For a long time we have practiced
The pure path of discipline and integrity
Based on the teaching of the Dharma King,

And now we have attained
The supreme fruit of noncorruption.
We are now real *śrāvaka*s
And cause everyone to hear the words "Buddha path."
We are now real arhats and shall be revered
Among the *deva*s, humans, *māra*s, and Brahmas
In all the worlds.
The Bhagavat, the Great Benefactor,
Benefits us with marvelous things
By his inspiration and compassion.
Who can repay him for it
Even in immeasurable *koṭi*s of *kalpa*s!
Even if one were to serve him
With one's hands and feet,
Bow one's head in reverence,
And give all kinds of offerings,
One could not repay him.
Even if one were to bear him
On one's head and shoulders
Out of deep respect, for as many *kalpa*s
As there are sands in the Ganges River,
One could not repay him.
Or even if one were to honor him
With delicious food,
Uncountable jeweled garments,
Beddings, various medicines,
Famed sandalwood from Mount Oxhead,
And various precious jewels;
19a Or by building temples,
Spreading jeweled clothing and other such things
For as many *kalpa*s as there are sands in the Ganges River,
One could not repay him.
The Buddhas have marvelous, immeasurable,
Limitless, inconceivable great transcendent powers.
They are the Kings of the Dharma.

Without depravities and unconditioned,
They are patient in all matters,
For the sake of the humble ones.
They teach the common people,
Who are attached to tangible things,
According to what is appropriate to them.
All of the Buddhas having attained
Complete mastery over the Dharma,
Perceive the various desires and intentions
Of sentient beings and explain the teachings
With innumerable illustrations,
According to what is appropriate to them.
Judging from the roots of good merit
That sentient beings have planted in former lives,
The Buddhas perceive who are mature
And who are not.
Considering this in various ways
And understanding the distinctions completely,
The Buddhas teach the single path,
Explaining it as three
In accordance with what is appropriate.

Chapter V

Herbs

Thereupon the Bhagavat addressed Mahākāśyapa and other great disciples saying: "Splendid! Splendid! O Kāśyapa! You have skillfully explained the real merit of the Tathāgata. It is exactly as you have said. The Tathāgata has immeasurable, unlimited, and incalculable merits. Thus even in a period of immeasurable *koṭi*s of *kalpa*s you will never fully be able to explain all of his merits.

"O Kāśyapa! You should know that the Tathāgata is the king of all the teaching. What he teaches is never false. He explains all the teaching using his wisdom and skillful means and what he teaches leads everyone to the stage of omniscience.

"The Tathāgata perceives the goal of all teachings and knows the underlying mental disposition of all sentient beings, perceiving all with no obstructions. He completely understands all teachings and displays omniscience to all sentient beings.

"O Kāśyapa! Suppose in the great manifold cosmos there are mountains, rivers, valleys, and plains where many kinds of grasses, trees, shrubs, and herbs of different names and colors grow. Dense clouds thoroughly cover this great manifold cosmos and rain falls 19b
at the same time everywhere, moistening the small, medium, and large roots, stems, branches, and leaves of all the grasses, trees, shrubs, and herbs.

"The sizes of all the trees depend on whether their capacities are superior, mediocre, or inferior; and the rain falling from the same cloud makes them grow according to the nature of their various seeds. Flowers blossom in the same place and fruit ripens in the same place moistened by the same rain, yet there are differences among these grasses and trees.

"O Kāśyapa! You should know that the Tathāgata is exactly like this. He appears in this world like a great overspreading cloud.

His great voice resounds over the *deva*s, humans, and *asura*s in the world, just as the great cloud thoroughly covers the great manifold cosmos. He declares to the assembly:

> I am the Tathāgata, Arhat, Completely Enlightened, Perfect in Knowledge and Conduct, Well-Departed, Knower of the World, Unsurpassed, Tamer of Humans, Teacher of Devas and Humans, Buddha, Bhagavat. I set free those who have not been freed. I enlighten those who have not been enlightened and bring calm to those who have not been calmed. I cause those to obtain nirvana who have not yet obtained it. I am the one who knows the present and future worlds exactly as they are. I am the All-Knower, the All-Seer, the Knower of the Path, the One who discloses the path and explains it. All of you *deva*s, humans, and *asura*s! Come and listen to my teachings.

"At that time innumerable thousands of myriads of *koṭi*s of sentient beings approach the Buddha and listen to his teaching. Then the Tathāgata, perceiving the faculties of sentient beings—whether they are sharp or dull, diligent or idle—explains the teachings according to their capacities in a variety of immeasurable ways, gladdening and benefiting them all.

"Having heard his teaching, all of these beings are at peace in this world and are born into a good existence in the future. Through this they will receive peace of mind and be able to hear the teaching. Having already heard the teaching they will become free from obstructions and be able to gradually enter the path to the Dharma according to their capacities.

"Just like the great cloud that rains upon all the grasses, trees, shrubs, and herbs, whose seeds are watered and which grow according to their capacities, the Tathāgata teaches the Dharma of one aspect and character; that is to say, the character of liberation, dispassion, and cessation which ultimately leads to omniscience.

"Those sentient beings who hear, hold, and recite the teachings of the Tathāgata and practice it accordingly will nevertheless not perceive the merit that they have obtained.

"Why is this? Only the Tathāgata knows the seed, character, disposition, and capacity of sentient beings. Only he knows what they contemplate, think, and practice; how they contemplate, think, and practice; what teachings they contemplate, think, and practice; and what teaching they obtain through what teaching. 19c
Only the Tathāgata exactly perceives and knows without obstructions the various states in which sentient beings reside.

"It is just like the grasses, trees, shrubs, and herbs that do not know their own natures, whether they are superior, mediocre, or inferior. Yet the Tathāgata knows the teachings of one aspect and character, the character of liberation, dispassion, cessation, complete nirvana, and eternal tranquility which ultimately leads to emptiness.

"The Buddha knows this and perceives the aspirations of sentient beings. For this reason, in order to protect them, he does not immediately teach omniscience.

"O Kāśyapa! It is a rare thing that all of you know that the Tathāgata teaches according to your capacities and that you believe and accept it.

"Why is this? Because the Dharma taught by all the Buddha Bhagavats, according to what is appropriate to sentient beings, is difficult to understand and difficult to know."

Thereupon the Bhagavat, wanting to elaborate on the meaning of this further, spoke these verses:

> The King of the Dharma,
> The destroyer of delusive existence,
> Appears in the world
> And keeping in mind the aspirations of sentient beings
> Teaches the Dharma in various ways
> According to the wishes of sentient beings.
> The Tathāgata is greatly distinguished,
> And his wisdom is profound.
> He has been silent for a long time
> And intentionally has not taught the essential in haste.

Those who are wise
Will be well convinced when they hear it;
Those who are not wise will have doubts
And remain confused for a long time.
That is why, O Kāśyapa, the Tathāgata teaches
According to the capacities of sentient beings,
And enables them to attain the correct perspective
By using various illustrations.
O Kāśyapa, you should know
That it is as if a great cloud
Arises in the world
And covers everything.
This beneficent cloud contains moisture
And bright lightning flashes from it.
The sound of its thunder shakes the earth afar
And gladdens the people.
It conceals the sun
And cools the earth.
The spreading cloud hangs so low,
As if it could be touched.
Everywhere, equal, and immeasurable
The rain pours down and moistens the earth.
Grasses, herbs, large and small trees,
All kinds of crops, seedlings, sugarcane, and grapes
Growing in the depths of the mountains,
In rivers and in precipitous valleys,
Are all watered and completely nourished by the rain.
The dry earth is moistened everywhere
And the herbs and trees grow up thickly.
Out of this cloud the same rain
Waters these grasses, trees, and shrubs
Each according to their capacities.
All the trees, small, medium, or large
Are able to grow in accordance with their capacities.
The luster and colors of the roots, stems,

Branches, leaves, and flowers
Are all freshened by the same rain.
Each of these, although receiving the same moisture,
Reaches a greater or lesser size
In accordance with their different
Dispositions, characteristics, and natures.
The Buddha is exactly like this.
He appears in the world
As a great cloud 20a
Which covers everything universally.
Once appearing in this world
He illuminates and explains
The essence of the teachings
For the sake of sentient beings.
The Great Seer, the Bhagavat, expounds this
To the assembly of all the *deva*s and humans.
I am the Tathāgata, the Best of Humans.
I appear in the world to nourish sentient beings
Just as the great cloud
Moistens all the withered trees.
I cause everyone to be rid of suffering
And attain ease of heart,
Worldly happiness, and the joy of nirvana.
So, *deva*s and humans, listen carefully!
Come, all of you,
And look at the Highest One!
I am the Bhagavat.
No one is equal to me.
I appear in this world
To bring peace of mind to sentient beings
And to teach the Dharma of immortality
To the great assembly.
This Dharma has a single flavor
Of liberation and nirvana.
I expound its meaning with the same subtle voice,

Always making the Mahayana
The subject of my illustrations.
I see everywhere, and regard all as equal.
I have no feelings of like or dislike;
For me there is no this or that.
Nor do I have either love or hate.
I have no attachments and make no distinctions,
And so always teach the Dharma equally to all;
And teach the same thing to one person
As I teach to everyone else.
I always teach the Dharma and nothing else.
Going or coming, sitting or standing,
I never tire of satisfying the world,
Just like the rain that gives nourishment universally.
I tirelessly pour down the rain of the Dharma
Equally on those who are noble or humble,
Superior or inferior, who keep or break the precepts,
Who have good or bad conduct, right or wrong views,
Sharp or dull faculties.
According to their power to understand,
All sentient beings who hear my teaching
Dwell in various stages.
Those living among humans,
*Deva*s, noble emperors, Śakra, and Brahma kings
Are like the small herbs.
Those who know the incorruptible Dharma,
Who are able to attain nirvana,
Have the six transcendent powers, and
Have attained the three sciences.
Those who live alone in mountain forests
Always practicing meditation, and
Who attain the enlightenment of the *pratyekabuddha*s
Are like the medium-sized herbs.
Those who seek the stage
Of the Bhagavat, thinking that

They will become Buddhas,
And practice persistence and meditation,
Are like the large herbs.
The heirs of the Buddhas
Who concentrate on the path of the Buddha,
Who always cultivate compassion within themselves
And know definitely without a doubt
That they will become Buddhas,
Are like the small trees.
Those who are comfortable with transcendent powers, 20b
Who turn the irreversible wheel [of the Dharma]
And save innumerable hundreds
Of thousands of *koṭi*s of sentient beings,
Are the bodhisattvas
Who are like the large trees.
The Buddha's equal teaching
Is like the rain of one flavor.
The sentient beings accept it
According to their different capacities,
Just as the grasses and trees
Each differently absorb the rain.
The Buddha reveals the single teaching
With illustrations, using skillful means
And explains it with various explanations,
And yet it is just a drop in the ocean
Compared to the Buddha's wisdom.
I pour down the rain of the Dharma,
Fulfilling the world,
And the sentient beings
Practice the Dharma of one flavor
According to their capacities.
Just as the shrubs, herbs, and trees
Flourish in accordance with their capacities,
Reaching either a greater or lesser size,
The teaching of the Buddhas

Is always of one flavor
And fulfills the entire world.
Anyone who practices it little by little
Obtains the fruit of the path.
The *śrāvaka*s and *pratyekabuddha*s
Living in mountain forests,
Who, in their last bodies,
Hear the Dharma and attain its fruit,
Are just like the flourishing herbs.
The bodhisattvas who are firm in wisdom,
Who completely understand the triple world,
And seek the highest vehicle,
Are just like the flourishing small trees.
Those who abide in meditation,
Attain transcendent powers,
Listen to the teaching regarding the emptiness
Of every existence with great joy,
And save sentient beings
By emitting innumerable rays of light,
Are just like the flourishing large trees.
In this way, O Kāśyapa,
The Dharma that the Buddha teaches
Is just like the great cloud that enriches human flowers
With the rain of one flavor,
So that each attains its fruits.
O Kāśyapa!
You should know that I reveal the Buddha path
Using various explanations and illustrations
And that this is my skillful means.
All of the Buddhas are just like this.
I will now teach the highest truth for your sake:

> There are no *śrāvaka*s who attain nirvana.
> What you practice is the bodhisattva path;
> And if you practice step by step,
> You will all become Buddhas.

Chapter VI

Prediction

At that time, after the Bhagavat had spoken these verses, he addressed the great assembly, proclaiming: "This disciple of mine, Mahākāśyapa, in the future will be able to meet three hundred myriads of *koṭi*s of Buddha Bhagavats to whom he will pay homage, respect, veneration, and praise; and he will extensively expound the immeasurable great teachings of these Buddhas. In his last body he will become a Buddha called Raśmiprabhāsa, a Tathāgata, 20c
Arhat, Completely Enlightened, Perfect in Knowledge and Conduct, Well-Departed, Knower of the World, Unsurpassed, Tamer of Humans, Teacher of Devas and Humans, Buddha, Bhagavat.

"His world will be called Avabhāsaprāpta in the *kalpa* called Mahāvyūha. The lifespan of this Buddha will be twelve intermediate *kalpa*s. The True Dharma will last in the world for twenty intermediate *kalpa*s and the Semblance Dharma will also last for twenty intermediate *kalpa*s.

"His world will be adorned and there will be no dirt, shards, thorns, excrement, or other impurities. The earth will be level without irregularities, hollows, or hills. The earth will be made of lapis lazuli with jeweled trees in rows. Golden cords will line the borders of these roads, which will be scattered with precious flowers, and everywhere will be pure.

"In his world there will be immeasurable thousands of *koṭi*s of bodhisattvas as well as innumerable *śrāvaka*s. All malice will be far removed; and even though Māra and his minions will be there, they will all protect the Buddha-Dharma."

Thereupon the Bhagavat, wanting to explain the meaning of this further, spoke these verses:

> I tell you, O monks,
> That I see with the Buddha-eye

That Kāśyapa in the future
Will become a Buddha
After innumerable *kalpas* have passed.
In the future he will meet and pay homage
To three hundred myriads of *koṭis* of Buddha Bhagavats
And practice the pure path of discipline and integrity,
Seeking for the wisdom of the Buddhas.
Having offered respect to the highest and best of humans
And having completely grasped the ultimate wisdom,
He will become a Buddha while in his last body.
His land will be pure.
The earth will be made of lapis lazuli,
And many jeweled trees will be in rows
Along roads bordered with golden cords,
And those who see it will be gladdened.
The air will be always filled
With a pleasant fragrance,
And many beautiful flowers
Will be strewn about.
Various wonderful things
Will adorn this earth,
Which will be level
Without hills or hollows.
There will be an incalculable number
Of bodhisattvas there
Who will have the power of self-control,
Be versed in transcendent powers,
And who will preserve the sutras of the Mahayana
Taught by the Buddhas.
The multitude of *śrāvakas*,
Bearing their last bodies, free from corruption,
Heirs of the Dharma King,
Will also be unreckonable;
Their number will be impossible to calculate
Even with the divine eye.

The lifespan of this Buddha
Will be twelve intermediate *kalpas*.
The True Dharma will last in the world
For twenty intermediate *kalpas*.
And the Semblance Dharma will also last
For twenty intermediate *kalpas*.
Thus will things be with
The Bhagavat Raśmiprabhāsa.

At that time Mahāmaudgalyāyana, Subhūti, and Mahākātyāyana were all charged with excitement, and with palms pressed together they attentively gazed at the Bhagavat, never turning their eyes from him. They immediately spoke these verses in unison: 21a

O Bhagavat, Great Hero!
O King of the Dharma of the Śākyas!
Bestow the Buddha's words upon us
Out of your compassion for us.
If, knowing the depths of our hearts,
You give us your predictions,
It will be like cooling our fevers
By sprinkling us with the Dharma of immortality.
It is as though someone coming
From a country suffering from famine
Were suddenly to find
A great king's feast spread before him,
Yet is stricken with doubt
And does not venture to eat,
Until, being instructed by the king,
He dares at last to do so.
We are exactly like this.
We have been constantly thinking
About the faults of the inferior vehicle,
And so we had no knowledge of the way
To obtain the highest wisdom of the Buddha.
Although we hear the Buddha's voice

Saying that we will become Buddhas,
We still have doubt in our minds
As if we dare not eat the meal.
If we receive the Buddha's prediction
It will immediately put us at ease.
The Bhagavat, the Great Hero,
Always wants to put the world at ease;
And so we entreat you to bestow
Upon us your predictions,
As though to starving people
Waiting for permission to eat.

Then the Bhagavat, knowing what lay in the thoughts of the great disciples, addressed the monks saying: "This Subhūti in the future will meet, respect, venerate, praise, and pay homage to three hundred myriads of *koṭi*s of *nayuta*s of Buddhas; and he will always practice the pure path of discipline and integrity, and complete the bodhisattva path. In his last body he will become a Buddha called Yaśasketu, a Tathāgata, Arhat, Completely Enlightened, Perfect in Knowledge and Conduct, Well-Departed, Knower of the World, Unsurpassed, Tamer of Humans, Teacher of Devas and Humans, Buddha, Bhagavat.

"His land will be called Ratnasaṃbhava in the *kalpa* called Ratnāvabhāsa. The land will be even and the earth will be made of crystal and adorned with jeweled trees. It will be without pits, pebbles, thorns, or the filth of excrement. The earth will be covered with precious flowers and will be everywhere pure.

"The people in this world will all live in wonderful towers with jeweled terraces. The *śrāvaka*s, the disciples there will be innumerable and limitless, beyond calculation and metaphor, and there will also be innumerable thousands of myriads of *koṭi*s of *nayuta*s of bodhisattvas.

"The lifespan of this Buddha will be twelve intermediate *kalpa*s. The True Dharma will last in the world for twenty intermediate *kalpa*s and the Semblance Dharma will also last for twenty intermediate *kalpa*s. This Buddha will always dwell in the air, teaching the Dharma for the multitude, and he will save incalculable bodhisattvas and *śrāvaka*s."

Thereupon the Bhagavat, wanting to explain the meaning of this further, spoke these verses:

O monks! 21b
I shall now make something known to you.
You should attentively listen
To what I have to say.
My great disciple Subhūti
Will become a Buddha called Yaśasketu.
He will pay homage to innumerable
Myriads of *koṭi*s of Buddhas,
And, following the Buddha's practice,
He will gradually come to complete the great path.
He will attain the thirty-two marks
In his last body,
And his form will be fine and beautiful
Just like a jeweled mountain.
His Buddha world will be ultimately pure.
Of the sentient beings who see it
There will be none who do not rejoice.
There the Buddha will bring
Incalculable sentient beings to enlightenment.
In the midst of his Dharma
There will be many bodhisattvas
With keen faculties,
Who turn the irreversible wheel [of the Dharma].
This world will always
Be graced with bodhisattvas.
There will also be
Incalculable numbers of *śrāvaka*s.
All of them will have perfected the three sciences,
And the six transcendent powers,

Will abide in the eight liberations,
And have great dignity and virtue.
The Buddha will expound the Dharma
And reveal immeasurable,
Unthinkable, transcendent powers.
All the *deva*s and humans,
As numerous as the sands of the Ganges River,
Will listen to the Buddha's words
With palms pressed together.
The lifespan of this Buddha
Will be twelve intermediate *kalpa*s.
The True Dharma will last in the world
For twenty intermediate *kalpa*s,
And the Semblance Dharma will also last
For twenty intermediate *kalpa*s.

Thereupon the Bhagavat addressed the monks, saying: "I will now tell you that this Mahākātyāyana in the future will honor, respect, and pay homage to eight thousand *koṭi*s of Buddhas with offerings. After the *parinirvāṇa*s of these Buddhas, he will erect stupas, each of which will be one thousand *yojana*s in height and five hundred *yojana*s in both width and depth. These stupas will all be constructed of the seven precious treasures—gold, silver, lapis lazuli, mother-of-pearl, agate, pearls, and rubies. He will pay homage to these stupas with many flowers and necklaces, fragrant ointments, scented powders, burning incense, canopies, flags, and banners.

"After this he will also pay homage to two myriads of *koṭi*s of Buddhas in exactly the same way and, having done so, he will perfect the bodhisattva path and become a Buddha called Jāmbūnadābhāsa, a Tathāgata, Arhat, Completely Enlightened, Perfect in Knowledge and Conduct, Well-Departed, Knower of the World, Unsurpassed, Tamer of Humans, Teacher of Devas and Humans, Buddha, Bhagavat.

"His land will be level. The earth will be made of crystal and it will be adorned with jeweled trees. The roads will be bordered with golden cords and beautiful flowers will cover the earth. It will be pure everywhere and those who see it will rejoice.

"There will be none of the four troubled states of being, namely the hells, hungry ghosts, animals, and *asura*s. There will be many *deva*s and humans, and immeasurable myriads of *koṭi*s of *śrāvaka*s and bodhisattvas will grace this world. 21c

"The lifespan of this Buddha will be twelve intermediate *kalpa*s. The True Dharma will last in the world for twenty intermediate *kalpa*s and the Semblance Dharma will also last for twenty intermediate *kalpa*s."

At that time the Bhagavat, wanting to explain the meaning of this further, spoke these verses:

O monks, listen carefully!
What I shall say
Is nothing but the truth.
This Kātyāyana
Will pay homage to the Buddhas
With various wonderful offerings.
After the *parinirvāṇa*s of those Buddhas,
He will erect stupas constructed
Of the seven precious treasures
And offer respect to their relics
With flowers and incense.
In his last body
He will attain the wisdom of the Buddha
And will achieve complete enlightenment.
His world will be pure
And he will save incalculable
Myriads of *koṭi*s of sentient beings.
He will be venerated in the ten directions.
There is nothing that surpasses
This Buddha's ray of light,
So this Buddha
Will be called Jāmbūnadābhāsa.

There will be innumerable, uncountable
Bodhisattvas and *śrāvakas* gracing this world,
Who have shaken free from every state of being.

Thereupon the Bhagavat again addressed the assembly saying: "I will now tell you that this Mahāmaudgalyāyana will respect, venerate, and pay homage to eight thousand Buddhas with various offerings; and after the *parinirvāṇas* of these Buddhas, he will erect stupas, each of which will be one thousand *yojanas* in height and five hundred *yojanas* in both depth and width. These stupas will be constructed with the seven precious treasures—gold, silver, lapis lazuli, mother-of-pearl, agate, pearls, and rubies. He will offer them various flowers, necklaces, fragrant ointments, scented powders, burning incense, canopies, flags, and banners.

"After this he will pay homage to two hundred myriads of *koṭis* of Buddhas in exactly the same way, and will become a Buddha called Tamālapatracandanagandha, a Tathāgata, Arhat, Completely Enlightened, Perfect in Knowledge and Conduct, Well-Departed, Knower of the World, Unsurpassed, Tamer of Humans, Teacher of Devas and Humans, Buddha, Bhagavat.

"His world will be called Mano'bhirāma in the *kalpa* called Ratiprapūrṇa. The land will be level. The earth will be made of crystal, adorned with jeweled trees, and strewn with flowers of pearls. It will be pure everywhere and those who see it will rejoice. There will be many *devas* and humans, innumerable bodhisattvas, and *śrāvakas*.

"The lifespan of this Buddha will be twenty-four intermediate *kalpas*. The True Dharma will last in this world for forty intermediate *kalpas* and the Semblance Dharma will also last for forty intermediate *kalpas*."

Then the Bhagavat, wanting to elaborate on this meaning, spoke these verses:

22a This disciple of mine, Mahāmaudgalyāyana,
Having abandoned this body,
Will meet eight thousand and then two hundred
Myriads of *koṭis* of Buddha Bhagavats.

For the sake of the Buddha path
He will pay them homage and respect them,
And always practice holy conduct (*brahmacarya*)
Of discipline and integrity
In the presence of these Buddhas.
He will uphold the Buddha-Dharma
For immeasurable *kalpa*s.
After the *parinirvāṇa*s of these Buddhas
He will erect stupas
Constructed with the seven precious treasures
On which golden banners
Will be long displayed.
He will pay homage to
These stupas of the Buddhas
With flowers, incense, and music.
After having mastered
The bodhisattva path step by step,
In a land called Mano'bhirāma,
He will become a Buddha
Called Tamālapatracandanagandha.
The lifespan of this Buddha
Will be twenty-four intermediate *kalpa*s.
He will always expound the Buddha path
For the sake of *deva*s and humans.
There will be countless *śrāvaka*s,
As numerous as the sands of the Ganges River,
Who will have perfected the three sciences,
And six transcendent powers,
And have great dignity and virtue.
There will be innumerable bodhisattvas,
Resolute and persevering, who will never turn away
From the wisdom of the Buddhas.
After the *parinirvāṇa* of this Buddha
The True Dharma will last
For forty intermediate *kalpa*s,

And the Semblance Dharma
Will also be like this.
All of my disciples,
Five hundred in number,
Who are endowed with dignity and virtue,
Will also receive my prediction.
In the future they will all become Buddhas.
I will now explain the relationships
That you and I have formed in past lives.
All of you, listen carefully!

Chapter VII

The Apparitional City

The Buddha addressed the monks, saying: "Once upon a time, immeasurable, limitless, inconceivable, incalculable *kalpa*s ago, there was a Buddha called Mahābhijñājñānābhibhū Tathāgata, an Arhat, Completely Enlightened, Perfect in Knowledge and Conduct, Well-Departed, Knower of the World, Unsurpassed, Tamer of Humans, Teacher of Devas and Humans, Buddha, Bhagavat. His land was called Susaṃbhavā in the *kalpa* called Mahārūpa.

"O monks, it has been an extremely long time since this Buddha entered nirvana. Suppose there were a man who ground the earth of the entire great manifold cosmos into powdered ink, and he were to then pass through a thousand worlds to the east, where he let fall a single particle of ink, the size of a speck of dust.

"After passing through another thousand worlds, he let fall another particle; and he continued in this way until he had completely used all the ink.

"What do you think about this? Do you think that a mathematician or a mathematician's pupil would be able to count those worlds to the last particle or not?"

"O Bhagavat! No, they could not."

"O monks! Suppose that all the worlds this man passed through, whether letting fall a particle or not, were all ground into dust,
and one speck of this dust were equal to one *kalpa*. The time since 22b
the *parinirvāṇa* of this Buddha surpasses this number by immeasurable, limitless, incalculable hundreds of thousands of myriads of *koṭi*s of *kalpa*s; and through the power of the Tathāgata's wisdom and insight, I can see his distant past, as if it were today."

Thereupon the Bhagavat, wanting to elaborate on the meaning of this further, spoke these verses:

I recall that in the past,
Immeasurable *kalpa*s ago,
There was a Buddha, the most honored among two-legged beings,
Called Mahābhijñājñānābhibhū.
Suppose there was a man
Who vigorously ground up in its entirety
The earth of the great manifold cosmos
And turned it all to powdered ink.
After passing through one thousand worlds,
He let fall one particle of ink;
And in this way
He continued to let fall particles
Until he had used up all the ink.
If all these worlds,
Those where he let fall a particle
And those where he did not,
Were to be ground into specks of dust,
And one speck of dust were equal to a single *kalpa,*
Their number would be surpassed
By the number of *kalpa*s
That have passed since that Buddha's *parinirvāṇa,*
So incalculable has this number of *kalpa*s been.
With the Tathāgata's unobstructed wisdom,
I know of these bodhisattvas and *śrāvaka*s
And the *parinirvāṇa* of this Buddha;
It is as if I see his *parinirvāṇa* today.
O monks, you should know
That with the knowledge of the Buddha,
Which is pure and subtle,
Incorrupted and without obstructions,
I perceive what happened immeasurable *kalpa*s ago.

The Buddha addressed the monks, saying: "The lifespan of this Buddha Mahābhijñājñānābhibhū was five hundred and forty myriads of *koṭis* of *nayutas* of *kalpas*. When that Buddha was seated on the terrace of enlightenment after having defeated Māra's army, he tried to obtain highest, complete enlightenment, yet the Dharma of the Buddhas did not appear to him. In this way, even after having sat cross-legged for one to ten intermediate *kalpas*, undisturbed in body and mind, the Dharma of the Buddhas still did not appear to him.

"At that time a group of thirty-three *devas* first prepared for that Buddha a lion seat one *yojana* in height under the *bodhi* tree, for this Buddha was to attain highest, complete enlightenment on that seat. As soon as the Buddha sat on this seat, all the Brahmas rained down various heavenly flowers for a hundred *yojanas* around; periodically a fragrant breeze would blow away the withered flowers and they would rain down fresh ones.

"In this way they unceasingly paid homage to the Buddha for a full ten intermediate *kalpas*, raining down these flowers continuously until his *parinirvāṇa*. The *devas* of the four quarters constantly struck heavenly drums to honor the Buddha, and in the same way all the other *devas* made divine music for a full ten inter- 22c
mediate *kalpas* until his *parinirvāṇa*.

"O monks! The Dharma of the Buddhas appeared to the Buddha Mahābhijñājñānābhibhū after ten intermediate *kalpas* had passed, and he attained highest, complete enlightenment.

"This Buddha had had sixteen children before he renounced household life. The eldest child was called Jñānākara. Each child had various kinds of rare toys. After hearing about their father's attainment of highest, complete enlightenment, they all put aside their toys and set out for where the Buddha was. Weeping sad tears, their mothers saw them off. Their grandfather, the wheel-turning sage king, went with them, along with a hundred ministers and hundreds of thousands of myriads of *koṭis* of people.

"When they arrived at the terrace of enlightenment, they all wanted to approach the Tathāgata Mahābhijñājñānābhibhū, and pay homage and respect, honor, and praise him. They came up to him and bowed until their foreheads touched his feet, and then circled around him. Attentively, with palms pressed together, they gazed at the Bhagavat and spoke these verses:

> The Bhagavat of great, virtuous dignity,
> In order to bring sentient beings to the path,
> After immeasurable *koṭi*s of *kalpa*s
> And perfecting all the vows,
> Finally became a Buddha.
> How wonderful!
> There is nothing more auspicious!
> The Bhagavat is truly extraordinary!
> He sat tranquil for ten intermediate *kalpa*s
> With his body and limbs immobile.
> His mind was always calm and never distracted.
> He has attained ultimate, eternal tranquility,
> And is firmly established
> In the incorruptible Dharma.
> Now seeing the Bhagavat,
> Who has serenely attained the Buddha path,
> We receive benefit and celebrate
> With great joy.
> Sentient beings, ever suffering,
> Are blind and without a teacher.
> They are unaware of the path that leads
> To the extinction of suffering,
> Ignorant of the way to seek liberation.
> From one blind state to the next,
> Those in the troubled states of being daily increase
> While the *deva*s decrease.
> They never hear the Buddha's name.
> Now the Buddha has attained the highest,
> Serene, and incorruptible Dharma.
> Thus we and the *deva*s and humans,
> Shall obtain the greatest benefit.
> Therefore we all bow and pay homage
> To the highest Lord.

"At that time the sixteen princes, having praised the Buddha in verse, requested that the Bhagavat turn the wheel of the Dharma, saying:

> O Bhagavat, teach the Dharma! Put all the *devas* and people at ease and benefit them through your compassion! 23a

"They spoke further in verse, saying:

> O Hero of the World,
> The One Who Has No Equal,
> Who is adorned with a hundred merits,
> And has attained the highest wisdom!
> We entreat you to teach
> For the sake of the world,
> And bring us and all the other
> Sentient beings to the path.
> Illuminate and reveal this wisdom
> So that we may attain it.
> If we can become Buddhas,
> So can the other sentient beings.
> The Bhagavat knows
> The deep-seated intentions of sentient beings
> And the paths they practice,
> As well as the power of their wisdom.
> May the Bhagavat, being wholly aware
> Of their positive intentions,
> Accumulated merits, and past deeds,
> Turn the highest wheel of the Dharma.

The Buddha addressed the monks, saying: "When the Buddha Mahābhijñājñānābhibhū attained highest, complete enlightenment, five hundred myriads of *koṭi*s of Buddha worlds in each of the ten directions quaked in six ways. The dark places between the worlds, where the rays of the sun and moon had been unable to penetrate, were brightly illuminated. The sentient beings there were able to see each other and said:

> How is it possible that sentient beings have suddenly appeared here?

"Moreover, those worlds from the heavenly palaces up to the palaces of the Brahmas, also quaked in six ways. The great ray of light shone everywhere, filling the worlds with a radiance that surpassed the light of the *deva*s.

"At that time the palaces of Brahmas in the five hundred myriads of *koṭi*s of worlds in the east were illuminated twice as brightly as usual. The great Brahmas each thought:

> The palaces are illuminated now as never before. What has caused this phenomenon?

"At that time all of the great Brahmas approached each other to discuss this matter. In that assembly there was a great Brahma called Sarvasattvatrātar who spoke to the assembly of Brahmas in verse, saying:

> This illumination of our palaces
> Has never occurred before!
> Let us find out
> The reason for this!
> This great ray of light
> Has illuminated the ten directions.
> Has a *deva* of great merit been born,
> Or has a Buddha appeared in the world?

"Then the great Brahmas of the hundred myriads of *koṭi*s of worlds went toward the west with their palaces to enquire about this phenomenon, carrying heavenly flowers in their robes. They
23b saw the Tathāgata Mahābhijñājñānābhibhū on the terrace of enlightenment, sitting on the lion seat under the *bodhi* tree. He was respectfully surrounded by humans and such nonhumans as *deva*s, *nāga* kings, *gandharva*s, *kiṃnara*s, and *mahoraga*s. They also saw the sixteen princes requesting the Buddha to turn the wheel of the Dharma. Then the great Brahmas bowed until their foreheads touched the Buddha's feet and then circled around him

one hundred thousand times. They scattered heavenly flowers on the Buddha, and the flowers they scattered were piled as high as Mount Sumeru. They also paid homage to the Buddha's *bodhi* tree, which was ten *yojana*s in height. Having reverently offered him flowers, they presented their palaces to the Buddha, saying:

> Please accept the palaces we now offer you, and benefit us through your compassion!

"Then the great Brahmas spoke these verses wholeheartedly and in unison before the Buddha:

> The Bhagavat, who is truly extraordinary,
> Is extremely difficult to meet.
> He is endowed with immeasurable qualities
> And seeks to protect all.
> The Great Teacher of Devas and Humans
> Feels compassion for the world
> And causes all sentient beings
> In the ten directions
> To be universally benefited.
> All of us, who have come from
> Five hundreds of myriads of *koṭi*s of worlds,
> Have given up the pleasure of deep meditation
> In order to pay homage to the Buddha.
> To the Bhagavat we now present our palaces,
> Which the merits of our previous lives
> Have caused to be completely adorned.
> Please accept them through your compassion!

"Thereupon, having praised the Buddha in verse, the great Brahmas each said this:

> O Bhagavat! We entreat you to turn the wheel of the Dharma, open the path to nirvana, and guide sentient beings to it.

"Then the great Brahmas attentively spoke these verses in unison:

O Hero of the World, the most honored among two-legged beings!
We entreat you to expound the Dharma
And bring the suffering beings to the path
Through the power of your great compassion.

"Then the Tathāgata Mahābhijñājñānābhibhū silently consented.

"Furthermore, O monks, the great Brahmas in the five hundred myriads of *koṭi*s of worlds in the southeast saw their palaces illuminated with a ray of light that had never occurred before. Joyful and ecstatic, they were struck with wonder. They assembled to discuss this matter. At that time there was a great Brahma called Adhimātrakāruṇika. He spoke to the assembly of Brahmas in verse saying:

What is the reason
That this phenomenon has appeared?
Even since the olden times,
This illumination of all of our palaces
Is without precedent.
Has a *deva* of great merit been born,
Or has a Buddha appeared in the world?
23c Since we have never seen such a phenomenon,
We should seek thoroughly for its source.
Even if we have to pass
Through thousands of myriads of *koṭi*s of worlds,
We should seek together for the source of this light.
Possibly a Buddha has appeared in the world
To save suffering sentient beings.

"Thereupon five hundred myriads of *koṭi*s of great Brahmas went toward the northwest with their palaces, carrying heavenly flowers in their robes, to enquire about this phenomenon. They saw the Tathāgata Mahābhijñājñānābhibhū on the terrace of enlightenment, sitting on the lion seat under the *bodhi* tree. He was respectfully surrounded by humans and such nonhumans as *devas*, *nāga* kings, *gandharvas*, *kiṃnaras*, and *mahoragas*. They also saw the sixteen princes requesting the Buddha to turn the wheel of the Dharma.

"Then all the Brahmas bowed until their foreheads touched the Buddha's feet and then circled around him one hundred thousand times. They scattered heavenly flowers on the Buddha, and the flowers they scattered were piled up as high as Mount Sumeru. They also paid homage to the Buddha's *bodhi* tree. Having reverently offered the Buddha flowers, they presented their palaces to him, saying:

> Please accept the palaces we now offer you and benefit us through your compassion!

"Then the great Brahmas spoke these verses wholeheartedly and in unison before the Buddha:

> O Great Sage, Deva of Devas!
> We now bow to the one
> Whose voice is as beautiful as the *kalaviṅka* bird's
> And who has compassion for sentient beings.
> The Bhagavat is truly extraordinary
> And can only be seen once
> In an extremely long time.
> One hundred and eighty *kalpas*
> Have passed away fruitlessly,
> And no Buddhas have appeared during this time.
> The worlds have been filled
> With people in the three troubled states of being,
> And the *devas* have decreased.
> The Buddha has now appeared in the world
> To be the eyes of sentient beings.
> He will be the refuge of the world
> And will seek to protect all.
> As the father of sentient beings,

He is the compassionate benefactor.
Because of our past merits,
We now have the good fortune to be able
To meet the Bhagavat!

"Thereupon, having praised the Buddha in verse, the great Brahmas said this:

O Bhagavat! We entreat you to turn the wheel of the Dharma out of your compassion for all and save sentient beings.

"Then the great Brahmas spoke these verses wholeheartedly and in unison:

O Great Sage! Make us very happy!
Turn the wheel of the Dharma,
Reveal the character of all *dharma*s,
Save the suffering beings!
If sentient beings hear this Dharma
They will attain the path and be born as *deva*s.
The beings in the troubled states of being will decrease
24a While those who persevere in the good will increase.

"Then the Tathāgata Mahābhijñājñānābhibhū silently consented.

"Furthermore, O monks, the great Brahmas in the five hundreds of thousands of *koṭi*s of lands in the south each saw their palaces illuminated as they had never been before. Joyful and ecstatic, they were struck with wonder. They immediately assembled to discuss this matter together, asking:

Why have our palaces been illuminated?

"At that time there was a great Brahma, called Sudharma. He spoke to the assembly of Brahmas in verse saying:

Our palaces are illuminated
With brilliant light.
There must be a reason for this,

And we should seek its source.
We have not seen such a phenomenon
During the past hundreds of thousands of *kalpa*s.
Has a *deva* of great merit been born,
Or has a Buddha appeared in the world?

"Thereupon five hundred myriads of *koṭi*s of great Brahmas went toward the north with their palaces, to enquire about this phenomenon, carrying heavenly flowers in their robes. They saw the Tathāgata Mahābhijñājñānābhibhū on the terrace of enlightenment, sitting on the lion seat under the *bodhi* tree. He was respectfully surrounded by humans and such nonhumans as *deva*s, *nāga* kings, *gandharva*s, *kiṃnara*s, and *mahoraga*s. They also saw the sixteen princes requesting the Buddha to turn the wheel of the Dharma.

"Then all the great Brahmas bowed until their foreheads touched the Buddha's feet and then circled around him one hundred thousand times. They scattered heavenly flowers on the Buddha, and the flowers they scattered piled up as high as Mount Sumeru. They also paid homage to the Buddha's *bodhi* tree. Having revered the Buddha with flowers, they offered their palaces to him, saying:

Please accept the palaces we now offer you, and benefit us through your compassion!

"Then the great Brahmas spoke these verses wholeheartedly and in unison before the Buddha:

O Destroyer of Afflictions!
It is extremely difficult to meet a Bhagavat.
We are now meeting the Buddha for the first time
Since one hundred and thirty *kalpa*s have passed away.
Please satisfy sentient beings,
Who are suffering from hunger and thirst,
By pouring down the rain of the Dharma!
O One Possessed of Immeasurable Wisdom,

Whom we have never met before!
Today we have encountered
The one who appears as rarely
As the *uḍumbara* flower blooms.
Our palaces are beautifully adorned
By this ray of light.
We entreat you to accept them
Out of your great compassion!

24b "Thereupon, having praised the Buddha in verse, the great Brahmas said this:

O Bhagavat! We request that you turn the wheel of the Dharma, thus causing the *devamāras*, Brahmas, *śrāmaṇas*, and brahmans to be at ease and saving them all!

"Then the great Brahmas spoke these verses wholeheartedly and in unison:

We entreat you, O Best of Devas and Humans,
To turn the wheel of the highest Dharma,
Beat the drum of the great Dharma,
Blow the conch of the great Dharma,
Rain the rain of the great Dharma everywhere,
And save incalculable sentient beings!
We have all come to request
That you expound it
With your profound voice!

"Then the Tathāgata Mahābhijñājñānābhibhū silently consented.

"The very same thing happened in the worlds from the southwestern to the lower regions, as well as those in other directions.

"Then all the great Brahmas in the five hundred myriads of *koṭis* of lands in the upper region saw their palaces illuminated with a light that had never existed before. Joyful and ecstatic, they were struck with wonder. They immediately assembled to discuss this matter together, asking:

Why have our palaces been illuminated?

"There was a great Brahma in that assembly called Śikhin. He spoke to the assembly of Brahmas in verse, saying:

Why have all our palaces
Been brilliantly illuminated
With this light of virtuous dignity
And adorned in this unprecedented way?
We have never seen such a wonderful phenomenon!
Has a *deva* of great merit been born,
Or has a Buddha appeared in the world?

"Thereupon five hundred myriads of *koṭis* of great Brahmas went into the lower regions with their palaces to enquire about this phenomenon, carrying heavenly flowers in their robes. They saw the Tathāgata Mahābhijñājñānābhibhū on the terrace of enlightenment sitting on the lion seat under the *bodhi* tree. He was respectfully surrounded by humans and such nonhumans as *devas*, *nāga* kings, *gandharvas*, *kiṃnaras*, and *mahoragas*. They also saw the sixteen princes requesting the Buddha to turn the wheel of the Dharma.

"Then all the great Brahmas bowed until their foreheads touched the Buddha's feet and then circumambulated him one hundred thousand times. They scattered heavenly flowers on the Buddha, and the flowers they scattered were piled up as high as Mount Sumeru. They also paid homage to the Buddha's *bodhi* tree. Having reverently offered him flowers, they presented their palaces to the Buddha saying:

Please accept the palaces we now offer you, and benefit us through your compassion!

"Then all the great Brahmas spoke these verses wholeheart- 24c
edly and in unison before the Buddha:

How splendid it is to meet the Buddhas,
The Great Sages who deliver the world,

Who diligently work to get sentient beings
Out of the hell of the triple world!
The Best of Devas and Humans,
Who has universal wisdom,
Out of compassion for everyone
Opens the gate to immortality
And extensively saves all.
Since olden times, immeasurable *kalpa*s
Have passed away in vain
Without the presence of the Buddha.
In the time before the Bhagavat appears,
The ten directions are in constant darkness.
Those in the three troubled states of being increase
And the *asura*s also flourish.
The *deva*s decrease all the more,
And when they die
Many of them fall into those troubled states.
Having never heard the teaching from the Buddha,
All of them always behave badly,
And their physical power and wisdom decreases.
Because of their erring deeds
They lose happiness or any notion of it.
Abiding in the teaching of false views
They know nothing of good conduct.
Deprived of the Buddhas' inspiration,
They always fall into the troubled states of being.
After a very long time, the Buddha has now
Appeared as the Eye of the World.
It is out of compassion for sentient beings
That the Buddha appears in the world.
Transcending everything, the Buddha
Has attained complete enlightenment.
We are all extremely happy,
And all the other beings joyfully acclaim
This unprecedented experience.

All our palaces are beautifully adorned
By this ray of light.
We now offer them to the Bhagavat.
Please accept them out of your compassion!
By the universal transference of this merit,
May we and all other beings
Together attain the Buddha path!

"Thereupon the five hundred myriads of *koṭi*s of great Brahmas, having praised the Buddha in verse, each spoke to him, saying:

O Bhagavat! We strongly entreat you to turn the wheel of the Dharma, give ease to many, and enable them to attain the path.

"Then all the great Brahmas spoke these verses:

O Bhagavat! Turn the wheel of the Dharma,
Beat the drum of the Dharma of immortality,
Save the suffering sentient beings,
And reveal the path to nirvana!
We strongly entreat you to accept our request;
And out of your compassion
And with your wonderful voice,
Expound the Dharma
That you have perfected
Over immeasurable *kalpa*s.

"And then the Tathāgata Mahābhijñājñānābhibhū acceded to 25a
the request made by all the great Brahmas from the ten directions and the sixteen princes. He then immediately turned three times the Dharma wheel of twelve spokes that no *śrāmaṇa*s, brahmans, *devamāra*s, Brahmas, or any other being in the world could turn. He taught:

This is suffering. This is the origination of suffering. This is the cessation of suffering, and this is the path that leads to the cessation of suffering. (i.e., the Four Noble Truths)

"He also extensively taught the Dharma of the twelve-linked chain of dependent origination, saying:

> Conditioned states are dependent on ignorance. Consciousness is dependent on conditioned states. Name and form are dependent on consciousness. The six sense fields are dependent on name and form. Contact is dependent on the six sense fields. Feelings are dependent on contact. Craving is dependent on feelings. Grasping is dependent on craving. Becoming is dependent on grasping. Birth is dependent on becoming. And old age, sickness, death, anxiety, sorrow, suffering, and distress are dependent on birth.
>
> When ignorance ceases, then conditioned states cease. When conditioned states cease, then consciousness ceases. When consciousness ceases, then name and form cease. When name and form cease, then the six sense fields cease. When the six sense fields cease, then contact ceases. When contact ceases, then feelings cease. When feelings cease, then craving ceases. When craving ceases, then grasping ceases. When grasping ceases, then becoming ceases. When becoming ceases, then birth ceases. When birth ceases, then old age, sickness, death, anxiety, sorrow, suffering, and distress cease.

"When the Buddha explained this Dharma to the great assembly of the *deva*s and humans, at that time six hundred myriads of *koṭi*s of *nayuta*s of people, because they were not attached to any existent thing, became free of all corruption. All of them perfected profound meditations, the three sciences, the six transcendent powers, and were endowed with the eight liberations.

"When he taught the Dharma for the second, third, and fourth time, thousands of myriads of *koṭi*s of *nayuta*s of sentient beings, equal to the sands of the Ganges River, who were not attached to any existent thing, became free of all corruption. Innumerable, immeasurable, incalculable *śrāvaka*s followed in their turn.

"At that time the sixteen princes who were still young renounced household life and became *śrāmaṇera*s. All their faculties were sharp, and their wisdom was penetrating. They had paid homage to hundreds of thousands of myriads of *koṭi*s of Buddhas, practiced the pure path of discipline and integrity, and sought highest, complete enlightenment.

"They all spoke to the Buddha, saying:

> O Bhagavat! All of these immeasurable thousands of myriads of *koṭi*s of *śrāvaka*s of great merit have all attained perfection. O Bhagavat! You should also expound the teaching of highest, complete enlightenment to us! Hearing it, we shall all practice it. O Bhagavat! We aspire for the wisdom and insight of the Tathāgata. The Buddha himself knows what is deep in our minds.

"At that time eight myriads of *koṭi*s of people in the assembly who served the noble emperor saw the sixteen princes renounce household life and appealed to the emperor to allow their own renunciation. The emperor immediately gave his permission.

"Then the Buddha accepted the request of the *śrāmaṇera*s. After twenty thousand *kalpa*s had passed he taught to the fourfold assembly this Mahayana sutra called the *Lotus Sutra,* the instruction for bodhisattvas and treasured lore of the Buddhas.

"After the Buddha taught this sutra, all the sixteen *śrāmaṇera*s
preserved, recited, and understood it in order to achieve highest, 25b
complete enlightenment. When the Buddha taught this sutra, all the sixteen *śrāmaṇera*s, the bodhisattvas, completely accepted it. There were also some among the *śrāvaka*s who believed it. But all the other thousands of myriads of *koṭi*s of sentient beings became confused.

"The Buddha continuously taught this sutra for eight thousand *kalpa*s without stopping. After teaching this sutra, he immediately entered a quiet place and abided in meditation for eighty-four thousand *kalpa*s.

"At that time each of the sixteen *śrāmaṇera*s, the bodhisattvas, knowing that the Buddha had entered the quiet place and was abiding tranquilly in meditation, ascended the Dharma seat and extensively taught and explained the *Lotus Sutra* to the fourfold assembly for eighty-four thousand *kalpa*s. Each of them saved six hundred myriads of *koṭi*s of *nayuta*s of sentient beings equal in number to the sands of the Ganges River. By revealing and teaching it, they gladdened these sentient beings and awoke in them the thought of highest, complete enlightenment.

"Having arisen from *samādhi* after eighty-four thousand *kalpa*s had passed, the Buddha Mahābhijñājñānābhibhū approached the Dharma seat and sat down with complete mindfulness. He addressed everyone in the great assembly, saying:

> These sixteen *śrāmaṇera*s, bodhisattvas, are extraordinary. All their faculties are sharp and their wisdom is penetrating. In times past they have paid homage to immeasurable thousands of myriads of *koṭi*s of Buddhas and have constantly practiced the pure path of discipline and integrity under them. They preserved the wisdom of the Buddhas and revealed it to sentient beings, causing them to enter into it. All of you should approach and pay them homage again and again. Why is this?
>
> If there are any *śrāvaka*s, *pratyekabuddha*s, and bodhisattvas who are able to believe and preserve the teaching in this sutra expounded by these sixteen bodhisattvas and not disparage it, they will all attain the wisdom of the Tathāgata, highest, complete enlightenment.

The Buddha addressed the monks, saying: "These sixteen bodhisattvas always willingly taught this *Lotus Sutra*. Each bodhisattva has inspired six hundred myriads of *koṭi*s of *nayuta*s of sentient beings equal in number to the sands of the Ganges River. In life after life, they remained with these bodhisattvas and, hearing this teaching from them, they believed and understood. For this reason they were able to meet four myriads of *koṭi*s of Buddha Bhagavats during a period uninterrupted up to the present.

"O monks! I shall now tell you that these sixteen *śrāmaṇera*s, disciples of that Buddha Mahābhijñājñānābhibhū, have now attained highest, complete enlightenment and presently teach the Dharma in the lands of the ten directions. There are immeasurable hundreds of thousands of myriads of bodhisattvas and *śrāvakas* who have become their attendants.

"Two of these *śrāmaṇeras* have became Buddhas in the east. One is called Akṣobhya in the land called Abhirati and the other is called Merukūṭa. In the southeast there are two Buddhas. One is called Siṃhaghoṣa and the other is called Siṃhadhvaja. In the south there are two Buddhas called Ākāśapratiṣṭhita and Nityaparinirvṛta. There are also two Buddhas in the southwest. One is 25c
called Indradhvaja and the other is called Brahmadhvaja. In the west there are two Buddhas called Amitāyus and Sarvalokadhātūpadravodvegapratyuttīrṇa. There are two Buddhas in the northwest. One is called Tamālapatracandanagandhābhijña. The other is called Merukalpa. In the north there are two Buddhas. One is called Meghasvaradīpa and the other is called Meghasvararāja. In the northeast there is a Buddha called Sarvalokabhayacchambhitatvavidhvaṃsanakara. And the sixteenth one is myself, Buddha Śākyamuni, who in this *sahā* world achieved highest, complete enlightenment.

"O monks! When we were *śrāmaṇeras*, each of us inspired immeasurable hundreds of thousands of myriads of *koṭis* of sentient beings equal in number to the sands of the Ganges River. Those sentient beings who heard the teaching from me attained highest, complete enlightenment. There are sentient beings who still abide in the stage of a *śrāvaka* and whom I will inspire to attain highest, complete enlightenment. By means of this teaching, they will gradually enter the Buddha path. Why is this?

"The wisdom of the Tathāgatas is hard to believe and hard to understand. Those incalculable sentient beings equal in number to the sands of the Ganges River who were inspired at that time were you, O monks, and those disciples who will be *śrāvakas* in the future after my *parinirvāṇa*.

"After my *parinirvāṇa* there will be disciples who will not hear this sutra and will neither know nor understand the bodhisattva practice; yet through the merit they have acquired, the thought of extinction will awake in them and they will enter *parinirvāṇa*.

"I will become a Buddha in another land with a different name. Although the idea of extinction has awoken in these disciples and they have entered *parinirvāṇa,* in that land they will still seek the wisdom of the Buddhas and will then be able to hear this sutra. They can obtain *parinirvāṇa* only through the Buddha vehicle. There are no other vehicles except the one taught through the skillful means of the Tathāgatas.

"O monks! When the Tathāgata realizes that the time of his *parinirvāṇa* is approaching, knowing that the assembly is pure, firm in belief and understanding, has penetrated the teaching of emptiness, and has deeply entered meditation, he will then gather the assembly of bodhisattvas and *śrāvaka*s together and teach this sutra to them. In this world there is no second vehicle through which one can attain *parinirvāṇa;* only through the single Buddha vehicle can one attain it.

"You should know, O monks, that the Tathāgata through skillful means deeply penetrates the dispositions of sentient beings. Knowing their inclination toward the inferior teachings and that they are deeply attached to the desires of the five senses, he teaches nirvana for their sake. If they listen, they will accept it.

"Suppose in a desolate, fearful place there were a dangerous road five hundred *yojana*s long. There is a large group that wants to travel along this road to reach a place where there is great treasure. They have a leader who is wise and penetrating and who knows the passable and impassable parts of this dangerous road very well. Although he wants to guide these people past the dan-
26a ger, they become exhausted along the way. Addressing the leader they say:

> We are extremely tired and frightened. We cannot go any further. We are still far away from our destination, and we want to turn back.

"The leader, knowing many skillful means, thinks:

> These people are to be pitied. How could they want to turn back and abandon the great treasure?

"After thinking this the leader, through his skillful means, magically creates a city three hundred *yojanas* away along the dangerous road. He addresses the people, saying:

> Do not be frightened. Do not turn back! You may now stay in this great city and be at your leisure. If you enter this city, you can be comfortable and at ease. Once you are able to go on and reach the treasure site, then you can depart once more.

"Then the exhausted people rejoice greatly and praise this unprecedented experience, saying:

> We are now free of this evil road and will be comfortable and at ease.

"Then they proceed to the apparitional city and enter it. They believe that their hardships are over and feel at ease. Then the leader realizes that they are rested and their fatigue has gone. He immediately makes the apparitional city vanish and says to the people:

> All of you, come along! The treasure site is near. I made that great apparitional city only in order to let you rest.

"O monks! The Tathāgata is exactly like this. Now for your sake he has become a great leader who knows the long, dangerous, and evil road of birth, death, and desire's confusion. You should leave it and be saved.

"If sentient beings hear only about the single Buddha vehicle they will then want neither to see nor approach a Buddha. They will think that the Buddha path is long and attainable only after enduring severe and protracted suffering. The Buddha, knowing their minds, knowing that they are weak-willed and of lowly aspiration, teaches them the two nirvanas through skillful means in order to let them rest halfway to the goal. If there are sentient beings who abide in either of these two stages, the Tathāgata immediately teaches:

What you have accomplished is not complete. The stage you abide in is close to the wisdom of the Buddhas. You should observe and consider that the nirvana you have obtained is not the true one. It is only through the power of the Tathāgata's skillful means that the single Buddha vehicle is explained as three.

"The Buddha is just like that leader who conjured a great apparitional city to let the people rest. Knowing that they were rested, he addressed them, saying: "The treasure site is near. This city is not real. It is only my invention."

Thereupon the Bhagavat, wanting to elaborate on the meaning of this further, spoke these verses:

The Buddha Mahābhijñājñānābhibhū sat
On the terrace of enlightenment for ten *kalpa*s,
But still the Dharma of the Buddhas
Did not appear to him,
And he did not attain the Buddha path.
The *deva*s, *nāga* kings, *asura*s, and others
Constantly rained down heavenly flowers
In order to pay homage to that Buddha.
26b The *deva*s beat heavenly drums
And played various kinds of music.
The fragrant winds blew the withered flowers away
And then they rained down fresh, beautiful ones.
After ten intermediate *kalpa*s had passed,
He then attained the Buddha path;
And all the *deva*s and humans
Became joyful and ecstatic.
The sixteen princes of that Buddha,
Surrounded by thousands of
Myriads of *koṭi*s of attendants,
Came to the place where the Buddha was.
Having bowed until their foreheads touched his feet,
They requested him to turn the wheel of the Dharma

Saying:

> O Noble Lion!
> Fill us and everyone else with the rain of the Dharma!
> It is extremely difficult to meet a Bhagavat,
> Since he appears only once in a very long time!

To get the attention of the beings,
The Buddha shook the entire world.
The palaces of the Brahmas in the five hundred
Myriads of *koṭis* of lands in the east
Were illuminated as never before.
All of the Brahmas, seeing this phenomenon,
Came to the place where the Buddha was.
They reverently scattered flowers
And offered him their palaces.
Requesting the Buddha
To turn the wheel of the Dharma,
They praised him in verse.
The Buddha knew that the right time
Had not yet arrived,
And although he had been asked,
He sat in silence.
The other three directions, the four remaining quarters,
And the upper and lower regions were all like this.
All the Brahmas scattered flowers,
Offered their palaces, and requested the Buddha
To turn the wheel of the Dharma,
Saying:

> It is extremely difficult to meet a Bhagavat.
> We entreat you to open wide the gate to immortality
> And turn the wheel of the highest Dharma
> Through your great compassion!

The Bhagavat, having immeasurable wisdom,
Accepted their request

And expounded various teachings,
Such as the Four [Noble] Truths
And the twelve-linked chain of dependent origination,
saying:

> Beginning with ignorance
> And ending with old age and death,
> All these derive from birth.
> You should know about such miseries!

When the Buddha expounded this teaching,
Six hundred myriads of *koṭi*s of trillions of people
Attained the complete extinction of all suffering,
And became arhats.
At the time of the second teaching,
Thousands of myriads of people,
Equal in number to the sands of the Ganges River,
Unattached to any existent thing,
Also attained arhatship.
After that an incalculable number
Of beings attained the path.
26c Even if one were to count
For myriads of *koṭi*s of *kalpa*s,
One could not finish counting their number.
Then the sixteen princes renounced
Household life and became *śrāmaṇera*s.
They all asked the Buddha to expound
The teaching of the Mahayana, saying:

> Let us and all of our attendants
> Attain the Buddha path!
> We entreat you to let us obtain
> The Bhagavat's eye of wisdom, supreme in purity!

The Buddha, knowing the minds of his children
And their past conduct, taught the six perfections
And various transcendent powers

Through incalculably numerous explanations
And various illustrations.
Explaining the true teaching
And the path to be practiced by the bodhisattvas,
He taught this *Lotus Sutra* in verses
Equal in number to the sands of the Ganges River.
After the Buddha taught this sutra,
He entered meditation in a quiet place
And sat with complete concentration in the same spot
For eighty-four thousand *kalpa*s.
Those *śrāmaṇera*s, knowing that the Buddha
Had not arisen from meditation,
Taught the highest wisdom of the Buddhas
To immeasurable *koṭi*s of beings.
Each sat on the Dharma seat
And explained this Mahayana sutra.
After the great *parinirvāṇa* of that Buddha,
They propagated the Dharma and inspired others.
Each *śrāmaṇera* saved
Six hundred myriads of *koṭi*s of sentient beings,
Equal in number to the sands of the Ganges River.
Those who heard the teaching
After the Buddha's *parinirvāṇa*
Were always born together with their teachers
In various other Buddha lands.
These sixteen *śrāmaṇera*s
Completely cultivated the Buddha path
And now, in the ten directions,
They have attained highest, complete enlightenment.
Then those who heard the Dharma
In the presence of each of these Buddhas
And those who are in the *śrāvaka* stage
Will gradually be taught the Buddha path.
I am one of the sixteen.
I have also taught you in the past.

Therefore through skillful means
I will now also lead you to the goal
Which is the wisdom of the Buddhas.
Through these former causes and conditions,
I will now teach the *Lotus Sutra*
In order to let you enter the Buddha path.
Do not be worried or frightened!
Suppose there were a dangerous road
In a deserted wasteland far away,
Where there are many harmful beasts.
27a There is neither water nor grass.
It is a fearful place for human beings.
Innumerable thousands of myriads of beings
Wish to pass along this dangerous way.
But that road is very long,
Some five hundred *yojana*s.
Then there is a leader,
Endowed with deep wisdom and knowledge,
Discerning and resolute,
Who saves the people from various calamities
When they meet with danger.
The people all get tired
And address the leader, saying:

> We are all now totally exhausted.
> We want to turn back from here!

The leader thinks:

> These people are really to be pitied.
> How could they possibly want to return
> And lose the great treasure!

He immediately thinks of skillful means
And how he should now use his transcendent powers;
And he makes a great apparitional city

With houses adorned and surrounded
With gardens, moats, and ponds.
There are fortified gates and tall towers,
And it is full of men and women.
When the apparition is complete,
He immediately consoles the people, saying:

> Do not be afraid!
> When you enter the city,
> You can each do as you please.

All the people enter the city.
They are very happy and feel at ease,
Thinking they have been saved.
When the leader knows they are rested,
He gathers them together and addresses them, saying:

> You should now proceed,
> For this is just an apparitional city!
> Seeing that you were extremely fatigued
> And that you wanted to turn back
> After coming halfway,
> I made this apparitional city through skillful means.
> You should now strive
> To reach the treasure site together.

I am exactly like this.
I am the leader of all.
Perceiving that those seeking the way
Have become timid, have stopped halfway,
And are unable to walk to the end of the dangerous road
Of birth, death, and desire's confusion,
I use skillful means and teach nirvana
So that they may rest, saying:

> You have extinguished suffering,
> And you have completed what must be done.

Knowing that they have reached nirvana
And attained arhatship, the Buddha immediately
Gathers the great assembly together
And teaches the True Dharma.
27b All the Buddhas explain and teach
The three vehicles through skillful means.
Although there is only the single Buddha vehicle,
They teach two in order to provide a place of rest.
For your benefit I now teach the truth:

> What you have attained is not the ultimate goal.
> You must call forth great efforts
> In order to obtain the omniscience of a Buddha.
> If you attain omniscience
> And the qualities of the Buddha,
> Such things as the ten powers,
> And become endowed with the thirty-two marks,
> Then you will have attained the ultimate goal.

The Buddhas, the Leaders, teach nirvana
In order to let beings rest in comfort.
When they know that they have rested,
They lead them to the wisdom of the Buddhas.

Chapter VIII

The Five Hundred Disciples Receive Their Predictions

At that time, Pūrṇa, the son of Maitrāyaṇī, after hearing the Buddha teach the Dharma according to what is appropriate to sentient beings through the wisdom of skillful means and bestow the prediction of highest, complete enlightenment on all the great disciples, and then hearing stories about past causes and conditions and that all the Buddhas have obtained perfect mastery of transcendent powers, obtained an unprecedented experience and became pure in mind and joyful. He immediately rose from his seat, went into the presence of the Buddha, bowed until his forehead touched the Buddha's feet, and then stood to one side gazing unwaveringly at the Buddha and thought this:

> The Bhagavat is truly marvelous. His actions are rare. He teaches the Dharma according to the natural capacities of the beings in the world through skillful means, wisdom, and insight. He leads sentient beings away from their various attachments. We have no words to describe the Buddha's qualities. Only the Buddha, the Bhagavat, is able to know our deep intentions and original vow.

Then the Buddha addressed the monks, saying: "Do you see Pūrṇa, the son of Maitrāyaṇī? I always praise him as the foremost among the teachers of the Dharma. I also always praise his various qualities. He diligently maintains and propagates my teaching and is able to gladden and benefit the fourfold assembly. He interprets the True Dharma of the Buddhas perfectly and greatly 27c
benefits those who practice the pure path of discipline and integrity together with him. With the exception of the Tathāgata no one else explains the doctrine more eloquently.

"You must not think that Pūrṇa is only now able to protect and propagate my teaching. He also protected and propagated the True Dharma of the Buddhas in the presence of ninety *koṭi*s of Buddhas in the past when he was always the foremost among the teachers of the Dharma. Moreover he was completely versed in the teaching of emptiness that the Buddhas taught, and attained the fourfold unobstructed wisdom. He has always been able to teach the Dharma clearly and purely. He never had any doubts and was endowed with the transcendent powers of the bodhisattvas.

"Throughout each life he always practiced the pure path of discipline and integrity. The people who lived in the same Buddha world all thought he really was a *śrāvaka*, yet Pūrṇa benefited immeasurable hundreds of thousands of sentient beings through this skillful means and also led and inspired immeasurable incalculable numbers of beings and caused them to attain highest, complete enlightenment. In order to purify the Buddha land he always did what the Buddhas have done and led and inspired sentient beings.

"O monks! Pūrṇa also was able to become the foremost among the teachers of the Dharma under the past seven Buddhas; and he is also the foremost of those who preach the Dharma under me. He will also be the foremost among the teachers of the Dharma under the future Buddhas in this auspicious *kalpa*. He will protect and propagate the Buddha-Dharma; and also in the future he will protect and propagate the Dharma of incalculable limitless Buddhas. He will lead, inspire, and benefit incalculable sentient beings and cause them to attain highest, complete enlightenment. In order to purify the Buddha lands he will always be diligent and persevering, leading and inspiring sentient beings.

"He will gradually perfect the bodhisattva path and, after immeasurable incalculable *kalpa*s, he will attain highest, complete enlightenment in this land. He will be called Dharmaprabhāsa, a Tathāgata, Arhat, Completely Enlightened, Perfect in Knowledge and Conduct, Well-Departed, Knower of the World, Unsurpassed, Tamer of Humans, Teacher of Devas and Humans, Buddha, Bhagavat. That Buddha's land will consist of all the worlds in the great manifold cosmos, equal in number to the sands of the Ganges River. The earth will be made of the seven treasures and it will be level, just like the palm of one's hand. There will be no mountains, valleys, or hollow places. This land will be filled with towers of the seven treasures. The heavenly palaces will be in the sky close at hand, and the humans and *deva*s will come and go between them, so that they will be able to see each other. There will be no troubled states of being nor any women. All the sentient beings will be born here spontaneously, without any sexual desires. They will attain great transcendent powers, emit rays of light from their bodies, and fly freely through the air.

"These beings will be firm in recollection, persevering, and wise. They will all be of golden hue and adorned with the thirty-two marks. The sentient beings in that land will always eat two meals: one being the meal of delight in the Dharma, and the other the meal of pleasure in meditation.

"There will be immeasurable incalculable thousands of myri- 28a
ads of *koṭi*s of *nayuta*s of bodhisattvas who have attained great transcendent powers and the fourfold unobstructed wisdom. They will be able skillfully to lead and inspire sentient beings. The number of *śrāvaka*s there will be impossible to calculate. They will all perfect the six transcendent powers, the three sciences, and the eight liberations.

"Such will be the immeasurable merits of this Buddha's land, being perfect in adornment. The *kalpa* will be called Ratnāvabhāsa and his land will be called Suviśuddha. This Buddha's lifespan will last for immeasurable incalculable *kalpa*s, and the Dharma will abide for a very long time. After the *parinirvāṇa* of that Buddha, stupas of the seven treasures will be erected everywhere throughout the land."

Then the Bhagavat, wanting to elaborate on the meaning of this further, spoke these verses:

O monks! Listen carefully!
The path that the heir of the Buddhas

Has practiced by learning skillful means
Cannot be conceived.
Because the bodhisattvas know
That sentient beings long for inferior teachings
And are afraid of great knowledge,
They make themselves either *śrāvaka*s
Or *pratyekabuddha*s.
They inspire those sentient beings
Using innumerable skillful means, saying:

> We are *śrāvaka*s and still very far away
> From attaining the Buddha path.

They save immeasurable sentient beings,
All of whom they cause to attain perfection;
And they even cause those who are lazy,
Or who have lowly intentions,
Gradually to become Buddhas.
These beings secretly carry out the bodhisattva practice
While outwardly calling themselves *śrāvaka*s.
Having little desire,
Their thoughts fixed on birth and death,
They in fact purify the Buddha lands.
These bodhisattvas show sentient beings
That they have the three poisons
And further they reveal the mark of false views.
In this way my disciples save
Sentient beings through skillful means.
If I fully disclosed
That they had taken on various forms,
The sentient beings hearing this
Would immediately become doubtful.
This Pūrṇa has now practiced the path
Under thousands of *koṭi*s of Buddhas in the past,
And he has propagated and protected
The teaching of these Buddhas.

Seeking the highest wisdom
Under all these Buddhas,
He showed that he was the foremost
Among the disciples,
And that he was knowledgeable and wise.
Fearless in his teaching,
He was able to gladden the people.
He never tired in performing
The actions of a Buddha.
He has already attained the great transcendent powers
And is endowed with the fourfold unobstructed wisdom.
Knowing whether the faculties 28b
Of sentient beings are sharp or dull,
He always teaches the pure Dharma.
Expounding such doctrines as these,
He has taught thousands of *koṭi*s of beings
And, by making them abide in the Mahayana teaching,
He himself has purified his Buddha land.
In the future he will also pay homage to
Incalculable innumerable Buddhas,
Protect and propagate the True Dharma,
And also purify his Buddha land.
He will always fearlessly teach the Dharma
Using his skillful means,
Save incalculable sentient beings,
And enable them to achieve omniscience.
Paying homage to all the Tathāgatas
And preserving the treasure house of the Dharma,
He will eventually become the Buddha
Called Dharmaprabhāsa.
His land will be called Suviśuddha
Which will consist of the seven treasures;
His *kalpa* will be called Ratnāvabhāsa.
There will be a large number of bodhisattvas there
Numbering immeasurable *koṭi*s.

His Buddha land will be filled
With bodhisattvas who have attained
Great transcendent powers,
And are endowed with dignity.
There will also be innumerable *śrāvaka*s
Who have perfected the three sciences,
The eight liberations,
And the fourfold unobstructed wisdom.
Such beings as these will form the sangha.
The sentient beings in his land
Will have already cut themselves off from sexual desires.
Everyone there will thus be pure and born spontaneously,
With bodies adorned with the thirty-two marks.
They will feast on delight in the Dharma
And pleasure in meditation,
Never thinking of eating anything else.
There will be neither women
Nor troubled states of existence.
The qualities of the monk Pūrṇa
Will be completely perfected
And there will be many wise people
In this pure land.
I am now only briefly explaining
These immeasurable things.

Thereupon there were twelve hundred arhats, who had attained complete mental discipline, who thought this: "We have joyfully attained an unprecedented experience. If the Bhagavat would give each of us a prediction like those he has given the other great disciples, we would be overjoyed!"

The Buddha, knowing their minds, addressed Mahākāśyapa, saying: "I shall now bestow the prediction of highest, complete enlightenment one by one on these twelve hundred arhats who are in my presence.

"My great disciple, the monk Ājñātakauṇḍinya who is in this assembly, will pay homage to sixty-two thousands of *koṭi*s of

Buddhas. He will thereafter become the Buddha called Samanta- 28c
prabha, a Tathāgata, Arhat, Completely Enlightened, Perfect in Knowledge and Conduct, Well-Departed, Knower of the World, Unsurpassed, Tamer of Humans, Teacher of Devas and Humans, Buddha, Bhagavat.

"The five hundred arhats beginning with Uruvilvakāśyapa, Gayākāśyapa, Nadīkāśyapa, Kālodāyin, Udāyin, Aniruddha, Revata, Kapphiṇa, Bakkula, Cunda, Svāgata, and the others will all attain highest, complete enlightenment. They will all have the same name, that of Samantaprabha."

Then the Bhagavat, wanting to elaborate the meaning of this further, spoke these verses:

The monk Kauṇḍinya
Will meet immeasurable Buddhas
And, after incalculable *kalpas* have passed,
He will attain perfect enlightenment.
He will always emit a great ray of light
And will be endowed with transcendent powers.
His fame will spread universally
Throughout the ten directions.
He will be honored by all beings
And will always teach the highest path;
He will therefore be called Samantaprabha.
His land will be pure,
And the bodhisattvas there
Will all be of great vigor.
They will all ascend marvelous towers
And roam in the lands of the ten directions;
They will present the most excellent offerings
To all of the Buddhas.
After having shown their reverence in this way,
They will be full of great joy
And immediately return to their own lands.
Such will be their transcendent powers.
The lifespan of this Buddha

Will be sixty thousand *kalpa*s
And the True Dharma will last
Twice as long as his lifespan.
The Semblance Dharma
Will last twice as long as this.
When the Dharma disappears,
The *deva*s and humans will grieve.
Those five hundred monks
Will become Buddhas each in their turn,
All having the same name Samantaprabha.
They will give predictions
One after the other, saying:

> After my *parinirvāṇa*
> So-and-so will become a Buddha.
> The world he inspires
> Will be exactly like mine today.
> The embellishments of their lands,
> All the transcendent powers,
> The assembly of bodhisattvas and *śrāvaka*s,
> The True and Semblance Dharma,
> The lifespan and duration of the *kalpa,*
> Will be just as I explained before.

O Kāśyapa! You now know
That the five hundred arhats
Whose minds are free,
And the remaining *śrāvaka*s
Will also be exactly like this.
You should teach those
Who are not in this assembly!

29a Thereupon the five hundred arhats, having obtained their predictions from the Buddha, were joyful and ecstatic. They rose from their seats, approached the Buddha, bowed until their foreheads touched his feet, repented of their faults, and reproached themselves, saying: "O Bhagavat! We have always thought we had attained complete nirvana. We now realize that we were ignorant. Why is this? We should have attained the wisdom of the Tathāgatas. Yet we were satisfied with little wisdom!

"O Bhagavat! Suppose there were a man who came to the house of a close friend and went to sleep after becoming intoxicated with wine. The intimate friend, having to go out on official business, sews a priceless jewel into the inside of his friend's garment and, giving it to him, leaves. But the man who was drunk and asleep is totally unaware of this. After getting up he leaves and roams around until he arrives in another country. Although he diligently seeks for food and clothing they are very difficult to obtain. He is satisfied if he just obtains a very meager amount. Later on the intimate friend happens to meet this man. Seeing him, he says:

> O poor fellow! How have you come to this state through lack of food and clothing? Once, on such-and-such a day in such-and-such a month and year, I sewed a priceless jewel into the inside of your garment, wanting to make things easier for you and to let you enjoy the desires of the five senses as much as you wished.
>
> It is still there, although you aren't aware of it, and you seek your livelihood with great effort and hardship! You have been very foolish. Sell this jewel and use it to buy what you need. From now on you will know neither poverty nor want and can live as you wish.

"The Buddha is exactly like this. When he was a bodhisattva he aroused in us the aspiration for omniscience. Nevertheless we forgot, we did not know or understand. We attained the path of the arhats and considered that we had attained nirvana. It was very hard for us to support ourselves and we were satisfied with little. But we never fully lost our wish for all-knowledge. Now the Bhagavat, perceiving our minds, has said this:

> O monks! What you have attained is not the complete nirvana. For a long time I have made you plant the various roots of good merit of a Buddha and shown you the marks of nirvana through

skillful means. That is why you consider yourselves to have actually attained nirvana!

"O Bhagavat! We now know that we are actually bodhisattvas and will obtain a prediction of highest, complete enlightenment. For this reason we are extremely happy at having obtained such an unprecedented experience."

At that time Ājñātakauṇḍinya and the others, wanting to elaborate on the meaning of this further, spoke these verses:

We have heard his voice
Giving the prediction of utmost ease.
Rejoicing in this unprecedented experience,
We bow to the Buddha whose wisdom is immeasurable.
We now repent of our faults
In the presence of the Bhagavat.
Although we had attained
Only a small measure of nirvana,
Out of the immeasurable treasures of the Buddha,
29b We were self-satisfied,
Just like ignorant fools!
Suppose there were a poor man
Who went to the house of a close friend
Whose family was very wealthy.
He was entertained with a feast
And had a priceless jewel sewn
To the inside of his garment.
The wealthy friend made him this gift
Without saying anything, and went away.
The poor man had fallen asleep
And did not know of this.
Shortly afterward this man gets up,
And after wandering around
Arrives in another country.
He manages to seek out
Enough food and clothing to live

But has great difficulty in supporting himself.
Yet he is satisfied to obtain a little
And does not desire anything better.
He is still unaware of the priceless jewel
Sewn inside his garment.
The intimate friend who gave him the jewel
Meets this poor man later
And bitterly reproaches him,
Showing him the jewel
That had been sewn into his garment.
The poor man, seeing this jewel, rejoices greatly
And with this rich treasure he enjoys
To his satisfaction the desires of the five senses.
We are exactly like this.
For a long time, the Bhagavat
Has led and inspired us
Through his compassion,
And planted in us the highest aspiration.
Because we were ignorant
We neither noticed nor knew;
We were satisfied with attaining
Only a small measure of nirvana
And did not seek for the rest.
Now the Buddha has enlightened us, saying:

> This is not the real nirvana.
> Attaining the highest wisdom of the Buddhas
> Is indeed the only real nirvana.

Now, having heard the predictions from the Buddha
And of the adorned lands,
And the subsequent predictions,
We universally rejoice in body and mind!

Chapter IX

The Predictions for Those Who Still Have More to Learn and for Those Who Do Not

At that time Ānanda and Rāhula thought this: "The delight we would feel if we were to receive our predictions is constantly before our minds!"

Then arising from their seats and going into the presence of the Buddha, they bowed until their foreheads touched his feet, and spoke to him in unison, saying: "O Bhagavat! We should also be qualified to receive our predictions! Both of us take refuge only in the Tathāgata. Moreover we are well known by the *deva*s, humans, and *asura*s throughout the entire world! Ānanda has always attended the Tathāgata, preserving the treasure house of the Dharma; and Rāhula is the son of the Buddha. If the Buddha would bestow upon us the prediction of highest, complete enlightenment then our vows would be fulfilled and our wishes also realized!"

Then two thousand disciples, *śrāvaka*s, some who still had 29c
more to learn, and some who did not, all arose from their seats and with their right shoulders bared went into the presence of the Buddha. Attentively, with palms pressed together, they gazed at the Bhagavat, all having the same wish as Ānanda and Rāhula, and stood to one side. Then the Buddha addressed Ānanda, saying: "In the future world you will become a Buddha called Sāgaradharabuddhivikrīḍitarājābhijña, a Tathāgata, Arhat, Completely Enlightened, Perfect in Knowledge and Conduct, Well-Departed, Knower of the World, Unsurpassed, Tamer of Humans, Teacher of Devas and Humans, Buddha, Bhagavat. You will pay homage to sixty-two *koṭi*s of Buddhas, preserve the treasure house of the Dharma and ultimately attain highest, complete enlightenment.

Further, you will inspire twenty thousands of myriads of *koṭi*s of bodhisattvas, equal in number to the sands of the Ganges River, causing them to attain highest, complete enlightenment.

"Your land will be called Avanāmitavaijayantā. It will be pure and the earth will be made of lapis lazuli. The *kalpa* will be called Manojñaśabdābhigarjita. The lifespan of this Buddha will be for immeasurable, incalculable thousands of myriads of *koṭi*s of *kalpa*s. Their number would be incalculable even if one were to count for immeasurable, innumerable thousands of myriads of *koṭi*s of *kalpa*s. The True Dharma will abide in the world twice as long as his lifespan and the Semblance Dharma will abide in the world twice as long as the True Dharma.

"O Ānanda! The virtues of this Buddha Sāgaradharabuddhivikrīḍitarājābhijña will be praised by immeasurable thousands of myriads of *koṭi*s of Buddha Tathāgatas in the ten directions, equal in number to the sands of the Ganges River."

Thereupon the Tathāgata, wanting to elaborate on the meaning of this further, spoke these verses:

> I now tell the assembly
> That Ānanda, the preserver of the Dharma,
> Will pay homage to the Buddhas
> And ultimately attain complete enlightenment.
> He will be called the Buddha
> Sāgaradharabuddhivikrīḍitarājābhijña.
> His land will be pure
> And called Avanāmitavaijayantā
> He will lead and inspire bodhisattvas
> In numbers equal to the sands of the Ganges River.
> This Buddha will be endowed
> With great virtue and dignity, and his fame
> Will fill the ten directions.
> His lifespan will be immeasurable
> Due to his compassion for sentient beings.
> The True Dharma will abide

Twice as long as his lifespan
And the Semblance Dharma will abide
Twice as long as the True Dharma.
Countless sentient beings
Within the Dharma of this Buddha,
Equal in number to the sands of the Ganges River,
Will plant the seed of the Buddha path."

At that time the eight thousand bodhisattvas in the assembly, in whom the thought of enlightenment (*bodhicittta*) had recently awakened, all thought this: "Since we have never heard the great bodhisattvas receive predictions like this, why should 30a
the *śrāvaka*s now obtain it?"

Then the Bhagavat, knowing what the bodhisattvas were thinking, spoke to them, saying: "O sons of a virtuous family! The thought of highest, complete enlightenment once awoke simultaneously in Ānanda and myself in the presence of the Buddha Dharmagaganābhyudgatarāja. Ānanda always wanted to hear a great deal about the Dharma, and I always made diligent efforts. For this reason I was shortly able to attain highest, complete enlightenment, whereas Ānanda preserves my teaching and in the future will uphold the treasure house of the Dharma of all the Buddhas. He will lead, inspire, and perfect the bodhisattvas. Since this was his original vow, he has obtained this prediction!"

Ānanda, while facing the Buddha in the audience, heard his own prediction and about the adornments of his land. His vow fulfilled, he rejoiced greatly at attaining such an unprecedented experience. With his unobstructed penetration he immediately remembered the treasure house of the Dharma of the past immeasurable thousands of myriads of *koṭi*s of Buddhas as if he had just heard of it today; and he also became aware of his original vow.

Thereupon Ānanda spoke these verses:

The Bhagavat is truly extraordinary.
He has enabled me to recollect the Dharma
Of incalculable numbers of Buddhas of the past,

Just as if I had first heard of the matter today.
I now have no further doubts.
I am established in the Buddha path.
I have become an attendant of the Tathāgata
And, as an attendant, I will preserve
The Dharma of all the Buddhas, using skillful means.

Then the Buddha addressed Rāhula, saying: "In the future you will become a Buddha called Saptaratnapadmavikrama, a Tathāgata, Arhat, Completely Enlightened, Perfect in Knowledge and Conduct, Well-Departed, Knower of the World, Unsurpassed, Tamer of Humans, Teacher of Devas and Humans, Buddha, Bhagavat. You will pay homage to the Buddha Tathāgatas, whose number is equal to that of the grains of dust in the ten worlds; and you will always become the eldest son of all the Buddhas just as you are my eldest son now.

"The adornments of the land, the number of disciples led and inspired, the duration of the True and Semblance Dharma of this Buddha Saptaratnapadmavikrama will be just like those of the Buddha Sāgaradharabuddhivikrīḍitarājābhijña, without the slightest difference. You will also become the eldest son of this Buddha and after that attain highest, complete enlightenment."

At that time the Bhagavat, wanting to elaborate on the meaning of this further, spoke these verses:

When I was a prince,
Rāhula was my eldest son.
And now that I have perfected the Buddha path,
He accepts my teaching as the heir of the Dharma.
In the future he will meet
Immeasurable *koṭis* of Buddhas.
Becoming the eldest son of all these Buddhas,
He will wholeheartedly seek
The Buddha path.
Only I am able to discern
Rāhula's unseen practice.

But now that he has become my eldest son, 30b
He reveals it to the sentient beings.
His thousands of myriads
Of *koṭis* of merits are uncountable and incalculable;
He will become established in the Buddha-Dharma
And seek the highest path.

Then the Bhagavat perceived that the minds of those two thousand people, some of whom had more to learn and some of whom did not, were sincere, mild, and receptive. They were all attentively gazing at the Buddha. The Buddha said to Ānanda: "Do you not see these two thousand people, some of whom have more to learn and some of whom do not?"

Ānanda replied: "Yes, I see them."

The Buddha said: "O Ānanda! All of these people will pay homage to the Buddha Tathāgatas, whose number is equal to that of the grains of dust in fifty worlds. They will respect, honor, and preserve the treasure house of the Dharma and will later all become Buddhas simultaneously in the worlds in the ten directions. They will all have the same name, Ratnaketurāja, a Tathāgata, Arhat, Completely Enlightened, Perfect in Knowledge and Conduct, Well-Departed, Knower of the World, Unsurpassed, Tamer of Humans, Teacher of Devas and Humans, Buddha, Bhagavat. Their lifespans will last one *kalpa*. The adornments of their lands, the number of *śrāvaka*s and bodhisattvas, and the duration of the True and Semblance Dharma will be the same for all."

Thereupon the Bhagavat, wanting to elaborate on the meaning of this further, spoke these verses:

Now in my presence
These two thousand *śrāvaka*s
Have all received their predictions.
In the future they will all become Buddhas.
The Buddhas they will revere
Will be equal to the number of grains of dust,
Just as mentioned above.

Preserving this treasure house of the Dharma,
They will later attain complete enlightenment.
They will all have the same name
And dwell in the lands of the ten directions.
All sitting at the exact same time,
On the terrace of enlightenment,
They will attain the highest wisdom.
All of them will be called Ratnaketurāja.
Their lands, the number of disciples,
Duration of the True and Semblance Dharma
Will all be the same without any difference.
Moreover, through their transcendent powers,
They will save sentient beings
Throughout the ten directions.
Their fame will spread universally
And they will gradually enter nirvana.

Then the two thousand people, some of whom had more to learn and some of whom did not, having heard their predictions from the Buddha, rejoiced ecstatically and spoke in verse:

O Bhagavat, the Light of Wisdom!
We have just heard you give us our predictions
And our minds are full of joy,
Just as if we had been sprinkled
With the Dharma of immortality.

Chapter X

The Expounder of the Dharma

Thereupon the Bhagavat by addressing Bodhisattva Bhaiṣajyarāja (Medicine King), through him addressed eighty thousand *mahāsattvas*, saying: "O Bhaiṣajyarāja! In this assembly do you see innumerable humans and nonhumans such as *devas*, *nāga* kings, *yakṣas*, *gandharvas*, *asuras*, *garuḍas*, *kiṃnaras*, *mahoragas*, monks, nuns, laymen, and laywomen, those seeking the *śrāvaka* vehicle, the *pratyekabuddha* vehicle, and the Buddha path? If, in the presence of the Buddha any beings such as these hear a single verse or line of the *Lotus Sutra,* and thereupon have even one thought of rejoicing in it, I will bestow upon them my prediction that they will attain highest, complete enlightenment."

The Buddha addressed Bhaiṣajyarāja, saying: "If, after the *parinirvāṇa* of the Tathāgata, any being hears even a single verse or line of the *Lotus Sutra,* and thereupon has even one thought of rejoicing in it, I will bestow upon them the prediction that they will attain highest, complete enlightenment.

"If there is anyone who preserves, recites, explains, or copies even a single verse of the *Lotus Sutra,* or who respects this sutra as if it were a Buddha, or who reverently offers it various flowers, perfumes, necklaces, fragrant ointments, scented powders, burning incense, canopies, flags, banners, clothing, or music, or who simply honors it with his palms pressed together, know, O Bhaiṣajyarāja, that this person has already paid homage to tens of myriads of *koṭis* of Buddhas of the past! Such people have completed their great vow in the presence of all the Buddhas and yet they have been born as humans out of their compassion for sentient beings.

"O Bhaiṣajyarāja! If anyone should ask you what kind of sentient being will become a Buddha in the future, you should inform them that it is those of this kind who will definitely become Buddhas in the future. Why is this?

"If there are any sons or daughters of a virtuous family who preserve, recite, explain, and copy even a single line of the *Lotus Sutra,* or who pay homage to this sutra with various offerings of flowers, perfumes, necklaces, scented powders and ointments, burning incense, canopies, flags, banners, clothing, or music, or who honor it with their palms pressed together, such people should be respected by the entire world. They should be revered in the same way as the Tathāgata is revered. Know that these people are great bodhisattvas who are to attain highest, complete enlightenment. Out of their compassion for sentient beings they wish to be born among them in order to expound and explain the *Lotus Sutra* far and wide. How much more to be honored are those who completely preserve the entire sutra and pay homage to it with various offerings!

"O Bhaiṣajyarāja! You should know that after my *parinirvāṇa* these people will set aside the rewards of their pure karma and be born in the troubled world out of their compassion for sentient beings, and in order to expound this sutra far and wide. After my *parinirvāṇa,* if there are any sons and daughters of a virtuous family who expound even a single line of the *Lotus Sutra* in private to even a single person, they should be acknowledged as the ambassadors of the Tathāgata. They have been dispatched by the Tathāgata and carry out the Tathāgata's work. As for those who extensively teach among the common people, know that they are yet greater ambassadors.

31a "O Bhaiṣajyarāja, if there are erring people during a *kalpa,* those with troubled thoughts who always disparage the Buddha in his presence, their fault is nonetheless slight. Yet if there are those who disparage the laity or ordained people who recite the *Lotus Sutra* even with a single evil word, their fault is extremely grave.

"O Bhaiṣajyarāja! Know that those who recite this *Lotus Sutra* adorn themselves with the adornments of a Buddha. This means that they will carry the Tathāgata on their shoulders and pay him homage wherever they go. They should be respected, revered, honored, and praised wholeheartedly with palms pressed together, through offerings of flowers, perfumes, necklaces, scented powders, ointments, burning incense, canopies, flags, banners, clothing, delicious food, music, and the best offerings that people can make. They should have heavenly jewels scattered upon them and offered to them. Why is this? Because these people joyfully expound the Dharma and those who hear it even for an instant will fully attain highest, complete enlightenment."

Thereupon the Bhagavat, wanting to elaborate upon the meaning of this further, spoke these verses:

> Those who want to abide in the Buddha path
> And perfect the wisdom of the Self-generated One,
> Should always diligently pay homage
> To those who preserve the *Lotus Sutra.*
> Those who want to quickly attain omniscience
> Should hold to this sutra
> And pay homage to those who preserve it.
> Know that anyone who preserves the *Lotus Sutra*
> Is an ambassador of the Buddha
> Who feels compassion for sentient beings.
> Those who preserve the *Lotus Sutra*
> Were born here in this world,
> Withholding themselves from the Pure Land
> Out of their compassion for sentient beings.
> Know that such people are born
> Where and when they will.
> They are born in this troubled world
> To extensively expound the highest Dharma.
> Such expounders of the Dharma should be revered
> With offerings of divine flowers, perfumes,
> Heavenly jeweled clothing, and exquisite celestial jewels.
> Those who preserve this sutra
> In the troubled world after my *parinirvāṇa,*

Should be paid homage with palms pressed together
Just as one pays homage to the Bhagavat.
These heirs of the Buddhas should be revered
With delicious food, various delicacies,
And a variety of clothing, in the hope of hearing
The teaching even for an instant.
If in the future there is anyone
Who preserves this sutra,
31b I will dispatch him to the world of humans
To carry out the Tathāgata's task.
If throughout one entire *kalpa*
There is anyone with erring thoughts
Who always disparages the Buddha
With an angry countenance, the consequences of
His grave errors will be incalculable.
If there is anyone who speaks
A hostile word even for an instant
About those who recite and preserve this *Lotus Sutra,*
His fault will be even greater.
If throughout one entire *kalpa*
There are people seeking for the Buddha path
Who praise the Buddha in my presence
With incalculable numbers of verses
And with palms pressed together,
The merits they attain will be immeasurable
Because of praising this Buddha.
If there are people who praise
Those who preserve the sutra,
Their merit will be even greater.
You must pay tribute to those who preserve the sutra
Throughout eighty *koṭi*s of *kalpa*s
With the best objects, sounds,
Fragrances, flavors, and materials.
If you are able to hear the teaching for even a moment,

After having paid tribute in this way,
You will then become delighted, thinking:

I have now attained great benefits.

O Bhaiṣajyarāja! I now tell you that
I have taught many sutras;
Among these sutras, however,
The *Lotus Sutra* is the utmost and best.

Then the Buddha spoke further to Bodhisattva Mahāsattva Bhaiṣajyarāja, saying: "There are immeasurable thousands of myriads of *koṭi*s of sutras I have taught in the past, which I teach now, and which I will teach in the future. Among them, however, this *Lotus Sutra* is the most difficult to accept and to understand.

"O Bhaiṣajyarāja! This sutra is the treasure house of the hidden essence of all the Buddhas. It must not be distributed or heedlessly bestowed upon the people. Since times long past all the Buddha Bhagavats have protected it and have never openly taught it. Moreover, people show great hostility to this sutra, even in the presence of the Tathāgata. How much more so after the *parinirvāṇa* of the Tathāgata!

"O Bhaiṣajyarāja! You should know that after the *parinirvāṇa* of the Tathāgata, those who copy, preserve, recite, and revere this sutra and expound it for the sake of others will be clothed with the Tathāgata's garments and treasured by the present Buddhas of the other directions. Such people will have the power of great faith, the power of aspiration, as well as the power of the roots of good merit. You should know that these people have dwelled together with the Tathāgata, and his hand has caressed their heads.

"O Bhaiṣajyarāja! Wherever this sutra is taught, read, recited, copied, or wherever it is to be found, one should build a seven-jeweled stupa of great height and width and richly ornamented. There is no need to put a relic inside. Why is this? Because the Tathāgata is already in it. This stupa should be respected, honored, praised and rendered homage with offerings of all kinds of flowers, 31c perfumes, necklaces, canopies, flags, banners, music, and songs. If there is anyone able to see this stupa and to pay it homage and honor it, know that such a one is nearing highest, complete enlightenment.

"O Bhaiṣajyarāja! Among the many people, either among the laity or the ordained, who practice the bodhisattva path, if they are unable to see, hear, recite, copy, preserve, and pay homage to this *Lotus Sutra,* know that they are people who are not yet properly practicing the bodhisattva path. If anyone is able to hear this sutra, such a one is skillfully practicing the bodhisattva path. Among sentient beings seeking the Buddha path, if there are those who see or hear this *Lotus Sutra* and, after hearing it, are drawn to it and preserve it, know that they are those who are approaching highest, complete enlightenment.

"O Bhaiṣajyarāja! Suppose there were a thirsty man seeking water. He drills in search of water on a high plain, yet he sees only dry earth and thus realizes that water is still far away. But he does not cease his efforts until he turns up moist earth and gradually reaches mud. Now he is sure that water must be near.

"The bodhisattvas are exactly like this. If they have not yet heard, understood, or been able to practice this *Lotus Sutra,* they should be known as people who are still far away from highest, complete enlightenment. If they hear, understand, contemplate, and are able to practice it, they realize that they are certainly nearing highest, complete enlightenment. Why is this? Because the highest, complete enlightenment of all the bodhisattvas is within this sutra. This sutra opens the gate of skillful means and reveals the marks of the truth. The treasure house of this *Lotus Sutra* is deep and remote. No one is able to discover its depths. That is why the Buddha now reveals it, inspiring and perfecting the bodhisattvas.

"O Bhaiṣajyarāja! If there are bodhisattvas who hear this *Lotus Sutra* and are confused and frightened, know that they are bodhisattvas in whom the thought of enlightenment has only recently awakened. If there are *śrāvaka*s who hear this sutra and are confused and frightened, know that they are people who have excessive pride.

"O Bhaiṣajyarāja! If there are any sons and daughters of a virtuous family who, after the *parinirvāṇa* of the Tathāgata, want to teach this *Lotus Sutra* to the fourfold assembly, how should they teach it? These sons and daughters of a virtuous family, after entering the abode of the Tathāgata, wearing the Tathāgata's garments, and sitting on his seat, should then extensively teach this sutra to the fourfold assembly. The Tathāgata's chamber is nothing but the great compassion toward all sentient beings. The Tathāgata's garments are the thoughts of gentleness and perseverance, and the Tathāgata's seat is the very emptiness of all existing things. After settling among them one should tirelessly and extensively expound this *Lotus Sutra* for the sake of the bodhisattvas and the fourfold assembly.

"O Bhaiṣajyarāja! I will dispatch transformed beings to other worlds who will gather the people together to hear the teaching.
I will also dispatch transformed monks, nuns, laymen, and lay- 32a
women to hear this teaching. All these transformed beings will hear the Dharma, believe and accept it, and not reject it.

"If an expounder of the Dharma resides in a secluded place, I will then dispatch many *deva*s, *nāga*s, *yakṣa*s, *gandharva*s, and *asura*s to hear his teaching. Although I will be in a different land, I will periodically let the expounders of the Dharma see me. If they forget a line of this sutra I will explain it again, enabling them to master it."

Thereupon, the Bhagavat, wanting to elaborate on the meaning of this further, spoke these verses:

> If you wish to rid yourself of idleness,
> You should listen to this sutra.
> This sutra is rarely heard,
> And it is also difficult to accept.
> Suppose there were a thirsty man
> Seeking for water by drilling

Into the earth on a high plain.
He sees only dry earth and knows
That water is still far away.
He gradually sees
The moist earth turn into mud
And knows with certainty
That water is near.
O Bhaiṣajyarāja!
You should know that those people
Who do not hear the *Lotus Sutra*
Are very far away
From the Buddha's wisdom.
If they hear this profound sutra
Which brings resolution to the *śrāvaka*s
And if they hear this King of Sutras
And attentively contemplate it,
Know that these people
Are close to the Buddha's wisdom.
If people want to expound this sutra,
They should enter the Tathāgata's chamber,
Put on the Tathāgata's garments,
And sit on the Tathāgata's seat.
They then should face the people without fear,
So that they may extensively
Illuminate and explain it to the assembly.
The Tathāgata's chamber is great compassion,
His garments are gentleness and perseverance,
And his seat is the emptiness of all existent things.
After settling among them,
They should expound the Dharma.
Even if, when they expound this sutra,
People disparage them with evil words,
Or attack them with swords, sticks, tiles, or stones,
Being mindful of the Buddha,
They should persevere.

I will manifest my pure and solid form
In thousands of myriads of *koṭi*s of lands
And teach the Dharma to sentient beings
For immeasurable *koṭi*s of *kalpa*s.
If after my *parinirvāṇa*
There is someone who is able to teach this sutra,
I will dispatch a transformed fourfold assembly
Of monks, nuns, laymen and laywomen
To pay homage to this expounder of the Dharma.
I will lead the sentient beings 32b
And gather them together
To let them hear the teaching.
If anyone wishes to do ill to them
With swords, sticks, tiles, or stones,
Then I will dispatch those transformed ones
In order to guard them.
If there is any expounder of the Dharma
Who recites this sutra
In a secluded, tranquil place
Where there is no sound of human beings,
I will then manifest my body of pure light.
If they forget a chapter or a verse,
I will teach it to them,
Enabling them to master it.
If anyone perfects these qualities
If he teaches the fourfold assembly
Or, in a solitary place, recites this sutra,
Such a person will be able to see me.
If anyone abides in a secluded place
I will dispatch *deva*s, *nāga* kings,
*Yakṣa*s, and *rākṣasa*s
To be an audience to their teaching.
Such people teach the Dharma willingly
And explain it without obstruction.
Because all the Buddhas protect them

They gladden the great community of people.
Anyone who closely attends an expounder of the Dharma
Will immediately attain the bodhisattva path.
Anyone who follows this expounder's instructions,
Will be able to meet Buddhas
Equal in number to the sands of the Ganges River.

Chapter XI

The Appearance of a Jeweled Stupa

At that time there appeared before the Buddha a seven-jeweled stupa, five hundred *yojana*s in height and two hundred and fifty *yojana*s both in length and width, which emerged from the ground and hovered in the air. It was adorned with various jewels, had five thousand railings, and thousands of myriads of chambers. It was decorated with innumerable flags and banners and hanging jeweled necklaces, and myriads of *koṭi*s of jeweled bells hung from the top. The fragrance of *tamāla* leaves and sandalwood trees exuded from all sides of the stupa, covering the world. The banners and umbrellas were composed of the seven jewels such as gold, silver, lapis lazuli, mother-of-pearl, agate, pearl, and ruby; and they rose as high as the palaces of the world-protectors of the four quarters.

The thirty-three *deva*s rained down heavenly *māndārava* flowers in homage to the jeweled stupa. The other thousands of myriads of *koṭi*s of humans, and such nonhumans as *deva*s, *nāga*s, *yakṣa*s, *gandharva*s, *asura*s, *garuḍa*s, *kiṃnara*s, and *mahoraga*s also respected, honored, revered, and praised the precious stupa by offering all kinds of flowers, perfumes, necklaces, flags, banners, and music.

Then a tremendous voice issued forth in praise from the jeweled stupa, saying: "Splendid, splendid! O Śākyamuni! The Bhagavat teaches the *Lotus Sutra* to the great assembly: the instruction for bodhisattvas and treasured lore of the Buddhas, which is the wisdom attainable by every sentient being! Just so! Just so, O 32c
Śākyamuni Bhagavat! What you teach is true!"

Thereupon the fourfold assembly saw the great jeweled stupa hovering in the air and also heard the voice that issued forth from the stupa. They all were pleased with the teaching and marveled at this unprecedented experience. They stood up from their seats, honored Śākyamuni with their palms pressed together, and withdrew to one side.

At that time there was a bodhisattva *mahāsattva* called Mahāpratibhāna who, realizing that the *deva*s, humans, and *asura*s of the entire world were puzzled, addressed the Buddha saying: "O Bhagavat! Why has this jeweled stupa emerged from the earth? And why has this voice come forth from it?"

Then the Buddha told Bodhisattva Mahāpratibhāna: "The Tathāgata is in this jeweled stupa. In the remote past, immeasurable, incalculable thousands of myriads of *koṭi*s of worlds away in the east there was a land called Ratnaviśuddha. In that land there was a Buddha called Prabhūtaratna. When this Buddha was practicing the bodhisattva path in his previous lives he made a great vow, saying:

> If I become a Buddha, after my *parinirvāṇa* if the *Lotus Sutra* is being taught anywhere in all the lands of the ten directions, my stupa shall appear there so that this sutra may be heard, and in order that I may bear testimony to it and praise it with the word "Splendid!"

"After the Buddha had perfected the path and immediately before his *parinirvāṇa,* he addressed the monks among the great assembly of *deva*s and humans, saying:

> After my *parinirvāṇa* anyone who wishes to pay me homage should build a great stupa!

"If there is anyone teaching the *Lotus Sutra* anywhere in the worlds of the ten directions, this Buddha makes a jeweled stupa emerge out of the ground in that place through his transcendent powers and the power of his vow. He is in the stupa giving praise with the words, 'Splendid, splendid!'

"O Mahāpratibhāna! The Tathāgata Prabhūtaratna has now emerged from the earth, within his stupa, so that he may hear the *Lotus Sutra* and give praise with the words, 'Splendid, splendid!'"

At that time Bodhisattva Mahāpratibhāna spoke to the Buddha through the Tathāgata's transcendent powers, saying: "O Bhagavat! We all want to see this Buddha's form."

The Buddha answered Bodhisattva Mahāsattva Mahāpratibhāna, saying: "This Buddha Prabhūtaratna made a great vow, saying:

> Whenever my jeweled stupa appears in the presence of a Buddha in order to hear the *Lotus Sutra,* if that Buddha wants to show my form to the fourfold assembly he should gather into one place all his magically created forms that are teaching the Dharma in the worlds of the ten directions. After that my form will appear.

"O Mahāpratibhāna! I shall now gather all my magically created forms who are teaching the Dharma in the worlds of the ten directions."

Mahāpratibhāna spoke to the Buddha, saying: "O Bhagavat! We also strongly wish to see the Bhagavat's magically created forms, to honor and pay homage to them!"

Then the Buddha emitted a ray of light from the tuft of white hair between his eyebrows; and they immediately saw the Buddhas
in five hundred myriads of *koṭi*s of *nayuta*s of lands in the eastern 33a
direction equal in number to the sands of the Ganges River. In these lands the soil was of crystal and adorned with treasure trees and jeweled garments; and these lands were full of innumerable thousands of myriads of *koṭi*s of bodhisattvas. Jeweled drapes were hung everywhere and were covered with jeweled nets. All the Buddhas in these lands were teaching the Dharma in most harmonious voices. They also saw immeasurable thousands of myriads of *koṭi*s of bodhisattvas, filling all the lands and teaching the Dharma to sentient beings.

The other directions to the south, north, and west, the four intermediary directions, and the upper and lower regions were also illuminated by the ray of light emitted from the tuft of white hair between the Buddha's eyebrows; and they were also exactly like this.

Then all the Buddhas in the ten directions each addressed the assembly of bodhisattvas, saying: "O sons of a virtuous family! We will now go to the place where Śākyamuni is in the *sahā* world and pay homage to the jeweled stupa of the Tathāgata Prabhūtaratna."

At that time the *sahā* world was immediately purified; the earth was of lapis lazuli, adorned with jeweled trees, its roads laid out like a chessboard and bordered with golden cords; and there were no villages, towns, cities, oceans, rivers, mountains, streams, forests, or groves. Very precious incense was burning, *māndārava* flowers were spread everywhere on the earth, and it was covered with jeweled nets and drapes from which jeweled bells hung. With the exception of this assembly the *deva*s and human beings were all moved to other lands.

Then the Buddhas each took one great bodhisattva as an attendant and arrived under a jeweled tree in the *sahā* world. Each jeweled tree was five hundred *yojana*s in height and adorned with branches, leaves, blossoms, and fruits in their proper turn. Under all these jeweled trees were lion seats five *yojana*s in height that were adorned with great jewels. The Buddhas each sat cross-legged on these seats. They sat one after another in this way, filling the great manifold cosmos. Yet the separate forms of Śākyamuni Buddha of even one direction had not all arrived yet.

At that time Śākyamuni Buddha, wanting to be able to receive all of his magically created forms, transformed and purified two hundred myriads of *koṭi*s of *nayuta*s of lands in each of the world-systems in the eight directions. There were no hells, hungry ghosts, animals, or *asura*s; and all the *deva*s and humans were moved to other lands.

In these transformed lands the earth was made of lapis lazuli and adorned with jeweled trees. These trees were five hundred *yojana*s in height and were adorned with branches, leaves, blossoms, and fruits in their proper turn. Under every tree was a jeweled lion seat five *yojana*s in height which was adorned with various jewels. There were no oceans, rivers, or great mountain kings such as Mount Mucilinda, Mount Mahāmucilinda, Mount Cakravāḍa,

Mount Mahācakravāḍa, or Mount Sumeru. The lands were all
made into one Buddha world throughout. The jeweled earth was
level and covered everywhere with jewel-studded drapes. Banners 33b
and umbrellas were set up, precious incense was burning, and
heavenly jeweled flowers covered the ground everywhere.

Then Śākyamuni Buddha again transformed and purified two hundred myriads of *koṭi*s of *nayuta*s of lands in each of the eight directions so that the Buddhas could come and sit. There were no hells, hungry ghosts, animals, or *asura*s; and the *deva*s and humans were moved to other lands.

In the transformed lands the earth was of lapis lazuli and adorned with jeweled trees. The trees were five hundred *yojana*s in height and were adorned with branches, leaves, blossoms, and fruits in their proper turn. Under these trees were jeweled lion seats that were five *yojana*s in height and decorated with great jewels. There were no oceans, rivers, or great mountain kings such as Mount Mucilinda, Mount Mahāmucilinda, Mount Cakravāḍa, Mount Mahācakravāḍa, or Mount Sumeru. The lands were all made into one Buddha world throughout. The jeweled earth was level and covered everywhere with jewel-studded drapes. Banners and umbrellas were set up, precious incense was burning, and heavenly jeweled flowers covered the ground everywhere.

Then the magically created forms of Śākyamuni Buddha, which had been teaching the Dharma in the hundreds of thousands of myriads of *koṭi*s of *nayuta*s of lands in the east, equal in number to the sands of the Ganges River, gathered here.

In this way all the Buddhas in the ten directions gradually came until all were assembled, sitting in the eight directions. At that time these Buddha Tathāgatas filled four hundred myriads of *koṭi*s of *nayuta*s of lands in each direction. Then sitting on the lion seats under the jeweled trees, the Buddhas each dispatched their attendants with hands full of jeweled flowers to inquire after the Buddha Śākyamuni, saying: "O son of a virtuous family! You should approach the Buddha Śākyamuni on Mount Gṛdhrakūṭa and give him a greeting, saying:

> Are you without illness and pain and are you full of vigor and at ease; and are the assemblies of bodhisattvas and *śrāvaka*s all at ease or not?

"Then, having paid homage to the Buddha by scattering him with these jeweled flowers, say this to him:

> The Buddha So-and-so wishes you to open this jeweled stupa.

All the other Buddhas dispatched their messengers like this."

Then the Buddha Śākyamuni saw that his magically created forms had already gathered and were each sitting on a lion seat. And he heard that all the Buddhas also wanted him to open the treasured stupa. Immediately rising, he hovered in the air and the entire fourfold assembly rose and gazed attentively at the Buddha with their palms pressed together.

Thereupon Śākyamuni Buddha opened the entrance to the seven-jeweled stupa with his right finger. There was a tremendous sound as if the bar and lock to the gateway of a large city were being pushed aside. Then immediately the entire gathering saw the Tathāgata Prabhūtaratna in the jeweled stupa sitting on a lion seat as if he were in meditation, his body whole and undecomposed.

33c They heard him say: "Splendid, splendid! The Buddha Śākyamuni is teaching the *Lotus Sutra* and I have come in order to hear it."

At that time the fourfold assembly saw the Buddha who had entered *parinirvāṇa* immeasurable thousands of myriads of *koṭi*s of *kalpa*s ago speaking those words. They praised this unprecedented experience and scattered heavenly jeweled flowers upon the Buddhas Prabhūtaratna and Śākyamuni.

Then from within the stupa the Buddha Prabhūtaratna offered half of his seat to the Buddha Śākyamuni, saying: "O Śākyamuni Buddha, please take a seat here!"

The Buddha Śākyamuni immediately entered the stupa and sat cross-legged on half of the seat. Thereupon the great assembly saw the two Tathāgatas sitting cross-legged on the lion seat in the seven-jeweled stupa and they each thought thus: "The Buddhas are seated far away. O Tathāgata, we entreat you to use your transcendent powers so that we may be in the air together with you."

The Buddha Śākyamuni immediately moved the entire fourfold assembly into the air through his transcendent powers and addressed them with a great voice, saying: "Who in the *sahā* world is able to extensively teach the *Lotus Sutra*? It is now the right time! The Tathāgata will enter *parinirvāṇa* before long and the Buddha wants to transmit this *Lotus Sutra* to you.

Thereupon the Buddha, wanting to further elaborate upon the meaning of this, spoke these verses:

Although the Great Sage, the Bhagavat,
Entered *parinirvāṇa* long ago,
He has been abiding in a jeweled stupa;
And he has now come for the sake of the Dharma.
Why is it that people
Do not strive for the Dharma?
Although this Buddha entered *parinirvāṇa*
Incalculable *kalpas* ago,
Because it is difficult to encounter,
He listens to the Dharma
Wherever it is taught.
The original vow of this Buddha was:

After my *parinirvāṇa*
I will always listen to the Dharma
Wherever it may be.

My magically created forms,
Incalculable as the sands of the Ganges River,
Have come to hear the Dharma
And see the Tathāgata Prabhūtaratna,
Who has entered nirvana.
Each Buddha-form, having abandoned his beautiful land,

Disciples, *deva*s, humans, *nāga*s,
And ritual tributes, has come here
So that the Dharma may abide forever.
In order to seat all these Buddhas,
I transferred immeasurable beings
And purified the lands
Through my transcendent powers;
And each of these Buddhas
Settled under a jeweled tree—
As lotus blossoms
Adorn a limpid, cool pond.
Under every jeweled tree was a lion seat
On which the Buddhas sat radiating light—
34a As a great bonfire
Blazes in the dark of the night.
They emitted a subtle fragrance from their bodies
Which filled the lands of the ten directions.
Sentient beings who smelled this fragrance
Were overcome with unsurpassed joy,
Like branches of a small tree
Being blown by a great wind.
Through this skillful means
I enable the Dharma to abide forever.
I tell the great assembly
That after my nirvana
Whoever can preserve and recite this sutra
Should now individually make a declaration
In the presence of the Buddhas.
Although the Buddha Prabhūtaratna
Entered *parinirvāṇa* long ago,
Through his great vow
He has roared the lion's roar.
The Tathāgata Prabhūtaratna,
I myself, and all the magically created forms
Who have gathered here

Should know this intention.
O heirs of the Buddhas!
Whoever is able to preserve the Dharma
Should make a great vow
So that it may abide forever.
Whoever is able to preserve
The teaching of this sutra
Will thus honor me
And Prabhūtaratna.
This Buddha Prabhūtaratna
Always roams the ten directions
In a jeweled stupa
In order to hear this sutra.
He also honors
All the transformed Buddhas
Who have come here and who adorn
All the worlds with light.
Whoever teaches this sutra will see me,
The Tathāgata Prabhūtaratna,
And the transformed Buddhas.
O sons of a virtuous family!
Each of you must carefully consider this.
This is indeed a difficult matter.
Make a great vow accordingly!
It is not really difficult
To teach all of the other sutras,
The number of which is
Equal to the sands of the Ganges River.
It is not difficult
To take Mount Sumeru
And throw it to another quarter,
Over innumerable Buddha worlds.
It is also not difficult
To shake free the manifold cosmos
With one toe and throw it

Far into another distant world.
It is not difficult to stand
On the highest summit of the world
And teach the other innumerable sutras
For the sake of sentient beings.
However, it will indeed be difficult
To teach this sutra in the troubled world
After the Buddha's nirvana.
It is not difficult for anyone
To grasp empty space
And wander around with it.
But it will certainly be difficult to copy
And preserve this sutra
And cause others to copy it
After my nirvana.
It is not really difficult
To put the great earth on a toenail
And ascend with it
To the world of Brahmas.
However, it will indeed be difficult
To recite this sutra,
Even for a moment,
In the troubled world
After the Buddha's nirvana.
It is not really difficult
To enter into the conflagration
At the time of the close of a *kalpa*
Carrying hay on your back
And yet not be burned.
34b It certainly will be difficult
To preserve this sutra
And teach it to even a single person
After my nirvana.
It is indeed not really difficult for anyone to preserve
The eighty-four thousand treasure houses of the Dharma,

And the twelvefold scriptures,
And teach them so that the listeners
Can attain the six transcendent powers.
It will indeed be difficult for anyone
To hear and accept this sutra
And to ask about its meaning
After my nirvana.
It is not really difficult for people to do
Such beneficial things as teaching the Dharma
And making thousands of myriads of *koṭi*s of
Immeasurable, incalculable sentient beings,
Numbering as many as the sands of the Ganges River,
Attain arhatship and perfect
The six transcendent powers.
It will certainly be difficult
To preserve such a sutra as this
After my nirvana.
I have extensively taught many sutras
In incalculable lands
From the beginning until now,
For the sake of the Buddha path;
And yet among them
This sutra is the best.
If anyone preserves it,
He preserves the form of the Buddha.
O sons of a virtuous family!
Those who preserve and recite this [*Lotus*] *Sutra*
After my nirvana
Must now individually make a declaration
In the presence of the Buddhas.
It is hard to preserve this sutra.
If anyone preserves it
Even for a single moment,
I shall truly rejoice.
All of the other Buddhas

Will do so also.
Such people as these
Are praised by the Buddhas.
They are courageous.
They are persevering.
They are known as those
Who follow the rules of good conduct
And carry out ascetic practices.
Subsequently they quickly attain
The highest Buddha path.
Those in the future
Who recite and preserve this sutra,
Are the true heirs of the Buddha
And abide in the stage of purity.
Those who can understand its meaning
After the Buddha's nirvana
Will become the Eyes of the World
For *deva*s and humans.
Those who teach it, even for a moment,
In the fearful world
Will be revered
By all the *deva*s and humans.

Chapter XII

Devadatta

The Buddha then addressed the assembly of bodhisattvas, and also the *devas*, humans, and the fourfold assembly, saying: "In the past, immeasurable *kalpas* ago, I tirelessly sought the *Lotus Sutra*. Throughout many *kalpas* I always became a king and made a vow to seek highest enlightenment. My mind became irreversible. Wanting to fulfill the six perfections I diligently carried out practices: unstintingly giving elephants, horses, the seven precious treasures, countries and cities, wives and children, male and female servants, my head, eyes, marrow and brains, the flesh of my body, hands, and feet, without stinginess, not even hesitating to give my own life.

"At that time the lifespan of the people in the world was immeasurable. In order to seek the Dharma I abandoned my king- 34c
dom and abdicated my throne to the crown prince. Beating a drum I proclaimed to the four directions that I was seeking the Dharma, saying:

> I will be as a servant for the rest of my life to whosoever can teach me the Mahayana.

"At that time there was a sage who came to this king and said:

> I possess the Mahayana teaching called the *Lotus Sutra*. If you faithfully obey me I will expound it to you.

"Having heard the sage, the king became joyful and ecstatic and, accompanying the sage, he did everything he was asked. He gathered fruits, drew water, collected firewood, and provided meals. He even provided his own body as a bed for the sage. Yet he never tired in either body or mind and in this way served the sage for one thousand years. For the sake of the Dharma he served him diligently, making certain the sage never lacked for anything."

At that time the Bhagavat, wanting to elaborate on the meaning of this further, spoke these verses:

> I remember that in the past, many *kalpa*s ago,
> Although I became king of the world,
> In order to seek the great Dharma
> I was never attached to the desires of the five senses.
> Striking a bell I declared this
> To the four directions:
>
> > If anyone possesses the great Dharma
> > And explains it to me,
> > I will become his servant.
>
> At that time there was a sage called Asita
> Who came to the great king and said:
>
> > I possess a subtle and true Dharma
> > That is rare in the world.
> > If you are able to practice it,
> > I will explain it to you!
>
> On hearing what the sage said
> The king became overjoyed.
> He immediately accompanied the sage
> And performed whatever he was asked.
> He gathered firewood and various fruits
> And respectfully offered them whenever requested.
> Because he longed for the True Dharma,
> He never tired in body or mind.
> For the sake of sentient beings
> He diligently sought everywhere the great Dharma.
> He never sought it for his own sake
> Nor for the desires of the five senses.
> For this reason, although a great king,
> He diligently sought and attained this Dharma,
> Ultimately becoming a Buddha.
> That is why I now tell you this.

The Buddha addressed the monks, saying: "The king at that time was I myself, and the sage was he who is now Devadatta. Through the virtuous friendship of Devadatta I was able to become endowed with the six perfections, benevolence, compassion, sympathetic joy, generosity, the thirty-two marks, the eighty excellent characteristics, reddish-gold skin, the ten powers, the four kinds of fearlessness, the four methods of gaining trust, the eighteen excellent qualities, the transcendent powers, and the power of the path. It is all due to the good and virtuous friendship of Deva- 35a
datta that I attained complete enlightenment and extensively saved innumerable sentient beings."

The Buddha addressed the fourfold assembly, saying: "After immeasurable *kalpas* have passed, Devadatta will then become a Buddha called Devarāja, a Tathāgata, Arhat, Completely Enlightened, Perfect in Knowledge and Conduct, Well-Departed, Knower of the World, Unsurpassed, Tamer of Humans, Teacher of Devas and Humans, Buddha, Bhagavat. His world will be called Devasopānā. At that time the Buddha Devarāja will abide in the world for twenty intermediate *kalpas* and extensively teach the True Dharma to sentient beings. Sentient beings equal in number to the sands of the Ganges River will attain arhatship. The thought of a *pratyekabuddha* has awakened in incalculable numbers of sentient beings. The thought of the highest path will awaken in sentient beings equal in number to the sands of the Ganges River, and they will become convinced of the nonarising of all *dharmas* and reside in the stage of nonretrogression.

"Then, after the *parinirvāṇa* of the Buddha Devarāja, the True Dharma will abide in the world for twenty intermediate *kalpas*. A seven-jeweled stupa, sixty *yojanas* in height and forty *yojanas* in both length and width, will be built for all his relics; and all the *devas* and humans will honor and revere this beautiful seven-jeweled stupa with various flowers, scented powders, burning incense, fragrant ointments, clothing, necklaces, banners, flags, jeweled canopies, music, and songs. Incalculable sentient beings will attain arhatship. Innumerable sentient beings will be enlightened as *pratyekabuddhas*; and the thought of enlightenment will awaken in an inconceivable number of sentient beings, and they will reach the stage of nonretrogression."

The Buddha addressed the monks, saying: "If, in the future, there are sons and daughters of a virtuous family who, upon hearing the Devadatta chapter of the *Lotus Sutra,* accept it with pure minds and without doubt, they shall not fall into the realms of hell or to the states of hungry ghosts or of animals, but will be born in the presence of the Buddhas in the ten directions. Wherever they may be, they will always hear this sutra. If they are born among humans or *devas*, they will enjoy a supreme and delightful contentment; and if in the presence of a Buddha, they will be born spontaneously in a lotus flower."

At that time, in the lower region there was a bodhisattva called Prajñākūṭa who was accompanying the Bhagavat Prabhūtaratna. He urged the Buddha Prabhūtaratna to return to their original land. The Buddha Śākyamuni addressed Prajñākūṭa, saying: "O son of a virtuous family! Wait for a moment! There is a bodhisattva called Mañjuśrī. Let us meet him together and discuss the True Dharma. After that you can return to your original land."

At that time Mañjuśrī, sitting on a thousand-petaled lotus flower as large as a carriage wheel, together with attendant bodhisattvas also seated on jeweled lotus flowers, emerged spontaneously out of the ocean from the palace of the *nāga* king Sāgara and floated in midair. Arriving at Mount Gṛdhrakūṭa they descended from the lotus flowers and went into the presence of the Buddhas, where they bowed until their foreheads touched the feet of both Bhagavats. Having honored them, Mañjuśrī approached Prajñākūṭa. They greeted each other and withdrew to sit at one side. Then Bodhisattva Prajñākūṭa asked Mañjuśrī, saying: "Your Eminence! How many sentient beings did you lead and inspire at the palace of the *nāga* king?"

Mañjuśrī answered: "The number is immeasurable and incalculable. It is not possible to express it in words nor is it possible to
35b calculate it with one's mind. Wait a moment and you will have proof!"

Before he had finished speaking, innumerable bodhisattvas emerged from the ocean, seated on jeweled lotus flowers. Arriving at Mount Gṛdhrakūṭa they floated in midair. All of these were bodhisattvas who had been led and inspired by Mañjuśrī. Those who had perfected the bodhisattva practices discussed the six perfections together. Those who were originally *śrāvaka*s explained the *śrāvaka* practices in the air; and now they all practice to understand the meaning of emptiness of the Mahayana.

Mañjuśrī said to Prajñākūṭa: "Thus did I lead and inspire people in the ocean!"

Thereupon Bodhisattva Prajñākūṭa spoke these verses in praise:

O One of great wisdom, virtue, and courage!
This assembly and I have now all witnessed that
You have led and inspired
Incalculable numbers of sentient beings.
You have expounded the essential character of *dharma*s
And revealed the teaching of the single vehicle.
You have extensively led many sentient beings,
Causing them to quickly attain enlightenment.

Mañjuśrī said: "In the ocean I always expounded only the *Lotus Sutra*."

Then Prajñākūṭa questioned Mañjuśrī, saying: "This sutra is profound and subtle. It is a jewel among sutras and rare in the world. If sentient beings diligently strive to practice this sutra, will they immediately become Buddhas or not?"

Mañjuśrī answered: "Yes, they will. There is the daughter of the *nāga* king Sāgara who is only eight years old. She is wise; her faculties are sharp; and she also well knows all the faculties and deeds of sentient beings. She has attained the power of recollection. She preserves all the profound secret treasures taught by the Buddhas, enters deep meditation, and is well capable of discerning all *dharma*s. She instantly produced the thought of enlightenment and attained the stage of nonretrogression. She has unhindered eloquence and thinks of sentient beings with as much compassion as if they were her own children. Her virtues are perfect. Her thoughts and explanations are subtle and extensive, merciful, and compassionate. She has a harmonious mind and has attained enlightenment."

The Bodhisattva Prajñākūṭa said: "I see the Tathāgata Śākyamuni who has been incessantly carrying out difficult and severe practices for immeasurable *kalpa*s, accumulating merit and virtue while seeking the bodhisattva path. Looking into the great manifold cosmos, there is not a single place even the size of a mustard seed where this bodhisattva has not abandoned his life for the sake of sentient beings. He attained the path to enlightenment only after this. It is hard to believe that this girl will instantly attain complete enlightenment."

Before he had finished speaking the daughter of the *nāga* king suddenly appeared in their presence. Bowing until her forehead touched their feet, she withdrew to one side and spoke these verses in praise:

The Buddha is deeply versed
In the characteristics of good and evil,
And he completely illuminates the ten directions.
His subtle and pure Dharma body
Is endowed with the thirty-two marks;
35c With the eighty good characteristics
Is his Dharma body adorned.
He is adored by *deva*s and humans,
And honored by *nāga*s.
There is no sentient being
Who does not pay him homage.
Moreover, that I will attain enlightenment
Upon hearing him
Can only be known by a Buddha.
I will reveal the teaching of the Mahayana
And save suffering sentient beings.

At that time Śāriputra spoke to the daughter of the *nāga* king, saying: "You say that you will soon attain the highest path. This is difficult to believe. Why is this? The female body is polluted; it is not a fit vessel for the Dharma. How can you attain highest enlightenment?

"The Buddha path is long. One can only attain it after diligently carrying out severe practices, and completely practicing the perfections over immeasurable *kalpa*s. Moreover, the female body has five obstructions. The first is the inability to become a great Brahma. The second is the inability to become Śakra. The third is the inability to become Māra, and the fourth is the inability to become a universal monarch (*cakravartin*). The fifth is the inability to become a Buddha. How can you with your female body quickly become a Buddha?"

Then the daughter of the *nāga* king presented to the Buddha a jewel worth the great manifold cosmos, and the Buddha accepted it. The daughter of the *nāga* king spoke to Bodhisattva Prajñākūṭa and the noble Śāriputra, saying: "I offered a jewel and the Bhagavat accepted it. Was that done quickly or not?"

They answered, saying: "It was done extremely quickly!"

The daughter said: "Through your transcendent powers watch me become a Buddha even more quickly than that!"

Then the assembly there all saw the daughter of the *nāga* king instantly transform into a man, perfect the bodhisattva practices, go to the *vimalā* world in the south, sit on a jeweled lotus flower, and attain highest, complete enlightenment, become endowed with the thirty-two marks and eighty excellent characteristics, and expound the True Dharma universally for the sake of all sentient beings in the ten directions.

Then the bodhisattvas, *śrāvaka*s, eight kinds of *deva*s, *nāga*s, and so on, humans and nonhumans of the *sahā* world, all saw in the distance that the daughter of the *nāga* king had become a Buddha and was universally teaching the Dharma for the sake of the humans and *deva*s in that assembly. They rejoiced greatly and honored her from afar.

On hearing the Dharma, incalculable numbers of sentient beings became enlightened and attained the stage of nonretrogression. Incalculable numbers of sentient beings received their predictions to the path and the *vimalā* world quaked in six ways. In the *sahā* world three thousand sentient beings attained the stage of nonretrogression, and three thousand sentient beings, in whom the thought of enlightenment had awakened, received their predictions. The Bodhisattva Prajñākūṭa, Śāriputra, and the entire assembly accepted and believed in silence.

Chapter XIII

Perseverance

At that time Bodhisattva Mahāsattva Bhaiṣajyarāja and Bodhisattva Mahāsattva Mahāpratibhāna made this declaration in the
presence of the Buddha, together with two thousand bodhisattvas:
"O Bhagavat! We entreat you not to be concerned since, after the 36a
Buddha's *parinirvāṇa* we will preserve, recite, and teach this [*Lotus*]
Sutra! In the troubled world to come, sentient beings will have
hardly any roots of good merit but will have excessive pride and
will be greedy to receive offerings. They will increase their roots
of bad merit and thus will be far away from liberation. It will be
difficult to lead and inspire them. Therefore, we will produce the
power of great patience and recite, preserve, teach, and copy this
sutra as well as pay it homage in various ways, even willingly giving up our bodies and lives."

Then in the assembly, five hundred arhats who had received their predictions addressed the Buddha, saying: "O Bhagavat! We also declare that in other lands we will extensively teach this sutra."

Moreover, eight thousand of those who had received their predictions, including those who had more to learn and those who did not, rose from their seats and with their palms pressed together, faced the Buddha and made this declaration: "O Bhagavat! We also will extensively teach this sutra in other lands. Why is this? Because in the *sahā* world there are many erring people, with excessive pride and superficial virtue, those who are quick to anger, deceitful, and untrue."

Thereupon the Buddha's aunt, the nun Mahāprajāpatī Gautamī, with six thousand nuns, some of whom had more to learn and some who did not, rose from their seats and with their palms pressed together gazed attentively at the Buddha, never turning their eyes away. Then the Bhagavat spoke to Mahāprajāpatī Gautamī, saying:

"Why are you anxiously staring at the Tathāgata? Are you thinking that I have not given you your prediction of highest, complete enlightenment? O Mahāprajāpatī Gautamī! I have previously said that all of the *śrāvaka*s would receive their predictions. Now if you wish to know your prediction, I will tell you that in the future you will become a great expounder of the Dharma, taught by sixty-eight thousand *koṭi*s of Buddhas. These six thousand nuns, some of whom have more to learn and some who do not, will all become expounders of the Dharma together. In this way you will gradually be able to complete the bodhisattva path and become a Buddha called Sarvarūpasaṃdarśana, a Tathāgata, Arhat, Completely Enlightened, Perfect in Knowledge and Conduct, Well-Departed, Knower of the World, Unsurpassed, Tamer of Humans, Teacher of Devas and Humans, Buddha, Bhagavat. O Mahāprajāpatī Gautamī! This Buddha Sarvarūpasaṃdarśana will give predictions of highest, complete enlightenment one by one to bodhisattvas totaling six thousand in number."

Then the nun Yaśodharā, the mother of Rāhula, thought this: "While giving the predictions, the only name the Bhagavat did not mention was mine."

The Buddha addressed Yaśodharā, saying: "In the future you will cultivate the bodhisattva practice of the teachings of hundreds of thousands of myriads of *koṭi*s of Buddhas. You will become a great expounder of the Dharma, and gradually complete the Buddha path. In a land called Bhadrā you will become a Buddha called Raśmiśatasahasraparipūrṇadhvaja, a Tathāgata, Arhat, Completely Enlightened, Perfect in Knowledge and Conduct, Well-
36b Departed, Knower of the World, Unsurpassed, Tamer of Humans, Teacher of Devas and Humans, Buddha, Bhagavat. This Buddha's lifespan will be for immeasurable, incalculable *kalpa*s."

At that time the nun Mahāprajāpatī Gautamī and the nun Yaśodharā together with their attendants all rejoiced greatly at having attained such an unprecedented experience. In the presence of the Buddha they immediately spoke in verse, saying:

O Bhagavat! As a great leader
You bring ease to *deva*s and humans.
Having heard our predictions,
Our minds are at peace
And we are content.

Having spoken this verse all the nuns addressed the Buddha, saying: "O Bhagavat! We also will extensively expound this sutra in other lands."

Then the Bhagavat saw eighty myriads of *koṭi*s of *nayuta*s of bodhisattva *mahāsattva*s, all of whom were at the stage of nonretrogression. They had turned the irreversible wheel of the Dharma and attained the power of recollection. Arising from their seats they went before the Buddha with their palms pressed together and with this wholehearted thought: "If the Bhagavat commands us to preserve and teach this sutra, then we will extensively expound this Dharma exactly as the Buddha has taught."

They also thought: "The Buddha now keeps silent and does not command us. What should we do?"

Then all of the bodhisattvas, respecting the Buddha's intention and also wanting to fulfill their original vow, uttered a lion's roar in the presence of the Buddha and declared: "O Bhagavat! After the Tathāgata's *parinirvāṇa* we will roam throughout the worlds of the ten directions enabling sentient beings to copy, preserve, and recite this [*Lotus*] *Sutra,* and to explain its meaning, practice it according to the Dharma, and remember it correctly. This will all be due to the Buddha's majestic power.

"O Bhagavat! We entreat you to protect us from afar while we are in other quarters."

Immediately after that, all of the bodhisattvas spoke these verses in unison:

We entreat you not to be concerned
Because we will extensively teach
In the fearful, troubled world,

After the Buddha's *parinirvāṇa*.
We will be patient
With those who are ignorant,
Those who disparage others with evil words,
Or who attack us with sticks and swords.
Monks in this troubled world
Will have false wisdom
And be deceitful.
They will think they have attained
What they have not, and their minds
Will be full of conceit.
Then there will be those who dwell
In tranquil forests wearing rags,
With the thought that they alone practice the true path,
And who look down on those who lead worldly lives.
There will be those who teach the Dharma
To laypeople only out of greed for offerings,
Yet they will be respected in the world
As if they were arhats endowed with
The six transcendent powers.
36c The minds of such people are in error;
They are always thinking about worldly matters;
And they enjoy pointing out our faults,
Playing the role of the forest dwellers,
Thus they will say such things as:

> All of these monks here
> Teach heretical doctrines
> Because they are greedy for profit!
> They have fabricated this sutra
> To deceive the people of the world,
> And they explain this sutra
> Out of desire for fame!

They always want to slander us
In the great assembly;

They slander us to the kings,
Ministers, brahmans, householders,
And to other monks, saying that we are evil.
They say:

> These are people of false views
> Who teach heretical doctrines.

Since we revere the Buddha,
We will be patient with their wickedness.
They will mockingly address us, saying:

> All you Buddhas!

We will be patient with
These scornful words.
In the troubled world of the Age of [the Decadent Dharma]
There are many fearful things.
People possessed by evil spirits
Will scorn and slander us.
But we shall wear the armor of patience
Because we trust and revere the Buddha;
And we will persevere under these difficulties
In order to teach this sutra.
We will not be attached to our bodies or lives
We only desire the highest path.
In the future we will preserve
What the Buddha has entrusted us with.
The Bhagavat himself must know
That the erring monks in the troubled world
Will not understand the Dharma
Taught by the Buddha through skillful means,
According to what is appropriate to sentient beings.
They will utter evil words with angry countenances,
And they will repeatedly expel us,
And keep us away from the monasteries and stupas.
There will be many evils such as this.

We will all endure in these matters
Because we remember the Buddha's decree.
If there are any people seeking this Dharma
In villages or cities, we will all go there
And teach the Dharma entrusted to us by the Buddha.
Because we are the Bhagavat's ambassadors,
Wherever we go we have nothing to fear.
We will skillfully teach the Dharma.
We entreat you, O Buddha, to be at ease.
In the presence of the Bhagavat,
And all of the Buddhas who have come
From the ten directions,
37a We make this declaration.
O Buddha! You know our intentions!

Chapter XIV

Ease in Practice

Thereupon the Prince of the Dharma, Bodhisattva Mahāsattva Mañjuśrī addressed the Buddha, saying: "O Bhagavat! These bodhisattvas are very rare. In respectful obedience to the Buddha they have made this great vow: 'In the troubled world to come, we will preserve, recite, and teach this *Lotus Sutra*!'

"O Bhagavat! How can these bodhisattva *mahāsattvas* teach this sutra in the troubled world to come?"

The Buddha addressed Mañjuśrī, saying: "If the bodhisattva *mahāsattvas* want to teach this sutra in the troubled world to come, they should abide in the four kinds of practices. The first is to establish the sphere of their bodhisattva practice and the sphere of their relationships and thereupon expound this sutra for the sake of sentient beings.

"O Mañjuśrī! What is the sphere of the practice of the bodhisattva *mahāsattva*? If a bodhisattva *mahāsattva* abides in the stage of perseverance, is gentle, tranquil, nonviolent, and unafraid; and furthermore if he remains unmoved with regard to existent things and perceives them in their true aspect, and neither acts nor discriminates, this is called the sphere of the practice of the bodhisattva *mahāsattva*.

"What is the sphere of the relationships of the bodhisattva *mahāsattva*? The bodhisattva *mahāsattva* should not consort with kings, princes, ministers, and chief officials. He should not consort with heretics, brahmans, Jains, and others, or with worldly writers, critics of poetry, materialists, or extreme materialists. Nor should he become acquainted with pranksters, boxers, wrestlers, clowns, and various jugglers, nor with outcastes and people who raise boars, sheep, chickens, and dogs, nor with hunters, fishermen, and those with evil conduct. A bodhisattva should teach such people the Dharma if they come to him, but expect nothing.

"Nor should a bodhisattva consort with monks, nuns, laymen, and laywomen who seek the *śrāvaka* vehicle. Nor should he greet
37b them. The bodhisattva should avoid their company in chambers, on roads, or while in lecture halls, and not remain with them. If they come, teach them the Dharma according to their capacities, but expect nothing!

"Moreover, O Mañjuśrī! The bodhisattva *mahāsattva* should expound the teaching without any thought of desire for, or wish to see, a woman's body.

"If a bodhisattva enters someone else's home he should not talk to young girls, maidens, and widows. A bodhisattva should also not approach the five kinds of impotent men nor be intimate with them. He should not enter someone else's home alone; and if for any reason he should enter it alone a bodhisattva should do nothing but singlemindedly contemplate the Buddha.

"If he should teach the Dharma to women he should not show his teeth when smiling nor reveal his chest. A bodhisattva should not be intimate with them even for the sake of the Dharma. How much less for other things!

"A bodhisattva should take no pleasure in keeping young disciples, *śrāmaṇera*s, or young boys. Nor should he take pleasure in having the same teacher as them. He should always take pleasure in meditation and, in a quiet place, practice to control his mind. O Mañjuśrī! This is what is known as the first sphere of relationships.

"Furthermore, the bodhisattva *mahāsattva*s perceive the emptiness of all *dharma*s in their true aspect. All things are unerring, unmoving, nonreturning, irreversible, and like empty space which lacks substance. They are beyond all language. They are not produced, nor do they emerge, nor do they arise. They do not have any name or mark, and in reality they have no substance. They are immeasurable, limitless, without obstacles or obstructions. They exist only through dependent origination, arising through error. That is why I teach the permanent joy of perceiving the aspects of all existent things in this way. This is what is known as the second sphere of relationships of a bodhisattva *mahāsattva.*"

At that time the Bhagavat, wanting to elaborate upon the meaning of this further, spoke these verses:

If, in the troubled world to come,
A bodhisattva with a fearless mind
Wants to teach this sutra,
He should enter the sphere
Of the bodhisattva practice
And the sphere of relationships.
He should always stay away from kings,
Princes, ministers, chief officials,
Dangerous pranksters, outcastes,
Heretics, and brahmans.
He should not consort
With excessively proud scholars,
Who are attached to scriptures of the inferior vehicle
Contained in the three baskets (Tripiṭaka);
Nor with monks who violate the precepts,
With those who call themselves arhats,
Nor with nuns who like to joke and laugh.
He should not become acquainted with laywomen
Who are attached to the desires of the five senses,
And seek nirvana in their present lives.
If these people come to the bodhisattva
With good intentions
In order to hear about the Buddha path,
The bodhisattva should then fearlessly
Teach them the Dharma
Without any expectations.
A bodhisattva should not 37c
Become intimately acquainted
With widows, maidens,
Or impotent men.

Nor should he consort
With slaughterers, butchers, hunters,
Or fishermen who kill for profit.
He should not consort
With people such as those
Who make a living
From selling meat
Or from pandering prostitutes.
He should never become acquainted
With dangerous wrestlers,
Or the varieties of jugglers or courtesans.
He should not teach the Dharma
To a woman alone in a quiet place.
When he teaches the Dharma
He should not joke or laugh.
If he enters a village to beg for food
He should be accompanied by a monk.
If there is no monk he should
Singlemindedly contemplate the Buddha.
This is what is known as
The sphere of the bodhisattva practice
And the sphere of relationships.
Within these two spheres
He can teach at ease.
He should not practice
The superior, mediocre, or inferior teachings,
The conditioned and the unconditioned,
Or the teaching of the real and the unreal.
Nor should he discriminate
Between men and women.
He should not acquire, comprehend,
Or perceive any phenomenon.
This is what is known
As the sphere of the
Bodhisattva practice.

All *dharma*s are empty and without substance,
Impermanent, without origination or cessation.
This is known as the sphere
Of the relationships of the wise.
Through the error of discrimination
One sees all existent things
As existing or nonexisting,
Real or unreal,
Produced or unproduced.
Being in a quiet place, the bodhisattva
Carries out practices to control his mind
And remains as firm and unmoved
As Mount Sumeru.
He should regard all *dharma*s
As being without substance,
Like empty space
Which has no firmness.
All *dharma*s are neither produced
Nor do they emerge;
They are immovable, nonreturning,
And always remain in their single character.
This is known as the sphere of relationships.
Any monk after my *parinirvāṇa*
Who enters the sphere of practice
And the sphere of relationships
Will not be disheartened
When he teaches this sutra.
A bodhisattva, at proper times,
Should enter a quiet chamber
And contemplate all *dharma*s
With correct thoughts,
According to the meaning.
Arising from meditation he should reveal
And expound this sutra
To kings, princes, ministers, and brahmans.

Then his mind will be at ease and unafraid.
O Mañjuśrī!
This is the bodhisattva
Who firmly abides in the Dharma from the beginning
And in the world to come will be able
To teach the *Lotus Sutra*.

"Furthermore, O Mañjuśrī, after the Tathāgata's *parinirvāṇa*, anyone who wants to teach this sutra in the Age of the Decadent
38a Dharma should abide in ease of practice. When he expounds or recites this sutra he should not take pleasure in talking about the faults of people or of the sutra. Nor should he slander other expounders of the Dharma or talk of the good and bad, strong and weak points of others.

"As for the *śrāvaka*s, a bodhisattva should not name them and point out their faults, nor name them and praise their virtues. Moreover, he should not feel any hatred; because if he skillfully practices ease of mind in this way, those who listen to him will not oppose his intentions. If he is asked difficult questions, he should not answer using the teaching of the inferior vehicle. He should take his explanation only from the Mahayana, which will enable them to attain omniscience."

At that time the Bhagavat, wanting to elaborate the meaning of this further, spoke these verses:

The bodhisattva should always willingly
Teach the Dharma at ease,
Establishing his seat in a pure place.
He should anoint his body with oil
To cleanse himself of dirt,
And put on new, clean clothing.
Both his outer garments and undergarments being pure,
Sitting comfortably on the Dharma seat,
He should teach according to the questions.
If there are any monks, nuns, laymen, and laywomen,
Or kings, princes, subjects, officials, and commoners,

Using subtle ideas he should teach them
With a composed countenance.
If they have difficult questions
He should answer in accordance with the meaning,
Expounding and illuminating it
With various explanations and illustrations.
Through these skillful means
He should awaken the thought of
Enlightenment in them all,
Gradually benefiting them,
And causing them to enter the Buddha path.
Ridding them of idle minds
And lazy thoughts,
As well as anxieties,
He should compassionately
Teach the Dharma.
He should continuously expound
The teaching of the highest path
Both day and night, using various explanations
And incalculable illustrations.
Revealing this to sentient beings
He will cause them all to rejoice.
He should not expect to receive any clothing,
Bedding, food and drink, or medicine.
He should only singlemindedly think
Of teaching the Dharma,
Gain mastery of the Buddha path,
And enable sentient beings also to attain it.
It is exactly this kind of offering
That brings great benefit and ease.
After my *parinirvāṇa* if there is any monk
Who is able to explain the *Lotus Sutra,*
His mind will be free from the obstructions of
Jealousy, anger, and anxiety.
He will also be without sorrows

And no one will slander him.
He will not be afraid of being
Attacked with swords and sticks;
And he will not be expelled from the sangha,
Because he abides in perseverance.
The wise skillfully compose
Their minds in this way
And can abide in ease,
As I have described above.
38b One would not be able to fully
Describe the qualities of such a person
Through calculations and illustrations,
Though they lasted for
Thousands of myriads of *koṭi*s of *kalpa*s.

"Furthermore, O Mañjuśrī, in the future when the Dharma becomes extinct, any bodhisattva *mahāsattva* who preserves and recites this sutra will not feel jealous or be deceitful, nor will he insult those who study the Buddha path by pointing out their good qualities or their deficiencies.

"If there are any monks, nuns, laymen, and laywomen who are seeking the *śrāvaka* vehicle, the *pratyekabuddha* vehicle, or the bodhisattva path, a bodhisattva will not worry them, causing them to have doubts by saying:

> You are very far away from the path and will never be able to attain omniscience. Why is this? Because you are negligent and idle in the path.

"Moreover, a bodhisattva also should not devise hollow sophistries concerning the teachings and argue about them. In him the thought of great compassion for all sentient beings should awaken, together with the thought that all Tathāgatas are compassionate fathers and that all bodhisattvas are great teachers. He should always deeply respect and pay homage to all of the great bodhisattvas in the ten directions. He should teach the Dharma equally to all sentient beings in accordance with the Dharma, explaining neither too much nor too little. Nor should he teach too much even to those who are deeply enthusiastic about hearing the Dharma.

"O Mañjuśrī! In the future world, when the Dharma is to be extinguished, this bodhisattva *mahāsattva,* having perfected the third sphere of ease in practice, will not be perplexed when he teaches this Dharma. He will become acquainted with good fellow students who will recite this sutra together. He will also acquire a great following who come to hear his teaching, preserve it after hearing it, recite it after preserving it, teach it after reciting it, copy it after teaching it, and enable others to copy, respect, honor, praise, and pay homage to the [*Lotus*] *Sutra.*"

Thereupon the Bhagavat, wanting to elaborate on the meaning of this further, spoke these verses:

> If anyone wants to teach this sutra,
> He should get rid of jealousy, anger,
> Pride, flattery, deceitfulness, and falsity.
> He should always practice honest conduct.
> He should not slander others
> Or make up fallacies about the Dharma.
> Nor should he cause others to be doubtful by saying:
>
> > You will not become a Buddha.
>
> This heir of the Buddha who teaches the Dharma
> Should always be gentle, patient,
> And compassionate to all.
> He should never have lazy thoughts.
> He should respect the great bodhisattvas
> In the ten directions who practice the path
> Out of their compassion for sentient beings,
> And think that they are his great teachers.
> He should think that all the Buddha
> Bhagavats are the most excellent fathers.

38c Destroying arrogance, he should teach
The Dharma without obstructions.
The third sphere of the teaching
Of ease in practice is like this.
The wise should preserve it.
Those who practice wholeheartedly and at ease
Will be honored by innumerable sentient beings.

"Furthermore, O Mañjuśrī, in the future world when the Dharma is to be extinguished, any bodhisattva *mahāsattva* who preserves this *Lotus Sutra* will awaken the thought of great kindness toward lay Buddhists and renunciants and also awaken the thought of great compassion toward nonbodhisattvas. He should think:

> People like these have really missed the Tathāgata's teaching of the Dharma according to their capacities through skillful means. They do not hear, know, or realize it. They do not ask, believe, or understand. Those people do not even ask questions about this sutra, believe it, or understand it. When I attain highest, complete enlightenment, wherever I am, I will lead them and enable them to abide in this teaching through my transcendent powers and power of wisdom.

"O Mañjuśrī! After the Tathāgata's *parinirvāṇa,* this bodhisattva *mahāsattva,* who has perfected the fourth sphere of the teaching of ease in practice, will be faultless when he teaches this Dharma. He will always be paid homage to, respected, honored, and praised by monks, nuns, laymen, laywomen, kings, princes, ministers, commoners, brahmans, and householders. The *deva*s in the sky will always accompany him in order to hear the Dharma. If he is in a village, city, secluded spot, or forest and the people want to come and ask difficult questions, the *deva*s will protect him both day and night, always for the sake of the Dharma, and he will cause all of those who listen to him to rejoice. Why is this? Because this sutra is preserved through the transcendent powers of all the Buddhas of the past, present, and future.

"O Mañjuśrī! Even the title of this *Lotus Sutra* cannot be heard in incalculable lands. How much more is it unable to be seen, accepted, preserved, and recited!

"O Mañjuśrī! Suppose a very powerful noble emperor wanted to subdue other countries with his might, but the lesser kings would not obey his command. In such a case the noble emperor gathers an army together to overcome them. He recognizes the soldiers who have committed brave deeds in war and, greatly rejoicing, he bestows boons according to their merit, such as estates, villages, cities, garments, ornaments, various treasures, gold, silver, lapis lazuli, mother-of-pearl, agate, coral, amber, elephants, horses, chariots, servants, and subjects, but he never gives them the precious jewel in his topknot. Why is this? Because only the noble emperor has this precious jewel in his topknot. If the emperor gives it away his attendants would certainly be very surprised and mistrustful.

"O Mañjuśrī! The Tathāgata is exactly like this. He has 39a
attained the land of the Dharma through his powers of concentration and wisdom. Thus he has become the king of the triple world. Since the *māra* kings will not obey him, the wise and noble generals of the Tathāgata come to do battle with them. The Tathāgata rejoices at the meritorious ones and teaches various sutras to the fourfold assembly, gladdening them. He bestows upon them the property of all the teachings about concentrations, liberations, faculties without corruption, and powers. He also bestows upon them the city of nirvana. Saying that they have attained nirvana, he leads their minds onward and gladdens them all. And yet he does not teach them the *Lotus Sutra*.

"O Mañjuśrī! It is just as if the noble emperor finally gives the jewel that has been long concealed in his topknot. Although he perceived the great merit of those soldiers and was deeply pleased, he did not rashly give them the marvelous jewel. The Tathāgata is also exactly like this. Since he is the great King of the Dharma in the triple world he inspires all the sentient beings through the Dharma. When he sees the wise and noble soldiers who have done battle with the *māra* of the five aggregates, the *māra* of desires, and the *māra* of death, who have great merit in battle, and have extinguished the three poisons, left the triple world, and broken out of Māra's net, he then rejoices greatly. He now teaches the *Lotus Sutra,* which is treated with hostility by the entire world and is difficult to believe in, and which he has never taught before, and enables sentient beings to attain omniscience.

"O Mañjuśrī! This *Lotus Sutra* is the ultimate teaching of all the Tathāgatas, the most profound among all the teachings, and conferred at the very end. It was in the same way that the very powerful and noble emperor gave the jewel after having preserved it for a long time.

"O Mañjuśrī! This *Lotus Sutra* is the secret treasure house of all the Buddha Tathāgatas, and the foremost among all the sutras. The Buddha has preserved it for a long time and he has not taught it indiscriminately. Now, for the first time he teaches it."

At that time the Bhagavat, wanting to elaborate on the meaning of this further, spoke these verses:

> Always practice patience
> And be compassionate toward all,
> Since only then can one expound
> A sutra praised by the Buddha!
> In the future those who preserve this sutra
> Should be compassionate and kind toward
> Lay Buddhists, renunciants, and nonbodhisattvas,
> Saying:
>
> > Those who have not heard this sutra
> > Or who do not believe in it
> > Have consequently lost a great opportunity.
> > When I attain the Buddha path
> > I will expound this teaching
> > Through various skillful means
> > And enable them to abide in it.
>
> Suppose there was a powerful, noble emperor
> Who bestows upon those soldiers meritorious in battle

Various gifts of elephants, horses, chariots, conveyances,
Ornaments, estates, villages, cities, garments,
Various treasures, servants, and wealth. 39b
He gives these gifts with joy.
If there is anyone who has been brave
And has performed difficult deeds,
The noble emperor gives
The precious jewel in his topknot.
The Tathāgata is exactly like this.
He is the emperor of all the teachings.
Out of his great compassion,
And through his treasury of wisdom
And great power of patience,
He inspires the world according to the Dharma.
Seeing all the sentient beings suffering,
Seeking liberation
And doing battle with the *māra*s,
He explains various teachings for the beings
And teaches various sutras
With his great skillful means.
Knowing that the sentient beings have
Finally attained the power to understand,
He teaches this *Lotus Sutra* only at the very end,
Just like the noble emperor
Who gave the jewel in his topknot.
This sutra is the utmost,
Superior to all the sutras.
I have constantly preserved it
And have not revealed it indiscriminately.
Now is the right time to teach it to you.
After my *parinirvāṇa*
Those seeking the Buddha path,
Who want to attain ease and expound this sutra,
Should become familiar with these four spheres
Of the teaching concerning ease in practice.

Those who recite this sutra will always
Be free from anxiety and illness,
And will have a noble countenance.
They will not be born into poverty,
Lowliness or ugliness.
Sentient beings will want to meet them
Just as they long to meet a wise seer,
And all of the *devaputras* will serve them.
Sticks and swords cannot hurt them,
And poison cannot harm them.
If people slander them
Those slanderers' mouths will be sealed up.
They will travel fearlessly
Like a lion king, and
The light of their wisdom
Will illuminate just like the sun.
If they dream they see only subtle things.
They see the Tathāgatas seated on lion seats,
Teaching the Dharma to the assembly
Of monks surrounding them.
They see *nāgas* and *asuras*,
As numerous as the sands of the Ganges River,
Honoring the Tathāgatas
With their palms pressed together.
Revealing themselves,
They teach the Dharma to these beings.
They also see the Buddhas, with golden bodies,
Emitting immeasurable rays of light
Which illuminate universally,
And expounding various teachings
With beautiful voices like Brahma's.
To the fourfold assembly
The Buddha teaches the highest Dharma.
Revealing themselves among them,
They praise the Buddha

With palms pressed together.
Hearing the Dharma they rejoice
And pay homage to the Buddha.
They attain the power of recollection
And achieve the wisdom of nonretrogression.
The Buddha, knowing their minds,
And that they have deeply entered the Buddha path,
Gives them a prediction of the highest,
Complete enlightenment, saying: 39c

> O son of a virtuous family!
> In the future you will attain immeasurable
> Wisdom and the great path of the Buddha.
> Your land will be pure and vast,
> Beyond all comparison.
> The fourfold assembly will also be there
> Listening to the Dharma with their palms
> Pressed together.

They who recite this sutra also see themselves
In mountain forests, practicing excellent teachings,
Experiencing the real aspect,
Deeply entering into concentration,
And looking at the Buddhas in the ten directions,
All of whom have golden bodies
Adorned with a hundred auspicious marks.
They will always have such pleasant dreams
And, hearing the Dharma taught,
They will teach it to others.
They will also dream about becoming
The king of a realm who abandons his palace
And retinue, and the highly pleasing
Desires of the five senses,
Approaches the terrace of enlightenment,
Sits on the lion seat under the *bodhi* tree,
Attains the wisdom of all the Buddhas

After seeking the path for seven days,
And who, arising, turns the wheel of the Dharma
After having attained the highest path.
They will teach the Dharma to the fourfold assembly
For thousands of myriads of *koṭi*s of *kalpa*s.
Explaining the true and incorruptible Dharma,
They will save innumerable sentient beings.
Later they will enter nirvana
Just as smoke dies away
When the flame of a candle is extinguished.
If anyone in the troubled world to come
Teaches this highest Dharma
They will attain great benefits
Like the merits mentioned above.

Chapter XV

Bodhisattvas Emerging from the Earth

At that time the bodhisattva *mahāsattvas*, who had arrived from other lands and whose number exceeded that of the sands of eight Ganges Rivers, stood up in the great assembly, bowed with their palms pressed together, and then spoke to the Buddha, saying: "O Bhagavat! If you give us permission to diligently strive to preserve, recite, copy and pay homage to this [*Lotus*] *Sutra* after the *parinirvāṇa* of the Buddha in this *sahā* world, then we will extensively teach it in this land."

Then the Buddha addressed the assembly of bodhisattva *mahāsattvas*, saying: "Enough, O sons of a virtuous family! There is no need for you to preserve this sutra. Why is this? In my *sahā* world there are bodhisattva *mahāsattvas*, equal to the sands of sixty thousand Ganges Rivers in number; and each of these bodhisattvas, in turn, has a retinue equal to the sands of sixty thousand Ganges Rivers. After my *parinirvāṇa* they can preserve, recite, and extensively teach this sutra."

When the Buddha said this all the lands of the great manifold
cosmos in the *sahā* world quaked and the earth split. From out of 40a
this crevice there simultaneously appeared incalculable thousands of myriads of *koṭis* of bodhisattva *mahāsattvas*. All of these bodhisattvas had golden bodies endowed with the thirty-two marks and radiating immeasurable rays of light. They had all previously been living in the space under the earth of the *sahā* world. Having heard the sound of Śākyamuni's teaching, all of these bodhisattvas emerged from below.

Each of those bodhisattvas presided over a great assembly and each led a retinue equal to the sands of sixty thousand Ganges

Rivers in number. How much more numerous were the bodhisattvas who emerged leading retinues equal in number to the sands of fifty thousand, forty thousand, thirty thousand, twenty thousand, or ten thousand Ganges Rivers! How much more numerous were the bodhisattvas who emerged leading retinues even equal to the sands of one Ganges River, half a Ganges River, a quarter of a Ganges River, or even just one thousandth of a myriad of a *koṭi* of a *nayuta* of the sands of a Ganges River! How many more retinues were there numbering thousands of myriads of *koṭi*s of *nayuta*s! How many more retinues were there numbering myriads of *koṭi*s! How many more were those numbering ten million, one million, or even ten thousand! How many more were those numbering one thousand, one hundred, or even ten! How much more numerous were bodhisattvas leading disciples numbering five, four, three, two, or even one! And how many more bodhisattvas were there who had eagerly practiced alone and far from the worldly life! The number of such bodhisattvas as these is incalculable and limitless, beyond all calculation and metaphor.

Having emerged from the earth, each of these bodhisattvas approached the Tathāgatas Prabhūtaratna and Śākyamuni, still seated in the beautiful seven-jeweled stupa in the air. Going up to them, they bowed until their foreheads touched the feet of both Bhagavats. Then, having bowed to the other Buddhas, each sitting on a lion seat under the jeweled trees, they circumambulated them to the right three times, honoring them with their palms pressed together. Having praised them with various bodhisattva eulogies, they withdrew to one side and joyfully gazed at the two Bhagavats. All these bodhisattva *mahāsattva*s, having emerged from the earth, praised the Buddhas with various bodhisattva eulogies. While they did, fifty intermediate *kalpa*s passed.

During this time the Buddha Śākyamuni sat in silence; and the fourfold assemblies were also silent while the fifty intermediate *kalpa*s passed. Because of the Buddha's transcendent powers, the great assemblies believed that the time that had passed was only half a day. Then, through the transcendent powers of the

Buddha, the fourfold assemblies also saw the bodhisattvas filling the air throughout immeasurable hundreds of thousands of myriads of *koṭis* of lands.

There were four leaders among those bodhisattvas gathered there. They were called Viśiṣṭacāritra, Anantacāritra, Viśuddhacāritra, and Supratiṣṭhitacāritra. These four bodhisattvas were the foremost leaders in the assembly. At the head of the great assembly, they each pressed their palms together, gazed at Śākyamuni Buddha, and inquired of him, saying: "O Bhagavat! Are you without illness or pain? Are you at ease in practice or not? Do those who should be saved accept your teaching easily or not? Do they not make you weary, O Bhagavat?"

Thereupon the four great bodhisattvas spoke these verses:

O Bhagavat! Are you at ease? 40b
Are you without illness or pain?
Are you fatigued with leading
And inspiring sentient beings?
Do the sentient beings accept
Your guidance easily or not?
Do they not tire the Bhagavat?

At that time the Bhagavat spoke to the great assembly of bodhisattvas, saying: "It is exactly like this, O sons of a virtuous family! It is exactly so! The Tathāgata is at ease and without illness or pain. It is easy to save sentient beings, and I am not fatigued. Why is this? Because sentient beings have continually received my guidance throughout many lives, and they have also planted roots of good merit by revering and honoring the Buddhas of the past.

"When these sentient beings first saw me and heard my teaching, all, except for those who had previously practiced and studied the inferior vehicle, immediately believed and accepted it and entered the Tathāgata's wisdom. Now I enable even such people as these to listen to this sutra and enter the Buddha's wisdom."

Then the great bodhisattvas spoke these verses:

Splendid, splendid!
O Bhagavat, Great Hero!
All the sentient beings
Can easily be brought to the path.
They can ask about
The profound wisdom of the Buddhas.
Hearing about it, they trust and accept it.
We rejoice about this.

At that time the Bhagavat praised the foremost of the great bodhisattvas, saying: "Splendid, splendid, O sons of virtuous family! Thoughts of joy regarding the Tathāgata have awakened in you."

Then Bodhisattva Maitreya and the assembly of bodhisattvas equal in number to the sands of eight thousand Ganges Rivers thought this:

> Looking far into the past, we have never seen or heard of such an assembly of great bodhisattva *mahāsattva*s, who have now emerged from the earth and are standing before the Bhagavat with their palms pressed together in reverence, asking the Tathāgata questions.

Then Bodhisattva Mahāsattva Maitreya, knowing the minds of the bodhisattvas whose number was equal to the sands of eight thousand Ganges Rivers, and wanting to clear up their confusion, faced the Buddha with the palms of his hands pressed together and addressed him in verse, saying:

We have never seen such a great assembly
Of incalculable thousands of myriads of *koṭi*s
Of bodhisattvas before.
We entreat you, O Best of Humans,
To explain it to us!
Where have they come from?
For what reason have they gathered here?
They look magnificent

And have great transcendent powers.
Their wisdom is beyond our comprehension.
They are firm in their resolve,
Have the power of great perseverance,
And an appearance that sentient beings
Desire to see.
Where have they come from?
Each of these bodhisattvas is leading
A retinue whose number is incalculable, 40c
Like the sands of the Ganges River.
Some great bodhisattvas are leading retinues
Equal in number to the sands
Of sixty thousand Ganges Rivers.
Great are the assemblies,
Singlemindedly seeking the Buddha path.
These great leaders, equal in number
To the sands of sixty thousand Ganges Rivers,
Have come all together to pay homage to the Buddha
And preserve this sutra.
The number of bodhisattvas leading retinues
Equal in number to the sands of fifty thousand
Ganges Rivers is even greater;
And the number of bodhisattvas who lead retinues
Equal in number to the sands of forty thousand,
Thirty thousand, twenty thousand, ten thousand,
One thousand, one hundred, even one, one half,
One third, one fourth, one myriadth of a *koṭi*
Of the sands of a Ganges River exceeds even these.
There are disciples who number
Thousands of myriads of *nayuta*s,
Myriads of *koṭi*s, or even half a *koṭi*.
Their numbers also exceed that mentioned above.
There are also disciples in retinues
Of one million, ten thousand,
One thousand, one hundred, fifty, ten,

Even three, two, or one in number.
There are also great bodhisattvas
Who have come without retinues,
Desiring to be in solitude.
The number of those
Who have come before the Buddha
Is far beyond any calculation.
If anyone counted the number of such a great assembly
With bamboo counting-sticks, he would not finish
Even after exhausting *kalpa*s greater in number
Than the sands of the Ganges River.
Who has taught the Dharma
To this assembly of bodhisattvas,
Endowed with great dignity and perseverance?
Who has inspired and perfected them?
Under whom did the thought of enlightenment
First awaken in them?
Which Buddha-Dharma do they praise?
Whose sutra have they preserved and practiced?
And which Buddha path have they followed?
Such bodhisattvas as these,
Endowed with transcendent powers
And the power of great wisdom,
Have all emerged out of the earth,
Which quaked in the four directions
And split asunder.
O Bhagavat! We have never seen
Such a thing before.
We entreat you to tell us the name
Of the land from where they have come.
We have been constantly traveling
In various regions,
Nevertheless we have never seen
Such a thing before.
We do not know even a single person

In this assembly.
All of a sudden
They have emerged from the earth.
We entreat you to explain the reason why.
All of the immeasurable hundreds of thousands
Of *koṭis* of bodhisattvas in this great assembly
Now wish to know about this matter. 41a
There must be underlying causes for this,
To explain all of these bodhisattvas.
O Bhagavat, He of Immeasurable Qualities!
We entreat you to clear up
The confusion of the assembly!

Thereupon the Buddhas who were the magically created forms of Śākyamuni Buddha arrived from other incalculable thousands of myriads of *koṭis* of lands and sat cross-legged on lion seats under the jeweled trees in the eight directions. Each attendant of these Buddhas had seen the great assembly of bodhisattvas as they emerged from out of the earth and floated in midair in the four directions of the great manifold cosmos. Each of them addressed his Buddha, saying: "O Bhagavat! Where has this great assembly of immeasurable, limitless, incalculable bodhisattvas come from?"

Then the Buddhas answered their attendants, saying: "O sons of a virtuous family! Wait a moment! There is a bodhisattva *mahāsattva* called Maitreya, who has received a prediction from the Buddha Śākyamuni that he will become a Buddha after Śākyamuni in the future. Since he has already asked about this, the Buddha will now answer him. You shall be able to hear the reason yourselves."

Then the Buddha Śākyamuni addressed Bodhisattva Maitreya, saying: "Splendid, splendid, O Ajita! You have asked the Buddha an important question. You should all singlemindedly don the armor of perseverance and be of firm will. The Tathāgata now wants to reveal the wisdom of the Buddhas, the inherent transcendent powers of the Buddhas, the lionlike dignified power of the Buddhas, the majestic and mighty power of the Buddhas."

Thereupon the Bhagavat, wanting to elaborate on the meaning of this further, spoke these verses:

You should be persistent
And wholeheartedly attentive,
For I want to explain it to you.
Do not have any doubts, for the wisdom
Of the Buddha is difficult to comprehend!
You should now awaken the power of faith,
And with perseverance abide in the good.
Now you will all be able to hear
What you have never heard before.
I will now put you at ease.
Have no doubts or fear!
The Buddha never speaks false words.
His wisdom is immeasurable.
The foremost Dharma that he has attained
Is profound and difficult to explain.
I will now expound this difficult teaching,
So you should listen wholeheartedly.

Then the Bhagavat, after speaking these verses, addressed Bodhisattva Maitreya, saying: "I will now proclaim it to all of you in this assembly. O Ajita! All of you have never seen these immeas-
41b urable, innumerable, incalculable great bodhisattva *mahāsattva*s who have emerged from out of the earth. Having attained highest, complete enlightenment in this *sahā* world, I led, inspired, and instructed these bodhisattvas, restrained their thoughts, and caused the thought of the path to awaken in them. When these bodhisattvas lived in the space under the earth of this *sahā* world, they recited various sutras, became well versed in them, and contemplated, analyzed, and correctly remembered them.

"O Ajita! All these sons of a virtuous family did not wish to be among the multitude where there is always much discussion. They always wanted to be in quiet places. They diligently strove without resting or relying upon *deva*s or humans. They always desired the profound wisdom without obstructions; they always wanted the Dharma of the Buddhas. They strove wholeheartedly in seeking the highest wisdom."

At that time the Bhagavat, wanting to elaborate on the meaning of this further, spoke these verses:

O Ajita! You should know
That all of these great bodhisattvas
Have practiced the wisdom of the Buddha
For innumerable *kalpa*s.
They have all been inspired by me,
And the thought of the great path
Has awakened in them.
They are my heirs.
Abiding in this world,
They always cultivated ascetic practices,
Wishing to be in quiet places.
Rejecting the clamor of the multitude,
They did not want to have much discussion.
All my heirs such as these
Constantly practiced my teaching
With vigor, day and night.
In order to seek the Buddha path
They lived in the space
Under the earth of this *sahā* world.
They were firm in recollection,
And they always diligently sought wisdom.
Explaining various subtle teachings
Their minds were free from fear.
Sitting under the *bodhi* tree
In the city of Gayā,
I attained highest, complete enlightenment,
And turned the wheel of the highest Dharma.
I then led and inspired them
So that the thought of the path

Awakened in them for the first time.
All of them are now at the stage of nonretrogression,
And will certainly become Buddhas with no residue.
I now teach the truth.
You should wholeheartedly believe that
From long, long ago I have been
Leading and inspiring all these bodhisattvas.

Then Bodhisattva Mahāsattva Maitreya and the innumerable
41c other bodhisattvas became doubtful and confused concerning this unprecedented experience. They thought this:

> How is it possible in such a short time for the Bhagavat to have inspired such an immeasurable, limitless, incalculable number of great bodhisattvas, enabling them to abide in highest, complete enlightenment?

Immediately they addressed the Buddha, saying: "O Bhagavat! When the Tathāgata was a prince he left the palace of the Śākyas, sat on the terrace of enlightenment which is not far from the city of Gayā, and attained highest, complete enlightenment. Since then more than forty years have passed. How is it possible, O Bhagavat, for you to have done such great Buddha acts in such a short period of time? Is it through the might of the Buddha and through the Buddha's qualities that you have inspired such an assembly of incalculable great bodhisattvas to achieve highest, complete enlightenment?

"O Bhagavat! Even if someone counted the number of the great bodhisattvas for thousands of myriads of *koṭi*s of *kalpa*s they would not be able to finish. There would be no end. From long ago these bodhisattvas have been planting roots of good merit in the presence of immeasurable, limitless Buddhas. They have perfected the bodhisattva path and have always practiced the pure path of discipline and integrity. It is, O Bhagavat, difficult to believe such things in this world.

"Suppose a handsome man with dark hair, twenty-five years of age, were to point to a hundred-year-old man and say:

He is my son.

"And the one-hundred-year-old man points to the young fellow and says:

He is my father and he raised me!

"This would be difficult to believe; and what the Buddha has now taught is exactly like this. It has not, in fact, been so long since the Buddha attained the path. Yet for the sake of the Buddha path this great assembly of bodhisattvas has been diligently striving for innumerable thousands of myriads of *koṭi*s of *kalpa*s. They have skillfully entered, abided in, and emerged from immeasurable thousands of myriads of *koṭi*s of *samādhi*s. They have attained great transcendent powers and practiced the pure path of discipline and integrity for a long time. They have gradually and ably practiced wholesome teachings and are skilled at discussions. They are jewels among humans and a great rarity in the entire world.

"Today the Bhagavat has correctly said that after he attained the path of the Buddha he caused the thought of enlightenment to awaken in the bodhisattvas for the first time. He then led, inspired, and instructed them to approach highest, complete enlightenment. O Bhagavat! Although it has not been so long since you attained Buddhahood yet you have really done these great meritorious acts.

"We believe the Buddha's words, spoken according to our capacities, and that what he says is never false. We are all well versed in the Buddha's knowledge. However, if the bodhisattvas in whom the thought of enlightenment has recently awakened hear this after the Buddha's *parinirvāṇa,* they will not accept it; and this will bring about conditions for erring deeds that destroy the Dharma. That is why, O Bhagavat, we entreat you to explain it to us and remove our doubts. Moreover, in the future, when the sons of a virtuous family hear this, they will also be free from doubt."

Thereupon Bodhisattva Maitreya, wanting to elaborate upon the meaning of this further, spoke these verses:

42a Long ago the Buddha left
The household of the Śākya clan,
And approached Gayā
Where he sat under the *bodhi* tree;
It has not been so long since that time.
The number of the Buddha's heirs
Is incalculable;
From long ago they have practiced the Buddha path
And attained transcendent powers and
The power of wisdom.
They have thoroughly studied
The bodhisattva path,
And are as undefiled by worldly affairs,
As the lotus blossom in the water.
They have emerged from out of the earth,
And all stood respectfully before the Bhagavats.
It is difficult to comprehend this matter,
How can we possibly believe it!
The Buddha attained the path
Only a short time ago,
Yet he has accomplished so much.
We entreat you to remove our doubts
And give a detailed explanation
According to the truth.
Suppose there were a young man
Just twenty-five years of age
Who pointed to a one-hundred-year-old man,
Who was wrinkled and had white hair, saying:

> This is my offspring.

The [old man] also says:

> This is my father.

The father is young, and the son is old.
No one in the world would believe it.

The Bhagavat's teaching is exactly like this.
He attained the path only a very short time ago,
Yet these bodhisattvas are firm in resolution
And without weak will;
They have been practicing the bodhisattva path
For immeasurable *kalpa*s.
They are skilled at difficult discussions,
And their minds are free from fear.
They are resolute and persevering.
They are handsome and dignified,
Praised by the Buddhas in the ten directions.
They are good at detailed explanations.
They did not want to be among the multitudes
For they always liked being in meditation,
And so they lived in the space under the earth
In order to seek the Buddha path.
Since we heard about this from the Buddha
We have no doubts about it;
But still we entreat you, O Buddha, to expound it
And make it clear for the future.
Anyone in whom doubts awaken
And who does not believe in this sutra
Will certainly fall into the troubled states of being.
That is why we now entreat you to explain
How in such a short time
You have led and inspired
These innumerable bodhisattvas
So that the thought of enlightenment
Has awakened in them
And they abide in the stage of nonretrogression.

Chapter XVI

The Lifespan of the Tathāgata

Thereupon the Buddha addressed the bodhisattvas and the entire great assembly, saying: "O sons of a virtuous family! You should believe the true words of the Tathāgata." 42b

He addressed the great assembly again, saying: "You should believe the Tathāgata's true words."

He repeated this to them, saying: "You should believe the Tathāgata's true words."

Then the great assembly of bodhisattvas, headed by Maitreya, addressed the Buddha with their palms pressed together, saying: "O Bhagavat! We entreat you to explain it. We will accept the Buddha's words."

After they had spoken in this way three times, they again said: "We entreat you to explain it. We will accept the Buddha's words."

Then the Bhagavat, realizing that the bodhisattvas continued to entreat him after those three times, addressed them, saying: "Listen carefully to the Tathāgata's secret and transcendent powers. The *deva*s, humans, and *asura*s in all the worlds all think that the present Buddha, Śākyamuni, left the palace of the Śākyas, sat on the terrace of enlightenment not far from the city of Gayā, and attained highest, complete enlightenment. However, O sons of a virtuous family, immeasurable, limitless, hundreds of thousands of myriads of *koṭi*s of *nayuta*s of *kalpa*s have passed since I actually attained Buddhahood.

"Suppose there were a man who ground five hundreds of thousands myriads of *koṭi*s of *nayuta*s of incalculable great manifold cosmos into particles. While passing through five hundred thousands of myriads of *koṭi*s of *nayuta*s of incalculable lands to the east, he dropped just a single particle; and in this way he continued to drop the particles as he went toward the east, until they were all gone.

"O sons of a virtuous family! What do you think about this? Can all of these worlds be calculated or not? Can one imagine all of these worlds, calculate, and know their number or not?"

Bodhisattva Maitreya and the others together addressed the Buddha, saying: "O Bhagavat! These worlds are immeasurable, limitless, incalculable, and beyond our powers of conception. Even all the *śrāvakas* and *pratyekabuddhas*, with their knowledge free from corruption, are not able to comprehend them, or know their number. Although we abide in the stage of nonretrogression we cannot understand it. O Bhagavat! Such worlds as these are incalculable and limitless."

Then the Buddha addressed the assembly of the great bodhisattvas, saying: "O sons of a virtuous family! I will now explain it clearly to you. Suppose all these worlds, whether or not a particle was left in them, were reduced to particles, and each particle represented a *kalpa*. The period of time since I became a Buddha would exceed this by hundreds of thousands of myriads of *koṭis* of *nayutas* of incalculable *kalpas*. Since then I have constantly been residing in the *sahā* world, teaching the Dharma and inspiring sentient beings. I have also been leading and benefiting sentient beings in incalculable hundreds of thousands of myriads of *koṭis* of *nayutas* of other worlds.

"O sons of a virtuous family! During this interim I explained
42c about the Buddha Dīpaṃkara and others. Furthermore, I also said
that they had entered *parinirvāṇa*. I have explained such things
through skillful means.

"O sons of a virtuous family! If any sentient being comes to me, I perceive the dullness or sharpness of his faith and other faculties with my Buddha-eye. According to the way I should bring them to the path, I, myself, proclaim different names and lifespans in various places. In each case I have also clearly stated that I would enter *parinirvāṇa*. Through various skillful means I have explained subtle teachings and have made the sentient beings rejoice.

"O sons of a virtuous family! To those beings whom the Tathāgata perceives as taking pleasure in the inferior teachings, who have few qualities and grave defilements, he teaches that the Buddha attained highest, complete enlightenment after he renounced household life in his young age. However, it has been a very long time indeed since I attained Buddhahood. I give such an explanation only to lead and inspire the sentient beings to enter the Buddha path through skillful means.

"O sons of a virtuous family! The sutras that the Tathāgata has expounded are all to save the sentient beings. Whether the Tathāgata teaches about himself or others, whether he reveals his form or that of others, whether he shows his acts or those of others, everything he says is true, never false.

"Why is this? Because the Tathāgata perceives all the marks of the triple world as they really are: that there is no birth and death, coming or going; that there is also no existence or extinction in the world, truth or falsehood, sameness or difference. The Tathāgata does not view the triple world as sentient beings in the triple world see it. The Tathāgata perceives such things clearly and without mistakes.

"Since sentient beings have various natures, desires, behaviors, thoughts, and distinctions, the Tathāgata, wanting to cause them to plant roots of good merit, has explained various teachings through a variety of examples, explanations, and illustrations. He has not desisted from doing Buddha acts even for a single moment and in this way it has been an extremely long time since I attained Buddhahood. My lifespan is immeasurable and incalculable. I abide forever without entering *parinirvāṇa*.

"O sons of a virtuous family! The lifespan that I first attained through practicing the bodhisattva path has not yet expired. It is twice as great as the number previously mentioned. Although I do not actually enter *parinirvāṇa* I proclaim that I do. It is through this skillful means that the Tathāgata leads and inspires sentient beings.

"Why is this? Because if the Buddha abides a long time in this 43a
world, those who have few qualities do not plant roots of good merit, acquire poor and superficial characters, are attached to the desires of the five senses, and enter into the web of illusions and

false views. If they see the Tathāgata always existing without extinction, they then become proud, self-willed, and negligent. The thought that the Buddha is difficult to meet and that he is to be respected cannot awaken in them. That is why the Tathāgata teaches through skillful means, saying:

> O monks! You should know that the appearance of the Buddhas in the world is very difficult to encounter.

"Why is this? Because some of those with little merit may not see the Buddha during the passage of immeasurable hundreds of thousands of myriads of *koṭi*s of *kalpa*s.

"For this reason I say:

> O monks! It is difficult to meet the Tathāgata.

"Hearing such words, the thought that it is very difficult to meet the Tathāgata will certainly awaken in these sentient beings. Longing and yearning for the Buddha, they will plant roots of good merit. For this reason, although the Tathāgata does not really pass into extinction, he nevertheless says he does.

"Furthermore, O sons of a virtuous family, the teaching of all the Buddha Tathāgatas is exactly like this. It is entirely true, never false, all for the sake of saving sentient beings.

"Suppose there were an excellent doctor. He is wise, knowledgeable, his prescriptions are effective, and he has skillfully cured a variety of diseases. This man has many sons, say ten, twenty, or even one hundred in number. For some reason, he has to go far off to another country and, while he is away, his children, whom he has left behind, drink some poison. The poison starts to take effect and they roll on the ground in agony.

"At this moment their father returns home. Some of the children who have taken the poison are delirious, while others are not. Seeing their father in the distance they all rejoice greatly and kneeling respectfully address him, saying:

> It is good that you have returned safely. In our ignorance we

> took this poison by mistake. We entreat you to cure and save us, and restore us to life.

"Seeing his children suffering in this way, the father searches for beneficial herbs possessed of good color, aroma, and flavor, according to the medical manual. Blending them together after grinding and sifting, he gives the mixture to the children and says:

> This is an extremely beneficial medicine with good color, aroma, and flavor. All of you take it! It will quickly remove your pain and you will never be afflicted again.

"Then the children who have not become delirious see this beneficial medicine of good color and aroma, and immediately take it. The affliction is completely removed and they are cured. The remaining children, those who are delirious, seeing their father coming to them, rejoice and ask him to seek a cure for their illness. Although he offers them the medicine, they will not take it. Why is this? The poison has so deeply penetrated them that they have become delirious. They do not think that the medicine with good color and aroma is good.

"The father thinks:

> These children are to be pitied. The poison has completely warped their minds. Although they rejoiced upon seeing me and sought a cure they will not take this beneficial medicine. I will now cause them to take this medicine through skillful means.

"Then he says to them:

> You should know that I am now old and feeble, close to death. I will now leave this beneficial medicine here. You should take it. Do not worry about not recovering.

"Having left these instructions he goes to another country and sends a messenger back home to tell them: 'Your father has already died.' Upon hearing that their father is dead, the children become very distressed and think:

43b If our father had lived he would have taken pity on us and protected us. But now, abandoning us, he has died in a distant country.

"They now consider themselves orphans having no one to rely upon. Through constant grieving their minds become clear, and only then do they realize that the medicine has fine color, aroma, and flavor. They immediately take it and the poison is completely driven out. The father, hearing that all his children have completely recovered, immediately returns and makes his appearance."

The Buddha then asked the bodhisattvas: "O sons of a virtuous family! Do you think there is anyone who would say that this good doctor is guilty of lying?"

The bodhisattvas replied: "No, we do not, O Bhagavat!"

The Buddha said: "I am just like this. Since I became a Buddha, immeasurable, limitless, hundreds of thousands of myriads of *koṭi*s of *nayuta*s of incalculable *kalpa*s have passed. Though for the sake of sentient beings, I use skillful means and say that I will enter *parinirvāṇa,* there is no one who could rightly say that I am guilty of falsehood."

Thereupon the Bhagavat, wanting to elaborate on the meaning of this further, spoke these verses:

Since I attained Buddhahood,
Immeasurable hundreds of thousands of myriads
Of *koṭi*s of incalculable *kalpa*s have passed.
I have been constantly teaching the Dharma,
Through these immeasurable *kalpa*s,
Leading and inspiring
Innumerable *koṭi*s of sentient beings
And enabling them to enter the Buddha path.
Using skillful means
I have manifested the state of nirvana
To bring sentient beings to this path;
Yet I have not actually entered nirvana,
But continually abide here expounding the Dharma.

Although I am always among these erring beings,
With my transcendent powers,
I prevent them from seeing me.
The sentient beings,
Seeing me enter perfect extinction
Earnestly revere my relics
And, filled with longing,
Yearn for me.
When the sentient beings become
Sincere, mild, and receptive,
And, wanting wholeheartedly to meet the Buddha,
Are willing to give unsparingly
Of their bodies and lives,
Then I, together with the sangha,
Will appear on Mount Gṛdhrakūṭa.
I will declare this to sentient beings:

> Although I am always here without extinction,
> Through the power of skillful means
> I manifest extinction and nonextinction.
> If there are any sentient beings in other worlds
> Who respect and believe in me,
> I will also teach them the highest Dharma.

Not knowing this, you only think
That I have entered *parinirvāṇa*.
I see all sentient beings 43c
Submerged in the ocean of suffering.
That is why, by not manifesting my form,
I cause them to yearn for me.
Then, after awakening this longing,
I appear and expound the Dharma;
Such are my transcendent powers.
For innumerable *kalpa*s
I have constantly resided
On Mount Gṛdhrakūṭa and elsewhere.

When sentient beings see themselves
Amidst a conflagration
At the end of a *kalpa,*
It is in fact my tranquil land,
Always full of *deva*s and humans.
All the gardens and palaces
Are adorned with various gems.
The jeweled trees abound with flowers and fruits,
And the sentient beings are joyful among them.
The *deva*s beat heavenly drums
Making constant and varied music.
They rain down *māndārava* flowers
Upon the Buddha and the great assembly.
Although my Pure Land never decays,
The sentient beings see it as ravaged by fire
And torn with anxiety and distress;
They believe it is filled with these things.
Because of their misdeeds
These erring sentient beings do not hear
The name of the three treasures
For incalculable *kalpa*s.
But all who cultivate merit,
And are receptive and honest,
Will see me residing here,
Expounding the Dharma.
For the sake of these sentient beings
I teach that the lifespan
Of the Buddha is immeasurable.
To those who, after a long time,
Finally see the Buddha,
I teach that it is difficult to meet him.
Such is the power of my wisdom.
The light of my wisdom illuminates immeasurably
And my lifespan is of innumerable *kalpa*s.
This has been achieved through long practice.

You wise ones, do not give in to doubt!
Banish all doubt forever!
The Buddha's words are true, never false.
It is like the physician
Who proclaimed his own death,
Although it was untrue.
He did this to cure his delirious sons,
Through excellent skillful means;
So no one could say he really spoke falsehood.
I, also, being the father of the world,
Cure those who suffer.
To the deluded and unenlightened I say that
I have entered nirvana,
Although, in fact, I am really here.
For if they were to see me,
They would become lazy and arrogant.
Attached to the desires of the five senses,
They would fall into the troubled states of being.
Always aware of which sentient beings 44a
Practice the path and which do not,
I teach the Dharma in various ways,
According to their ability to be saved.
I am always thinking:

> By what means can I cause sentient beings to be able to
> Enter the highest path
> And quickly attain the Dharma?

Chapter XVII

Description of Merits

Thereupon, when the great assembly heard the Buddha explain that his lifespan was of such a great number of *kalpa*s, an immeasurable, limitless, incalculable number of sentient beings were greatly benefited.

Then the Bhagavat addressed Bodhisattva Mahāsattva Maitreya, saying: "O Ajita! When I explained the great length of this Tathāgata's lifespan, sentient beings, equal to the sands of the six hundred and eighty myriads of *koṭi*s of *nayuta*s of Ganges Rivers in number, gained understanding of the truth of the nonorigination of all *dharma*s. Furthermore, a thousand times this number of bodhisattva *mahāsattva*s attained the power of recollecting what they hear; and bodhisattva *mahāsattva*s equal to the number of particles in one world attained unhindered eloquence. Moreover, there were bodhisattva *mahāsattva*s equal to the particles in one world who attained the power of tenacious memory which revolves hundreds of thousands of myriads of *koṭi*s of immeasurable times. There were also bodhisattva *mahāsattva*s equal to the number of particles in the great manifold cosmos who turned the irreversible wheel of the Dharma, and bodhisattva *mahāsattva*s equal to the number of particles in two medium-sized manifold cosmos who turned the purified wheel of the Dharma.

"Furthermore, there were bodhisattvas *mahāsattva*s equal to the number of particles in one small-sized cosmos who will be able to attain highest, complete enlightenment after eight births; bodhisattva *mahāsattva*s equal to the number of particles in the four fourfold continents who will attain highest, complete enlightenment after four births; bodhisattva *mahāsattva*s equal to the number of particles in the threefold four continents who will attain highest, complete enlightenment after three births; bodhisattva *mahāsattva*s equal to the number of particles in the twofold four continents who will attain highest, complete enlightenment after two births; and bodhisattva *mahāsattva*s equal to the number of particles in the four continents who will attain highest, complete enlightenment after one birth. Moreover there were sentient beings equal to the number of particles in the eightfold great manifold cosmos, in all of whom the thought of highest, complete enlightenment had awakened."

When the Buddha explained that these bodhisattva *mahāsattva*s had attained deep insight into the Dharma, *māndārava* and great *māndārava* flowers rained down from the sky, scattering over the Buddhas who were seated on lion seats under immeasurable hundreds of thousands of myriads of *koṭi*s of jeweled trees; and they scattered over Śākyamuni Buddha and the Tathāgata Prabhūtaratna, who had attained *parinirvāṇa* long ago, both of whom were sitting on the lion seat in a seven-jeweled stupa; they
44b also scattered over all of the great bodhisattvas and the fourfold assembly. Finely powdered sandalwood and aloeswood incense also rained down, and heavenly drums resounded in the sky with a deep and beautiful sound. One thousand kinds of heavenly garments, draped with strings of pearl, jewels, and wish-fulfilling gems (*maṇi*), rained down, filling the nine directions. Priceless incense burned in various jeweled incense holders, and its fragrance spread spontaneously throughout the great assembly as an offering. Above each Buddha there were bodhisattvas holding banners and umbrellas that extended upward to the Brahma world. These bodhisattvas praised the Buddhas by singing immeasurable verses with beautiful voices.

Then Bodhisattva Maitreya rose from his seat, leaving his right shoulder bared, faced the Buddha with the palms of his hands pressed together, and spoke these verses:

> The Buddha has taught this marvelous Dharma
> That we have never heard before.
> The Bhagavat has great powers

And his lifespan is immeasurable.
Innumerable heirs of the Buddha
Attained the benefit of the Dharma
After hearing the Bhagavat's explanation,
And became completely filled with joy.
Some attained the stage of nonretrogression,
And others the power of recollection.
Some attained unhindered eloquence,
And others the power of tenacious memory
Which revolves many *koṭis* of times.
There were also bodhisattvas,
Equal to the number of particles
In the great cosmos,
Who each turned the irreversible wheel
Of the Dharma.
There were also bodhisattvas,
Equal to the number of particles
In a medium cosmos,
Who each turned the purified
Wheel of the Dharma.
There were also bodhisattvas,
Equal to the number of particles
In a small cosmos,
Who after eight births
Will complete the Buddha path.
There were also bodhisattvas,
Equal to four times, three times,
And two times the number of particles
In the four continents,
Who after four, three, and two births
Will attain Buddhahood.
There were also bodhisattvas,
Equal to the number of particles
In the four continents,
Who will obtain omniscience

After one birth;
And sentient beings, having heard about
The great length of the Buddha's lifespan,
Attained immeasurable results
That were pure and without corruption.
There were also sentient beings,
Equal to the number of particles
In the eight worlds,
In whom, having heard about the lifespan of the Buddha,
The thought of highest enlightenment awakened.
44c The Bhagavat has taught the Dharma
That is immeasurable and inconceivable,
And from which come benefits
As limitless as space.
Heavenly *māndārava*
And great *māndārava* flowers rained down;
And Śakras and Brahmas
Came from innumerable Buddha lands,
Equal in number to the sands of the Ganges River.
Sandalwood and aloeswood powder,
Scattered like birds in the sky
Flying in all directions,
And rained down over the Buddhas.
Heavenly drums resounded spontaneously
And beautifully in the air;
And thousands of myriads of *koṭi*s
Of heavenly garments floated whirling down.
Precious incense was burned
In various jeweled incense holders,
Its fragrance naturally penetrating everywhere,
In homage to the Bhagavats.
The great assembly of these bodhisattvas
Held myriads of *koṭi*s of tall and beautiful
Seven-jeweled banners and umbrellas,
Which extended gradually to the Brahma world.

They hung jeweled flags and excellent banners
In the presence of each of these Buddhas,
And chanted thousands of myriads of verses
In praise of the Tathāgatas.
Such things had never been
Experienced before.
Hearing of the Buddha's
Immeasurable lifespan, all rejoiced;
And, the Buddha's name being heard
Throughout the ten directions,
Sentient beings were greatly benefited.
Everyone became endowed
With the roots of good merit,
And the thought of highest, complete enlightenment
Awakened in them.

At that time the Buddha addressed Bodhisattva Mahāsattva Maitreya, saying: "O Ajita! Those sentient beings who hear about the great length of the Buddha's lifespan, and can awaken even a single thought of willing acceptance, will all obtain immeasurable merit. If there are sons and daughters of a good family who, for the sake of highest, complete enlightenment, practice the five perfections of giving (*dāna*), good conduct (*śīla*), perseverance (*kṣānti*), effort (*vīrya*), and meditation (*dhyāna*), with the exception of the perfection of wisdom (*prajñā*), for eighty myriads of *koṭi*s of *nayutas* of *kalpa*s, their merit is not even a hundredth, a thousandth, a hundred thousandth of a myriad of a *koṭi* of the former person's merit. It is so small that it cannot be conceived of through calculation or illustration. If there are sons and daughters of a virtuous family who possess such merit as the former, they will never revert from highest, complete enlightenment."

Thereupon the Bhagavat, wanting to elaborate on the meaning of this further, spoke these verses:

Those who seek the Buddha's wisdom 45a
Will practice the five perfections

For eighty myriads of *koṭi*s
Of *nayuta*s of *kalpa*s.
Throughout these *kalpa*s they will pay homage to
The Buddhas, *pratyekabuddha*s, *śrāvaka*s,
And all the bodhisattvas by offering
Rare delicacies, excellent garments, and bedding,
Or by building monasteries out of sandalwood
Which are adorned with gardens.
Through offering such a variety of precious things
Throughout all of these *kalpa*s,
They will transfer the merits to the Buddha path.
Those who further maintain good conduct,
Which is pure and without corruption,
Will seek what the Buddhas
Have praised as the highest path.
Those who further practice perseverance
And abide in the stage of self-control,
Will be of constant mind,
Even if subjected to ill-treatment.
They will continue to endure
Even if they are scorned and persecuted
By those who think, through their excessive pride,
That they have attained the truth.
Those who make diligent efforts
And are firm in their intentions
For immeasurable *koṭi*s of *kalpa*s
Will be intent and never lazy;
And those who abide in tranquil places
For immeasurable *kalpa*s
Will always discipline their minds, avoiding sleep,
While either sitting or wandering.
For these reasons they will
Abide in various meditations,
Their minds firm and unwavering,
For eighty myriads of *koṭi*s of *kalpa*s.

Maintaining the merit of this concentration
They seek the highest path saying:

> I will attain omniscience.

Then they will achieve
This perfection of meditation.
Practicing thus for hundreds of thousands
Of myriads of *koṭi*s of *kalpa*s,
Their merits will be as mentioned above.
If those sons and daughters of a virtuous family,
Upon hearing me explain about my lifespan
In this way, are able to awaken
Even a single thought of willing acceptance,
Their merit exceeds that of the former.
Such will also be the merit
Of those who have no doubts whatsoever
And believe deeply even for a single moment.
Those bodhisattvas who practice the path
For a period of immeasurable *kalpa*s,
And who believe my explanation of my lifespan
When they hear it, are the ones 45b
Who fully accept this sutra,
Saying:

> Let us in the future devote a long life
> To saving sentient beings!
> Just as the present Bhagavat,
> King among the Śākyas, who roars the lion's roar
> On the terrace of enlightenment,
> Is fearless in teaching the Dharma,
> Let us in the future be respected by all
> And teach of the lifespan
> While seated upon the terrace of enlightenment.

Those who have profound thoughts, are pure,
Honest and learned, have good recollection,

And understand the Buddha's words in accordance
With what is appropriate,
Will have no doubts regarding this.

"Furthermore, O Ajita, those who hear of the great length of the Buddha's lifespan and understand the intent of these words will obtain limitless merit that will give rise to the highest wisdom of the Tathāgata. How much more merit will they gain who extensively hear this sutra, move others to listen to it, preserve it, move others to preserve it, copy it, or move others to copy it; and pay homage to the sutra by offering flowers, incense, necklaces, flags, banners, canopies, lamps of scented oil, and ghee! The merit of these people will be immeasurable and limitless. They will be able to achieve omniscience.

"O Ajita! Those sons and daughters of a virtuous family, who, hearing me teach the great length of the Buddha's lifespan, wholeheartedly accept it, will see the Buddha, who always dwells on Mount Gṛdhrakūṭa together with the great bodhisattvas and *śrāvakas*, teaching the Dharma to the assembly. Moreover, they will see the land of this *sahā* world, which is made of lapis lazuli, level and even. The network of roads is laid out like a chessboard, paved with Jāmbūnada gold and bordered with jeweled trees. All its foundations, towers, and balconies will be made of treasures and the multitude of these bodhisattvas will be dwelling in them. Those who can see such things should know that to be able to do so is a sign of their full and willing acceptance.

"Furthermore, after the Tathāgata's *parinirvāṇa*, those who hear this sutra do not disparage it and rejoice in their hearts, should know that this is a sign of their full and willing acceptance. How much more do those who recite and preserve this sutra show a sign of full and willing acceptance! Such are the people who hold the Tathāgata in respect.

"O Ajita! These sons and daughters of a virtuous family do not have to build stupas and monasteries for me, make chambers for the monks, or pay homage to the sangha with the four kinds of offerings. Why is this? Because these sons and daughters of a virtuous family

recite and preserve this sutra, which means they have already built stupas, made chambers for the monks, and paid homage to the sangha. They have already erected seven-jeweled stupas for 45c
the Buddha's relics, which are tall and wide, gradually narrowing to a pinnacle that reaches to the Brahma world. They have hung various banners, canopies, and variegated jeweled bells; offered flowers, incense, necklaces, scented powder, and ointment; burned incense; played drums, music, flutes, pipes, harps, and various dances; and adorned the stupas and relics of the Buddha by praising with verses and songs in beautiful voices. In this way they have already paid homage for immeasurable thousands of myriads of *koṭi*s of *kalpa*s.

"O Ajita! After my *parinirvāṇa*, those who hear this sutra and who can preserve it, copy it and move others to copy it, have already built chambers for monks, as well as thirty-two red sandalwood monasteries of the height of eight *tāla* trees, wide and fine, housing hundreds of thousands of monks. The monasteries they have built have gardens, ponds, paths for wandering, meditation caves, garments, food and drink, bedding, medicine, and are replete with all other necessities. Such hundreds of thousands of myriads of *koṭi*s of monks' chambers and towers will be incalculable. With these they pay homage to me and to the assembly of monks.

"I have explained that, for this reason, after the Tathāgata's *parinirvāṇa* those who preserve and recite this sutra, and explain it to others, who copy it or move others to copy it and who pay it homage to it no longer have to build stupas, monasteries, or erect chambers for the monks, or revere the sangha. How much less do those who preserve this sutra and practice the perfections of giving (*dāna*), good conduct (*śīla*), perseverance (*kṣānti*), effort (*vīrya*), meditation (*dhyāna*), and wisdom (*prajñā*) need to do so! Their merit is the highest, immeasurable and limitless. It is immeasurable and limitless in the same way that space is immeasurable and limitless in the ten directions—east, west, south, north, the four intermediate directions, and the zenith and nadir—and they will thus quickly obtain omniscience.

"Those who recite and preserve this sutra, who explain it for others, who copy it or move others to copy it, build monuments and make chambers for monks, revere and praise the sangha of *śrāvakas*, and praise the merits of the bodhisattvas in hundreds of thousands of myriads of *koṭis* of ways; those who explain this *Lotus Sutra* for the sake of others in accordance with its meaning through various illustrations, who preserve pure conduct and dwell together with gentle people, who are patient and have no anger, are firm in their intentions and always hold meditation in high regard, who attain profound *samādhi* and make vigorous efforts, persevere in all good practices, whose wisdom is keen and who answer difficult questions skillfully; O Ajita! Those sons and daughters of a virtuous family, who preserve and recite this sutra after my *parinirvāṇa* will attain good qualities like those mentioned above. You should know that such people have already set out for the terrace of enlightenment, are near to highest, complete enlightenment, and are seated under the *bodhi* tree.

"O Ajita! Wherever these sons and daughters of a virtuous
46a family sit, stand, or walk, there a monument should be built; and all of the *devas* and humans should pay homage to these monuments as they would do to those of the Buddha."

Thereupon the Bhagavat, wanting to elaborate on the meaning of this further, spoke these verses:

If after my *parinirvāṇa* there are people
Who preserve this sutra,
They will have immeasurable merits
As described above.
Such people have already given
Various kinds of offerings:
They have built stupas for the relics,
Adorned with the seven treasures,
With a pole on the top which is very tall and thick,
Gradually tapering upward,
Until it reaches the Brahma world.
These stupas have been adorned

With thousands of myriads of *koṭis* of jeweled bells
That ring with beautiful sounds as the wind blows.
For immeasurable *kalpas* such people
Have revered these stupas
By offering flowers, incense, necklaces,
Heavenly garments, and various kinds of music,
While burning scented ointments and butter-oil lamps
Which illuminate them on all sides.
In the troubled world of the Decadent Dharma,
Those who preserve this sutra
Will have already finished paying homage
In the way just described.
If they can preserve this sutra
It will be as if they had paid homage
In the presence of the Buddha;
And had built monasteries for monks
Out of sandalwood from Mount Oxhead,
And thirty-two buildings as tall
As eight *tāla* trees; and offered delicious food,
Excellent garments, bedding, hundreds of
Thousands of dwellings, gardens, ponds,
Paths for wandering, and meditation caves
All of fine quality.
Those who have the thought of willing acceptance,
Who preserve, recite, copy,
Or move others to copy this sutra,
And who pay it homage
By scattering flowers, incense, and scented powders on it,
And by constantly lighting lamps of
Fragrant oil made from *sumanas* flowers,
Campaka wood, and *atimukta* grass;
Those who pay it homage in this way
Will attain immeasurable merit.
Their merit will be as limitless
As empty space.

How much more is the merit
Of those who preserve this sutra,
Who carry out the practice of giving (*dāna*),
Good conduct (*śīla*), perseverance (*kṣānti*), and meditation (*dhyāna*),
Who never get angry or slander others,
Who honor monuments
And are humble before monks,
46b And who are free from pride,
Always contemplate wisdom,
Never get angry at difficult questions,
And teach in accordance
With the questioner's capacity!
If there is anyone
Who can carry out these practices,
Their merit will be immeasurable.
If one were to see such an expounder of the Dharma
Who has perfected merits like these,
One should scatter heavenly flowers over him
And provide him with heavenly garments,
Bow until one's forehead touches his feet,
And think of him as if he were a Buddha.
Furthermore, one should think
That before long the expounder of the Dharma
Will approach the terrace of enlightenment,
Attain the unconditioned state of noncorruption,
And extensively benefit *deva*s and humans.
Wherever he dwells, walks, or sits,
Or recites even a single verse,
A stupa should be built,
Made beautiful with adornments,
And paid homage in various ways.
Wherever the heirs of the Buddha may reside,
There the Buddha himself will take pleasure in its use
And will always be dwelling,
Walking, and sitting within.

Chapter XVIII

The Merits of Joyful Acceptance

Thereupon Bodhisattva Mahāsattva Maitreya addressed the Buddha, saying: "O Bhagavat! If sons and daughters of a virtuous family rejoice in hearing this sutra, how much merit do they acquire?"

And he spoke in verse, saying:

After the Bhagavat's *parinirvāṇa,*
If there is anyone who hears this sutra
And rejoices in it,
How much merit do they acquire?

Then the Buddha addressed Bodhisattva Mahāsattva Maitreya, saying: "O Ajita! After the Tathāgata's *parinirvāṇa*, suppose those monks, nuns, laymen, and laywomen and other wise ones, whether old or young, having rejoiced in hearing this sutra, take leave of the Dharma assembly and go to other places—either dwelling in 46c
monasteries or tranquil places, cities, towns, villages, or forests—and teach what they have heard to their parents, relatives, good friends, and acquaintances according to the various capacities of these people. Having heard the teaching, they will rejoice and go on to teach it to others. These people having heard it will also joyfully teach it to others in turn, and so it continues in this way until it reaches the fiftieth person.

"O Ajita! I will now explain about the merit which this fiftieth son or daughter of a virtuous family acquires from joyful acceptance. You should listen attentively!

"Suppose that in the four hundreds of myriads of *koṭi*s of incalculable worlds, there are sentient beings in the six transmigratory states and of the four modes of birth—born from an egg, born from the womb, from moisture, or born spontaneously—either with or without form, either with or without consciousness, either unconscious or not unconscious, having no legs, two, four, or many legs; and that, among the number of such beings, there is a person who seeks to acquire merit and gives pleasurable things to these beings, according to their desire. He gives each of those sentient beings gold, silver, lapis lazuli, mother-of-pearl, agate, coral, amber, and other treasures such as would fill this continent of Jambudvīpa, as well as elephant carts, horse carts, and palaces and towers made out of the seven treasures. Having performed such acts of giving for a full eighty years, this great donor thinks:

> I have already given these sentient beings such pleasurable things as they wished. Yet now these sentient beings are old and feeble. They are over eighty years old, with white hair and wrinkles, and they will die before long. I should now instruct them by means of the Buddha-Dharma.

"He immediately gathers these sentient beings together, inspires them by proclaiming the Dharma, and gladdens them by revealing its benefits. In an instant they all successively attain the first stage of the *śrāvaka*s called stream-winner (*srota-āpanna*), the second stage called once-returner (*sakṛdāgāmin*) the third stage called non-returner (*anāgāmin*), and finally the stage of the arhat, free from corruption, entering profound meditations, gaining complete mastery of all, and attaining the eight liberations.

"What do you think about this? Has this great donor acquired abundant merit or not?"

Maitreya addressed the Buddha, saying: "O Bhagavat! The donor's merit is extremely great, immeasurable and limitless. Even if this donor had only given all those pleasurable things to sentient beings, the merit would have been immeasurable. How much greater is this donor's merit after having caused them to attain arhatship!"

The Buddha addressed Maitreya, saying: "I will now clarify this for you. This person has given all these pleasurable things to the sentient beings in the six states of existence in four hundreds of myriads of *koṭi*s of incalculable worlds, and enabled them to attain arhatship. The merit he has attained cannot be compared with that of even the fiftieth person who, after hearing even a single verse of the *Lotus Sutra,* received it with joy. It would be even less than a hundredth, a thousandth, a hundred thousandth of a myriad of a *koṭi* of that person's merit.

"O Ajita! In this way the merit attained by even the fiftieth person who rejoiced in hearing this *Lotus Sutra* is immeasurable, limitless, and incalculable. How much more so is the merit of the 47a
first person who heard it in the assembly and rejoiced in it! His merit is even greater, it is immeasurable, limitless, and incalculable, and is not to be apprehended through metaphor.

"Furthermore, O Ajita, if anyone approaches the monasteries in order to listen to this sutra and hears it for even a single moment, whether seated or standing, through this merit they will be reborn into a place where they will gain beautiful and excellent elephant carts, horse carts, palanquins made out of rare treasures, and will ride on a heavenly vehicle. Moreover, if anyone sits in a place where the Dharma is taught, and if another comes along and they invite that person to sit down and listen, or if they offer that person part of their own seat, through this merit they will be reborn in the place where Śakra dwells, in the place where Brahmas dwell, or in a place where a noble emperor dwells.

"O Ajita! If anyone addresses others, saying:

> There is a sutra called the *Lotus Sutra.* Let us go together and listen to it!

"And if their instruction is accepted and the other person listens to it for even a single moment, then through this merit the former person will be reborn in the same place as the bodhisattva who has acquired the *dhāraṇīs*. They will have keen faculties and wisdom. For hundreds and thousands of myriads of lives they will never be deaf and dumb; nor will they have fetid breath. Their tongues will never be diseased, nor will they have diseases of the mouth. Their teeth will never be dirty, black, or yellow, nor gapped; nor will any be missing, irregular, or crooked. Their lips will not be drooping, pursed, or twisted; and their lips will never have cankers, scabs, be cracked, misshapen, thick or fat, black, or ugly. They will have no disagreeable features. Their noses will never be flat or thin, crooked or twisted. They will never be dark-complected, with a narrow or long face that is hollow-cheeked or twisted. They will have no mark that is displeasing to others. Their lips, tongues, and teeth will all be very beautiful. Their noses will be long, high, and straight. Their faces will be round, their eyebrows arched and long. Their foreheads will be broad and even. They will thus have a perfect human countenance. Wherever they may be born, life after life, they will meet a Buddha, hear the Dharma, and accept the teaching.

"Look, O Ajita! The merit of that person who moved others to listen to the Dharma is like this. How much more is the merit of those who singlemindedly listen, teach, and recite the sutra, explain it for others in the great assembly, and practice as they explain to others!"

Thereupon the Bhagavat, wanting to elaborate on the meaning of this further, spoke these verses:

If anyone hears this sutra
In the Dharma assembly,
And joyfully teaches others
Even a single verse,
And if in this way it is taught from one person
To another until it reaches the fiftieth one,
The merit that this last person will attain
Shall be as I will now explain:
Suppose there were a great donor
Who gave things to an immeasurable number
Of people as they wished
For a full eighty years.
47b He will see that they are old and feeble,
With white hair and wrinkled faces,
With gaps between their teeth and withered bodies,
And that they will die before long.
He will think that he should now

Teach them and enable them
To attain the fruits
Of the Buddha path.
He will teach nirvana, the True Dharma,
Through skillful means, saying:

> The world is impermanent
> Like splashes of water, bubbles, a mirage!
> The feeling of repulsion for it
> Should quickly awaken in you!

All of them, hearing this teaching,
Attain arhatship and perfect
The six transcendent powers, the three sciences,
And the eight liberations.
The merit of the fiftieth person
Who joyfully hears a single verse
Is so much greater than this great donor's
That it is beyond illustration.
The merit of those who successively hear
The *Lotus Sutra* in this way is immeasurable.
How much more is the merit of the first person
Who heard it with joy amid the Dharma assembly!
If there is a person who moves another
To listen to the *Lotus Sutra*, saying:

> This sutra is profound and difficult to encounter
> Even in thousands of myriads of *koṭi*s of *kalpa*s.

And if this person's urging is accepted
And the other one goes to hear it
And listens for a single moment,
The merit that the former person will acquire
Shall be as I will now explain:
Life after life they will have
No diseases of the mouth.
Their teeth will have no gaps,

Nor be yellow or black.
Their lips will be neither fat, thick,
Or thin; nor will they ever have
A disagreeable countenance;
And their tongues will never be
Dry, black, or short.
Their noses will be high, long, and straight.
Their foreheads will be broad and even.
Their faces will be completely handsome,
Pleasing to others who see them.
They will never have fetid breath.
And their mouths will always emit
The fragrance of a blue lotus flower.
I will now explain the merit
Of the one who approaches the monastery
Wanting to hear the *Lotus Sutra,*
And who joyfully listens to it
Even for a single moment:
Later they will be born among *deva*s and humans
And will acquire beautiful elephant and horse carts,
And palanquins made out of rare treasures,
And will ride on a heavenly vehicle.
If one is where the Dharma is taught
And invites another to sit there
And listen to the sutra,
Through the merit which is thus acquired,
One will attain the seats of Śakra,
Brahma, or the noble emperors.
How much more is the merit of a person
Who singlemindedly listens to this sutra,
Explains its meaning, and practices
47c In accordance with its teaching!
Their merit will thus be limitless.

Chapter XIX

The Benefits Obtained by an Expounder of the Dharma

Thereupon the Buddha addressed Bodhisattva Mahāsattva Satatasamitābhiyukta, saying: "If sons or daughters of a virtuous family preserve this *Lotus Sutra,* recite, explain, and copy it, they will attain eight hundred qualities of the eye, twelve hundred qualities of the ear, eight hundred qualities of the nose, twelve hundred qualities of the tongue, eight hundred qualities of the body, and twelve hundred qualities of the mind. These qualities will adorn the six sense faculties, purifying them all. Through the natural bodily eyes given them by their parents, which are thus purified, those sons and daughters of a virtuous family will see the mountains, forests, rivers, and oceans both within and beyond the great manifold cosmos, all the way from the lowest hell up as far as the highest summit of the universe. They will also see all the sentient beings there, perceive and know the causes and consequences of their deeds and of their states of birth."

Then the Bhagavat, wanting to elaborate upon the meaning of this further, spoke these verses:

> Listen to the qualities
> Of those in the great assembly
> Who can fearlessly teach
> This *Lotus Sutra*!
> Such people will attain
> The eight hundred qualities
> Of the excellent eye.
> Adorned with these qualities
> Their eyes are extremely pure.
> With the eyes given by their parents

They see both all the manifold cosmos,
Within and beyond Mount Meru, Sumeru, up to Mount
Cakravāḍa,
And many other mountains,
Forests, oceans, rivers, and streams,
Down to the lowest hell
And up to the summit of the universe.
There they see all the sentient beings;
Although they have not yet
Attained the divine eyes,
Their power of sight will be like this.

"Furthermore, O Satatasamitābhiyukta, if sons or daughters of a virtuous family preserve, recite, explain, or copy this sutra, they will attain the twelve hundred qualities of the ear. Through their pure ears they will hear both within and beyond the great manifold cosmos, down as far as the lowest hell and up as high as the summit of the universe; they will hear all kinds of voices and sounds, such as the sound of elephants, the neighing of horses, the sound of cows and carts, cries, weeping, the sound of conches and drums, gongs and bells, laughter, talking, male and female voices, the voices of boys and girls, righteous and unrighteous voices, the sounds of suffering and happiness, the voices of common and holy
48a people, pleasant and unpleasant sounds; the voices of *deva*s, *nāga*s, *yakṣa*s, *gandharva*s, *asura*s, *garuḍa*s, *kiṃnara*s, *mahoraga*s, the sounds of fire, water, wind, beings in the hells, animals, hungry ghosts, monks, nuns, *śrāvaka*s, *pratyekabuddha*s, bodhisattvas, and Buddhas.

"In short, although they do not have the divine faculty of hearing, they will always hear and know everything both within and beyond the great manifold cosmos, through the purified, natural bodily ears given by their parents. They distinguish all these various sounds and yet their faculty of hearing remains unharmed."

Thereupon the Bhagavat, wanting to elaborate on the meaning of this further, spoke these verses:

The ear, given by the parents,
Is pure and spotless;
With this natural ear
They hear the sounds of the manifold cosmos.
They hear the sounds of elephants,
Horses, carts and cows;
The sounds of gongs, bells, conches,
Drums, and *vīṇās*;
The sounds of harps, bamboo pipes, and flutes;
Pure and pleasing songs.
And even though they hear these,
They are not attached to them.
They hear innumerable kinds of human voices,
And yet they are able to discriminate them.
Furthermore, they hear divine sounds,
Subtle melodies, male and female voices,
The sounds of boys and girls.
They also hear the cries of the *kalaviṅka*
And *jīvakajīvaka* birds in the mountains,
Around the rivers, or in deep valleys.
They hear as well various sounds of pain
And suffering from the hells,
And sounds of hungry ghosts,
Who, suffering from hunger and thirst,
Are in search of food and drink.
When the *asuras* living along the ocean
Speak to each other and utter great cries,
Such expounders of the Dharma, living here,
Hear all of these various voices from afar,
And yet their faculty of hearing is unharmed.
Those expounders of the Dharma
Hear all birds and animals
In the ten directions calling to each other.
The expounders of the Dharma dwelling here
Also hear the voices in the Ābhāsvara

And Śubhakṛtsna Heavens above the Brahma world,
All the way up to the summit of the universe.
The expounders of the Dharma dwelling here
48b Hear all of the monks and nuns
Either reciting the sutra
Or explaining it to others.
They also hear such voices
As those of the bodhisattvas reciting the sutra,
Teaching it to others, compiling the collections,
And explaining their meaning to others.
Those who preserve this *Lotus Sutra*
Will all hear the Buddhas, the great seers,
Teaching the subtle Dharma to the great assembly
And leading and inspiring sentient beings.
They will hear all the sounds
Both within and beyond the manifold cosmos,
Down to the lowest hell
And up to the summit of the universe;
And yet their faculty of hearing
Remains unharmed.
Because their faculty of hearing is keen,
They are able to discriminate these sounds.
Although those who preserve this *Lotus Sutra*
Have not yet attained the divine faculty of hearing,
They can simply use the ears given by their parents.
Their qualities are exactly like this.

"Furthermore, O Satatasamitābhiyukta, if sons or daughters of a good family preserve this sutra, recite, explain, or copy it, they will perfect the eight hundred qualities of the nose. With this pure faculty of the nose they will smell all kinds of fragrances both within and beyond the great manifold cosmos, such as the fragrance of *sumanas, jāti, mallikā, campaka, pāṭala* flowers, and red, blue, and white lotus flowers, the scent of blossoming and fruit-bearing trees like sandalwood, aloeswood, and *tagara* wood, the aroma of the leaves of the *tamāla* tree, thousands of myriads of sorts of fragrances of blended incense, either powdered, shaped into balls, or made into scented ointments. Those who preserve this sutra will be able to distinguish all of these fragrances while remaining in a single place. They will be able to distinguish the scents of sentient beings such as elephants, horses, cows, sheep, men and women, boys and girls, grasses, trees, and shrubs or any kind of odor, either nearby or at a distance. They will also be able to unerringly distinguish all kinds of scents.

"Those who preserve this sutra, although they dwell here, can smell all kinds of divine fragrances in heaven, such as the fragrance of *pāracitraka* and *kovidāra* trees; *māndārava*, great
māndārava, *mañjūṣaka*, and great *mañjūṣaka* flowers, or the fra- 48c
grance of sandalwood and aloeswood powder and various kinds of powdered and blended incense. Among these divine fragrances, there is not one whose scent they cannot distinguish.

"They can smell the fragrance of the bodies of all the *deva*s. They can also smell from afar the fragrance that is emitted when Śakra, the king of *deva*s, is dwelling in his excellent palace, when he is enjoying the desires of the five senses, or the fragrance that is emitted when he is in the Sudharmā Hall teaching the Dharma to the thirty-three *deva*s, or the fragrance that is emitted when he plays in the garden, or the fragrance of the bodies of all the other male and female *deva*s.

"In this way their faculty of smell reaches up to the Brahma world and to the highest summit of the universe, wherein they can smell the bodies of the *deva*s and the incense the *deva*s burn. They can also smell from afar the fragrance of the *śrāvaka*s, *pratyekabuddha*s, bodhisattvas, and Buddhas and know where they are.

"Although they can smell all these fragrances, their faculty of smell will not be harmed or misled; and if they want to discriminate and explain these different fragrances to others, they remember them without error."

At that time the Bhagavat, wanting to elaborate the meaning of this further, spoke these verses:

Their faculty of smell is pure.
They can smell and discriminate
All kinds of good and bad odors
In this world, such as *sumanas*
And *jāti* flowers, *tamāla* leaves,
Sandalwood, aloeswood, and *tagara* trees,
And various fruits and flowers.
And they also know the fragrance
Of sentient beings, men and women.
The Dharma teachers, although dwelling afar,
Know where these fragrances come from.
They smell the scents of the noble emperors
Of great dignity, the lesser rulers
And their children, subjects and attendants,
And know where they are.
They can smell the fragrance of the rare jewels
That they wear, their underground treasuries,
And the noble emperor's bejeweled queens,
And also know where they are.
They can also smell the ornaments, garments,
And necklaces with which people adorn themselves
And the fragrances they anoint themselves with,
And know who wears them.
Those who preserve this *Lotus Sutra* can smell
The fragrance of the *deva*s and tell
Whether they are walking, sitting,
Playing, or transforming themselves.
Although they dwell here,
49a Those who preserve this sutra,
Know the location of the fragrances
Of various flowers, fruits, and oils in detail.
They can smell the scent of sentient beings,
Either deep in dangerous mountains,
Or where the sandalwood flowers are in bloom,
And know where they are.

Those who preserve this sutra
Can smell the scents of sentient beings,
Either on Mount Cakravāḍa,
In the ocean or underground,
And know exactly where they are.
They can also smell the scents of the male
And female *asura*s and their attendants;
And they can discriminate them,
When they are fighting or when at play.
They can also smell the odors of lions,
Elephants, tigers, wolves, buffaloes,
And water buffaloes dwelling in dangerous
Precipitous places in the wilderness,
And know where they are.
They can smell and discriminate exactly
The scent of a pregnant woman
And determine whether the embryo
Will be male or female,
Without sex organs, or nonhuman.
Through this power of smell
They know in the first instance
If the woman is pregnant,
And whether or not
It will be carried to full term;
And if she will give birth easily,
And to a happy child.
Through this power of the faculty of smell
They know what men and women are thinking,
Their desires, delusions, and anger,
Or whether they cultivate goodness.
They can also smell gold, silver,
And various rare treasures hidden underground,
As well as the contents of copper vessels,
And completely distinguish them.
They can smell various necklaces

And know whether they are valuable or not,
Even when their prices are undetermined,
Where they come from and where they are now.
They can smell and know all about
Divine flowers such as *māndārava*
And *mañjūṣaka* flowers and *pārijāta* trees.
They can also smell and discriminate
The difference between superior,
Mediocre, and inferior fragrances
Of heavenly palaces adorned
With various jeweled flowers.
They can also smell and know exactly
About those who take pleasure
In the heavenly gardens, excellent palaces,
Towers and Dharma halls.
Moreover, they can smell and know exactly
Whether the *deva*s are listening to the Dharma,
Are enjoying the desires of the five senses,
Or whether they are coming, going,
Walking, sitting, or lying.
They can also smell and know every detail of
The garments worn by the heavenly maidens,
Giving off the fragrance of beautiful flowers,
And where those maidens ramble in their play.
In this way their power of smell reaches
All the way up to the Brahma world.
They can smell and know exactly
The *deva*s entering meditation and
Emerging from meditation.
49b They can also smell
All the way from the Ābhāsvara
And Śubhakṛtsna Heavens
Up to the highest summit of the universe,
And know exactly
Who has been born there for the first time

And who has emerged.
Those who preserve this sutra can
Smell the monks and know exactly where they are,
If they are constantly persevering toward the Dharma,
If they are either sitting or walking,
Reciting this sutra;
Or if they are diligently
Meditating under forest trees.
They can also smell and know exactly
If a bodhisattva is firm in intention,
Meditating or reciting the sutra,
Or teaching the Dharma to others.
They can also smell and know exactly
If the Bhagavat is being honored by all,
And if he is teaching the Dharma
Out of his compassion for sentient beings.
Moreover, they can smell and know exactly
If the sentient beings in the presence
Of the Buddha are joyfully listening
To the sutra, and are practicing
According to the Dharma.
Those who preserve this sutra
Will attain a faculty of smell such as this,
Even before the bodhisattva's faculty of smell
That is attained from the incorruptible Dharma.

"Furthermore, O Satatasamitābhiyukta, if sons and daughters of a virtuous family preserve, recite, explain, or copy this sutra, they will attain the twelve hundred qualities of the tongue. All that they taste, whether of good or bad flavor, savory or bland, bitter or astringent, will, through their pure faculty of tongue, come to taste just like the heavenly nectar of immortality, and they will find nothing unpleasant.

"If they expound the teaching to the great multitude with their tongues, their voices will be profound and touch the heart. All those in this multitude will be gladdened and pleased.

"Furthermore, Śakra, Brahma and other *devaputras* and heavenly maidens, hearing a sequence of their teaching expounded with such profound voices, will all come to hear it. Dragons, the daughters of *nāgas*, *yakṣas*, the daughters of *yakṣas*, *gandharvas*, the daughters of *gandharvas*, *asuras*, the daughters of *asuras*, *garuḍas*, the daughters of *garuḍas*, *kiṃnaras*, the daughters of *kiṃnaras*, *mahoragas*, and the daughters of *mahoragas* will all approach, respect, and honor them in order to listen to their teaching. The monks, nuns, laymen, and laywomen, kings and princes, ministers and their attendants, and the lesser noble emperors and great noble emperors adorned with the seven treasures and their thousand princes and their attendants of the inner and outer households will enter the palace and listen to the teaching.

"Since these bodhisattvas expound the teaching skillfully, the brahmans, householders, and the people of their land will attend and honor such bodhisattvas until the end of their lives. All the
49c *śrāvakas*, *pratyekabuddhas*, bodhisattvas, and Buddhas will always wish to see them.

"Wherever this person may be, he will teach the Dharma in the presence of the Buddhas there. He will thus be able to preserve the Buddha-Dharma entirely as well as utter the profound word of the Dharma."

Whereupon the Bhagavat, wanting to elaborate on the meaning of this further, spoke these verses:

Such people, through their pure faculty of taste,
Will never taste bad flavors.
Whatever they eat
Will all become the nectar of immortality.
With their profound, subtle voice
They will teach the Dharma to the great assembly.
With various explanations and illustrations
Their teaching will touch the hearts of sentient beings.
All those who hear them will be gladdened
And honor them with the best offerings.

All the *devas*, *nāgas*, *yakṣas*, and *asuras*
Will come together and listen with respect
To the Dharma.
If these expounders of the Dharma want
Their subtle voice to penetrate
Throughout the manifold cosmos,
It will reach wherever they wish.
The great and lesser noble emperors,
And their thousand princes and attendants,
Will always come and listen to the Dharma
With their palms pressed together
And with respectful thoughts.
All the *devas*, *nāgas*, *yakṣas*,
Rākṣasas, and *piśācas*
With joyful minds will also always
Rejoice to come and honor them.
All the *devas*,
Such as Brahma, Māra, Īśvara, Maheśvara,
Will always come to them.
All the Buddhas and their disciples,
Hearing the sound of his teaching,
Will always remember and protect him,
And at times appear in his presence.

"Furthermore, O Satatasamitābhiyukta, those sons and daughters of a virtuous family who preserve, recite, explain, and copy this sutra will attain eight hundred qualities of the body. Their bodies will be as pure as clear lapis lazuli and sentient beings will gladly look upon them. Because of this purity of body, everything will appear therein: the sentient beings in the great manifold cosmos, when they are born or die, whether they are superior or inferior, whether they are fair or ugly, whether they are in the good or bad states of being. The mountain kings, such as Mount Cakravāḍa, Mount Mahācakravāḍa, Mount Meru, or Mount Mahāmeru, as well as all the sentient beings who dwell there, will all appear

in their body. All those who dwell down as far as the lowest hell and up as high as the summit of the universe will appear in their body. Wherever those *śrāvakas*, *pratyekabuddhas*, bodhisattvas,
50a or Buddhas are, the Buddhas teach the Dharma; and will appear with their physical images in their body."

Thereupon the Bhagavat, wanting to elaborate on the meaning of this further, spoke these verses:

> Their bodies are extremely pure
> Like clear lapis lazuli.
> All those sentient beings
> Who preserve the *Lotus Sutra*
> Will gladly look upon them.
> Just as all physical images
> Reflect in a clear mirror,
> The bodhisattvas will see in their own bodies
> Everything in this world.
> They alone see it,
> While no one else does.
> All those sentient beings, *devas*, humans,
> *Asuras*, hell-dwellers, hungry ghosts,
> Or animals in the manifold cosmos
> Will also appear in this body
> With their physical images.
> All the heavenly palaces
> Which reach as high as the top of the universe,
> Mount Cakravāḍa, Mount Meru, Mount Mahāmeru
> And the oceans will appear in their bodies.
> Those Buddhas, *śrāvakas*, or bodhisattvas,
> Heirs of the Buddhas,
> Who are either alone
> Or who teach the Dharma to the assembly,
> Will all appear in their body.
> Even though they have not yet attained
> The Dharma body,

Which is subtle and without corruption,
Everything in this world
Will appear in their pure physical bodies.

"Furthermore, O Satatasamitābhiyukta, a son or a daughter of a virtuous family who preserves, recites, explains, or copies this sutra, after the *parinirvāṇa* of the Tathāgata will attain twelve hundred qualities of the mind. Through their pure faculty of mind, on hearing but a single verse or a single line, they will become versed in the immeasurable and limitless meaning.

"If, after having understood this meaning, they teach a single line or a single verse for the period of one month, four months, or one year, all the teachings they expound will be entirely characterized by the mark of truth, in accordance with its meaning.

"If they teach the works on worldly affairs, treatises on political science or enterprise, all these will be in harmony with the True Dharma. They will completely know the minds of those sentient beings who pass through the six transmigratory states in the great manifold cosmos—their workings, shifts, and fallacies—even though they have not yet attained the uncorrupted wisdom. Their faculty of mind will be pure just like this.

"Whatever this person contemplates, judges, or expounds will be nothing but the True Buddha-Dharma, which has also been taught in the sutras by previous Buddhas."

Thereupon the Bhagavat, wanting to elaborate the meaning of this further, spoke these verses:

The minds of such people are pure 50b
And transparent without impurity.
Through their faculty of intellect
They will know the superior,
Mediocre and inferior teachings.
On hearing a single verse,
They will thoroughly penetrate
The immeasurable meaning.
Thus they will teach the Dharma little by little

For a period of one month,
Four months, or one year.
As the result of preserving the *Lotus Sutra,*
They will instantly know
What all the sentient beings,
Inside and outside this world,
Such as *deva*s, *nāga*s, humans, *yakṣa*s, *rākṣasa*s,
And those who dwell in the six transmigratory states,
Think in their various ways.
They will hear and completely preserve the Dharma
Which the innumerable Buddhas in the ten directions,
Who are possessed of the marks of a hundred merits,
Teach for the sake of sentient beings.
They contemplate the immeasurable meaning
And they teach the Dharma in immeasurable ways;
They will neither forget nor be confused
From the beginning to the end
Because they preserve the *Lotus Sutra.*
They will completely know
All aspects of all *dharma*s,
And discern the meaning
According to the sequence.
They will be versed in names and words
And expound in accordance with this knowledge.
What they teach is the Dharma
That has all been taught
By the Buddhas of the past.
Because they expound this Dharma,
They will have no fear among the people.
Those who preserve the *Lotus Sutra* possess
The pure faculty of mind just like this.
Even though they have not yet attained
The stage of noncorruption,
They will previously have had
The characteristics described above.

These people preserve this sutra
And dwell in the marvelous stage;
All the sentient beings will rejoice
And revere them.
They will illuminate and explain the teaching
With thousands of myriads of *koṭi*s of skillful words
Because they preserve the *Lotus Sutra*.

Chapter XX

Bodhisattva Sadāparibhūta

Thereupon the Buddha addressed Bodhisattva Mahāsattva Mahāsthāmaprāpta: "You should know that, as I have previously explained, those who revile, disparage, or slander monks, nuns, laymen, and laywomen who preserve the *Lotus Sutra* will sow a bitter harvest; as I have just taught, the merit attained by preserving the *Lotus Sutra* will result in the pure faculties of the eye, ear, nose, tongue, body, and mind.

"O Mahāsthāmaprāpta, in the past, immeasurable, limitless, inconceivable and incalculable *kalpa*s ago, there was a Buddha called Bhīṣmagarjitasvararāja, a Tathāgata, Arhat, Completely Enlightened, Perfect in Knowledge and Conduct, Well-Departed, Knower of the World, Unsurpassed, Tamer of Humans, Teacher of Devas and Humans, Buddha, Bhagavat. His land was called Mahāsaṃbhavā and the *kalpa* was named Vinirbhoga. The Buddha Bhīṣmagarjitasvararāja expounded the Dharma for the *deva*s, humans, and *asura*s in his world.

"To those who sought the *śrāvaka* vehicle he expounded the Dharma in accordance with the Four Noble Truths, ferried them from birth, old age, illness, and death, and ultimately led them to nirvana. To those who sought the *pratyekabuddha* vehicle, he expounded the Dharma in accordance with the twelve-linked chain of dependent origination. To the bodhisattvas he expounded the Dharma in accordance with the six perfections, with reference to highest, complete enlightenment, and led them to the Buddha's wisdom.

"O Mahāsthāmaprāpta, the lifespan of the Buddha Bhīṣmagarjitasvararāja was as *kalpa*s equal to forty myriads of *koṭi*s of *nayuta*s of sands of the Ganges River. The True Dharma abided for *kalpa*s equal to the number of particles in Jambudvīpa. The

Semblance Dharma abided for *kalpa*s equal to the number of particles in the four continents. After having benefited the sentient
beings, the Buddha entered *parinirvāṇa*. After the extinction of
the True and Semblance Dharmas, there appeared in this land
another Buddha who was also called Bhīṣmagarjitasvararāja, a
Tathāgata, Arhat, Completely Enlightened, Perfect in Knowledge
50c and Conduct, Well-Departed, Knower of the World, Unsurpassed,
Tamer of Humans, Teacher of Devas and Humans, Buddha, Bhagavat. In this way there appeared two myriads of *koṭi*s of Buddhas
one after another, all of whom had the same name.

"After the *parinirvāṇa* of the first Tathāgata Bhīṣmagarjitasvararāja, there were excessively proud and overbearing monks in the Age of the Semblance Dharma, after the True Dharma had been extinguished. At that time there was also a monk, a bodhisattva, called Sadāparibhūta (Never Despising).

"O Mahāsthāmaprāpta, why was he called Sadāparibhūta? Because whenever he saw any monk, nun, layman, or laywoman, he would praise and pay homage to them, saying:

> I deeply respect you. I dare not belittle you. Why is this? Because all of you practice the bodhisattva path, and will become Buddhas.

"Furthermore, this monk did not concentrate himself on reciting the sutras but only paid homage such that, even when he saw the fourfold assembly from afar, he would go up to them, praise, and pay homage to them, saying:

> I dare not belittle you, because you will all become Buddhas.

"In the fourfold assembly there were some whose minds were impure and who became angry, and reviled and disparaged him, saying:

> Where does this ignorant monk come from? He says that he himself does not belittle us and predicts that we shall all become Buddhas. We do not need such an idle prediction.

"In this way he wandered about for many years and was always reviled. But he never got angry and always said, 'You will become a Buddha.'

"Whenever he spoke these words, people would assail him with sticks or stones; he fled from them yet still proclaimed loudly at a distance:

> I dare not belittle you. You will all become Buddhas. 51a

"Since he always spoke these words, the excessively proud monks, nuns, laymen, and laywomen called him Sadāparibhūta. When this monk was about to die, he heard in the air twenty thousands of myriads of *koṭi*s of verses of the *Lotus Sutra* expounded previously by the Buddha Bhīṣmagarjitasvararāja and, completely preserving them, he attained the purity of the eye, and the purity of the ear, nose, tongue, body, and mind that were described before. After having attained these pure faculties, his lifespan increased two hundreds of myriads of *koṭi*s of *nayuta*s of years and he taught this *Lotus Sutra* to the people far and wide.

"Then those excessively proud monks, nuns, laymen, and laywomen in the fourfold assembly who had despised him and called him Sadāparibhūta saw that he had attained great transcendent powers, the power of joy in eloquence, and the power of great virtuous meditation. Hearing his teaching, all of them believed and followed him.

"Furthermore, this bodhisattva inspired a thousand myriads of *koṭi*s of sentient beings and caused them to abide in highest, complete enlightenment. After his death, he met two thousand *koṭi*s of Buddhas, all of whom were called Candrasūryapradīpa. In accordance with his teaching he expounded this *Lotus Sutra,* and for this reason met another two thousand *koṭi*s of Buddhas, all of whom were called Meghasvararāja. He preserved and recited this sutra in accordance with the teaching of these Buddhas and expounded it for the sake of the fourfold assembly. Thus he attained purity of the natural eye and purity of the ear, nose, tongue, body, and mind, and taught the Dharma to the fourfold assembly without fear.

"O Mahāsthāmaprāpta, this Bodhisattva Mahāsattva Sadāparibhūta respected, honored, praised, and paid homage to all these Buddhas. Having planted roots of good merit, he again met thousands of myriads of *koṭis* of Buddhas; and he expounded this sutra over again in accordance with the teaching of those Buddhas. Having perfected his merits he attained Buddhahood.

"O Mahāsthāmaprāpta, what do you think about this? Was Bodhisattva Sadāparibhūta of that time someone unknown to you? He was none other than I myself. If I had not preserved and recited this sutra and taught it to others in my previous lives, I would not have swiftly attained highest, complete enlightenment. Because I preserved and recited this sutra and taught it to others in the presence of previous Buddhas, I swiftly attained highest, complete enlightenment.

"O Mahāsthāmaprāpta, then the fourfold assembly of monks, nuns, laymen, and laywomen who became angry and disparaged me, did not, as a consequence, meet a Buddha for two hundred *koṭis* of *kalpas*, nor did they hear the Dharma or see the Sangha. They suffered greatly in the Avīci Hell for a thousand *kalpas*. After
51b having been freed from the consequences of their errors they finally met Bodhisattva Sadāparibhūta, who led and inspired them to highest, complete enlightenment.

"O Mahāsthāmaprāpta, what do you think about this? Were those in the fourfold assembly of that time who disparaged this bodhisattva persons unknown to you? They are the five hundred bodhisattvas in this assembly, beginning with Bhadrapāla, the five hundred nuns beginning with Siṃhacandrā, and the five hundred laymen beginning with Sugatacetanā, all of whom will never turn back on the path to highest, complete enlightenment.

"O Mahāsthāmaprāpta, know that this *Lotus Sutra* will greatly benefit the bodhisattva *mahāsattvas* and lead them to highest, complete enlightenment. For this reason, after the Tathāgata's *parinirvāṇa* the bodhisattva *mahāsattvas* should always preserve, recite, explain, and copy this sutra."

Thereupon the Bhagavat, wanting to elaborate on the meaning of this further, spoke these verses:

In the past there was a Buddha
Called Bhīṣmagarjitasvararāja.
He had immeasurable transcendent powers,
Led and guided all sentient beings,
And was paid homage by *deva*s, humans, and *nāga*s.
After the *parinirvāṇa* of this Buddha,
When the True Dharma faced extinction,
There was a bodhisattva called Sadāparibhūta.
At that time the fourfold assembly
Was becoming attached
To its own interpretation of the Dharma.
Bodhisattva Sadāparibhūta
Would approach them and say:

> I do not belittle you;
> Practice the path
> And you will all become Buddhas.

After hearing this,
All the people insulted and disparaged him;
But Bodhisattva Sadāparibhūta
Patiently bore this.
As he neared the time of his death,
When he had expiated his past errors,
He was able to hear this sutra,
And his six sense faculties became pure.
Through his transcendent powers
He prolonged his life
And explained this sutra far and wide,
Acting, once again, for the benefit of others.
Those who were attached
To their own interpretations of the Dharma
Were led and inspired by this bodhisattva

And were enabled to abide
Within the Buddha path.
After the end of his life,
Bodhisattva Sadāparibhūta
Met innumerable Buddhas.
Because he explained this sutra,
He attained immeasurable happiness.
Gradually accumulating his merits,
He quickly attained the Buddha path.
The Bodhisattva Sadāparibhūta of that time
Was none other than I.
Because the fourfold assembly,
Which was then attached to
Particular aspects of the Dharma,
Heard Bodhisattva Sadāparibhūta say:

You will all become Buddhas,

They have since met innumerable Buddhas.
Those people are none other
Than the five hundred bodhisattvas
And laymen and laywomen of pure belief
Who are now gathered before me
In this assembly to hear the Dharma.
In my previous lives I taught them
And led them to hear and accept this sutra,
51c Which is the ultimate Dharma.
I revealed it and taught it to others,
And caused them to abide in nirvana.
Throughout many lifetimes they preserved and kept
A sutra such as this.
Only after myriads of *koṭi*s of *koṭi*s
Of *kalpa*s have passed,
A time inconceivable,
Can they hear this *Lotus Sutra*.
Only after myriads of *koṭi*s of *koṭi*s

Of *kalpa*s have passed,
A time inconceivable,
Do the Buddha Bhagavats
Expound this sutra.
For this reason, all you practitioners
Who hear this sutra
After the nirvana of the Buddha
Should feel no doubt about it.
You must wholeheartedly
Expound this sutra far and wide.
You will then meet the Buddhas lifetime after lifetime
And quickly attain the Buddha path.

Chapter XXI

The Transcendent Powers of the Tathāgata

Thereupon the bodhisattva *mahāsattvas* equal to the number of particles in the great manifold cosmos, who had emerged from the earth, all in the presence of the Buddha gazed singlemindedly at his face with their palms pressed together, and spoke to the Buddha, saying: "O Bhagavat, after the *parinirvāṇa* of the Buddha, we will teach this sutra extensively in the lands of the Bhagavat's separate forms, at the time of his extinction. Why is this? Because we also wish to attain this true, pure, great Dharma, and to preserve, recite, explain, copy, and make offerings to it."

Then the Bhagavat manifested his great transcendent powers in the presence of Mañjuśrī and other immeasurable hundreds of thousands of myriads of *koṭis* of bodhisattva *mahāsattvas* who had long lived in this *sahā* world, such humans and nonhumans as monks, nuns, laymen, and laywomen, *devas*, *nāgas*, *yakṣas*, *gandharvas*, *asuras*, *garuḍas*, *kiṃnaras*, and *mahoragas*.

He put out his wide and long tongue which reached upward to the Brahma world. He emitted innumerable and immeasurable colored rays of light from all his pores and universally illuminated the worlds of the ten directions.

All the Buddhas sitting on the lion seats under the jeweled trees also put out their wide and long tongues and emitted immeasurable rays of light in the same way. Śākyamuni Buddha and the other Buddhas under the jeweled trees manifested transcendent powers while fully hundreds of thousands of years passed.

After this they drew back their tongues, coughed, and snapped their fingers together in unison. Those two sounds penetrated throughout the various Buddha worlds of the ten directions and the earth quaked in six ways.

Through the transcendent powers of the Buddha, all the sentient beings in these worlds—humans and such nonhumans as *deva*s, *nāga*s, *yakṣa*s, *gandharva*s, *asura*s, *garuḍa*s, *kiṃnara*s, and *mahoraga*s—saw all the Buddhas sitting on the lion seats under the immeasurable, limitless hundreds of thousands of myriads of *koṭi*s of jeweled trees in this *sahā* world.

They saw Śākyamuni Buddha sitting on the lion seat in the jeweled stupa, together with Tathāgata Prabhūtaratna. They also saw immeasurable, limitless hundreds of thousands of myriads of
52a *koṭi*s of bodhisattva *mahāsattva*s and the fourfold assembly respectfully surrounding Śākyamuni Buddha. After seeing this, they all rejoiced greatly at having attained this unprecedented experience. At the same time all the *deva*s spoke loudly while in the air, saying: "Beyond these immeasurable, limitless hundreds of thousands of myriads of *koṭi*s of incalculable worlds, there is a land called Sahā. In it is a Buddha called Śākyamuni. For the sake of the bodhisattva *mahāsattva*s he now teaches the Mahayana sutra called the *Lotus Sutra,* the instruction for bodhisattvas and treasured lore of the Buddhas. You should rejoice deeply. You should also honor and pay homage to Śākyamuni Buddha."

Hearing this voice in the air, all those sentient beings pressed their palms together, faced the *sahā* world and said: "We take refuge in Śākyamuni Buddha. We take refuge in Śākyamuni Buddha."

All of them scattered various kinds of flowers, incense, necklaces, banners, canopies, ornaments, jewels, and other beautiful things over the *sahā* world from afar. All that had been scattered formed together from the ten directions like a cloud and was transformed into a jeweled screen that covered all the Buddhas. Then the worlds of the ten directions became pellucid, without obstruction, as if they were one Buddha land.

Thereupon the Buddha addressed the great assembly of bodhisattvas, beginning with Viśiṣṭacāritra:

"The transcendent powers of the Buddhas are as immeasurable, limitless, and inconceivable as this. Yet if I were to use these transcendent powers to teach the benefits of this sutra so that it would be entrusted to you for immeasurable, limitless, hundreds of thousands of myriads of *koṭis* of incalculable *kalpa*s, I would not be able to reach the end of these qualities. To sum up, in this sutra I have clearly revealed and taught all the teachings of the Tathāgata, all the transcendent powers of the Tathāgata, all the treasure houses of the hidden essence of the Tathāgata, and all the profound aspects of the Tathāgata. For this reason, after the *parinirvāṇa* of the Tathāgata, you should wholeheartedly preserve, recite, explain, and copy it, and practice according to the teaching. Those who accept, recite, explain, and copy it, and practice according to the teaching, in whichever land they may be, in a place where the sutra abides—either in a garden, a forest, under a tree, in a monk's chamber, in a layman's house, in a palace, on a mountain, in a valley, or in the wilderness—in all of these places they should erect and pay homage to a monument. Why is this? Because you should know that these places are the terraces of enlightenment where all the Buddhas have attained highest, complete enlightenment, where all the Buddhas have turned the wheel of the Dharma, and where all the Buddhas entered *parinirvāṇa*."

Thereupon the Bhagavat, wanting to elaborate on the meaning of this further, spoke these verses:

> The Buddhas, world-inspirers,
> Abiding in their great transcendent powers,
> Manifest this immeasurable power 52b
> In order to gladden sentient beings.
> Their tongues reach up to the Brahma world
> And they emit innumerable rays of light
> From their bodies.
> They manifest this marvel
> For those who seek for the Buddha path.
> The coughing and snapping sounds
> Of the Buddhas are universally heard
> In the lands of the ten directions.

The earth quakes in six ways.
Because this sutra can be preserved
After the nirvana of the Buddha,
All the Buddhas rejoice and manifest
Their immeasurable transcendent powers.
Even if, for immeasurable *kalpa*s,
They praise those who preserve this sutra,
In order to entrust it,
They will not reach the limit of their merit.
The qualities of those people are
Limitless and endless,
Just like the boundless sky
In the ten directions.
Those who preserve this sutra
Have already seen me,
The Buddha Prabhūtaratna,
And the various magically created forms;
And today they see all the bodhisattvas
I have led and inspired up until now.
Those who preserve this sutra
Will gladden me, my magically created forms,
As well as the Buddha Prabhūtaratna
Who has entered nirvana.
They will also see, gladden, and pay homage to
The past and future Buddhas, and those who are present
In the ten directions.
Those who preserve this sutra
Will before long attain the Dharma,
The hidden essence,
Which was attained by the Buddhas
Seated upon the terrace of enlightenment.
Those who preserve this sutra
Will explain the meaning of the Dharma,
The names and phrases, joyfully and with undying vigor,
Like the wind in the sky

That has no obstruction whatsoever.
After the *parinirvāṇa* of the Tathāgata,
They will know the causes and conditions
And the sequences of the sutras
Taught by the Buddha,
And will explain the truth
In accordance with its meaning.
As the light of the sun and moon
Eliminates the darkness,
These people practicing in the world
Will extinguish the blindness of sentient beings,
Teaching innumerable bodhisattvas
To dwell ultimately in the single vehicle.
For this reason,
The wise, hearing of the benefits of these merits,
Should preserve this sutra 52c
After my nirvana.
Those people will be resolute and will
Unwaveringly follow the Buddha path.

Chapter XXII

Entrustment

Thereupon, having arisen from the Dharma seat and manifested his great transcendent powers, Śākyamuni Buddha caressed the heads of the innumerable bodhisattva *mahāsattva*s with his right hand, and addressed them, saying: "For immeasurable hundreds of thousands of myriads of *koṭi*s of incalculable *kalpa*s, I practiced this Dharma of highest, complete enlightenment, which is hard to attain. I now entrust it to you. You should wholeheartedly spread this teaching and so extensively benefit others."

Having caressed the heads of the bodhisattva *mahāsattva*s three times in this way, he further addressed them, saying: "For immeasurable hundreds of thousands of myriads of *koṭi*s of incalculable *kalpa*s, I practiced this Dharma of highest, complete enlightenment, which is hard to attain. I now entrust it to you. You should preserve and recite it. You should spread this teaching extensively. You should let all the sentient beings hear and know it. Why is this? Because with his great compassion, unstinting and unafraid, the Tathāgata gives the wisdom of the Buddha, the wisdom of the Tathāgata, and the knowledge of the self-arising one to the sentient beings. The Tathāgata is nothing but the great donor to all the sentient beings. You should accordingly practice the teaching of the Tathāgata. Never allow the thought of avarice to awaken in you! If there are sons and daughters of a virtuous family who believe in the wisdom of the Tathāgata in the future, you should expound this *Lotus Sutra;* and let them hear and know it so that they may attain the wisdom of the Buddha. If there are sentient beings who do not accept it, you should reveal, teach, benefit, and gladden them with the other profound teachings of the Tathāgata. If you do this, you will repay your indebtedness to the Buddha."

Having heard the Buddha teach this, all the bodhisattva *mahāsattvas* were filled with joy, inclined their bodies, bowed their heads with increased respect, and, with their palms pressed together, faced the Buddhas and uttered these words: "We will certainly do as the Bhagavat directs us. O Bhagavat, we entreat you to feel no anxiety."

All the bodhisattva *mahāsattvas* uttered these words three times in this way, saying: "We will do as the Bhagavat directs us. O Bhagavat, we entreat you to feel no anxiety."

At that time, in order to cause all the Buddhas who were his magically created forms and who had come from the ten directions to return to their own lands, Śākyamuni Buddha said this: "All the Buddhas should be at ease. The Buddha Prabhūtaratna will be restored as before."

When he said this, all the innumerable Buddhas in their magically created forms from the ten directions sitting on the lion seats
53a under the jeweled trees, the Buddha Prabhūtaratna, the great assembly of the limitless and incalculable bodhisattvas beginning with Viśiṣṭacāritra, the fourfold assemblies of the *śrāvakas* beginning with Śāriputra, and the *devas*, humans, and *asuras* in all the worlds, having heard what the Buddha had taught, rejoiced greatly.

Chapter XXIII

Ancient Accounts of Bodhisattva Bhaiṣajyarāja

Thereupon Bodhisattva Nakṣatrarājasaṃkusumitābhijña addressed the Buddha, saying: "O Bhagavat, why does Bodhisattva Bhaiṣajyarāja wander in this *sahā* world? O Bhagavat, this Bodhisattva Bhaiṣajyarāja has performed hundreds of thousands of myriads of *koṭi*s of *nayuta*s of difficult and arduous practices. Splendid, O Bhagavat! I entreat you to explain it even a little, so that all the *deva*s, *nāga*s, *yakṣa*s, *gandharva*s, *asura*s, *garuḍa*s, *kiṃnara*s, *mahoraga*s, humans, and nonhumans, and also the assemblies of the bodhisattvas who have come from the other lands and these *śrāvaka*s, will rejoice on hearing it."

Then the Buddha spoke to Bodhisattva Nakṣatrarājasaṃkusumitābhijña, saying: "In the remote past, beyond *kalpa*s as immeasurable as the sands of the Ganges River, there was a Buddha called Candrasūryavimalaprabhāsaśrī, an Arhat, Completely Enlightened, Perfect in Knowledge and Conduct, Well-Departed, Knower of the World, Unsurpassed, Tamer of Humans, Teacher of Devas and Humans, Buddha, Bhagavat. With this Buddha were eighty *koṭi*s of great bodhisattva *mahāsattva*s and an assembly of great *śrāvaka*s, as many as the sands of seventy-two Ganges Rivers. The lifespan of this Buddha was forty-two thousand *kalpa*s, and the lifespans of the bodhisattvas were also equal to this. In his land there were no women, no hell-dwellers, no hungry ghosts, no animals, no *asura*s, and no calamities. The land was level like the palm of one's hand and was made of lapis lazuli. It was adorned with jeweled trees, and was covered with jeweled canopies with various hanging, flowered banners. This world was filled with jeweled vases and incense burners. There were platforms made of the seven treasures. For each tree there was a platform, and each tree stood away from the platform a distance of no more than a bowshot. All the bodhisattvas and *śrāvakas* sat under these jeweled trees. On the top of every jeweled platform were hundreds of *koṭis* of *devas* who played divine music and sang in praise and homage to the Buddha. Then the Buddha expounded the *Lotus Sutra* for Bodhisattva Sarvarūpasaṃdarśana and numerous other bodhisattvas and *śrāvakas*. Bodhisattva Sarvarūpasaṃdarśana devoted himself entirely to severe practices. Following the teachings of the Buddha Candrasūryavimalaprabhāsaśrī, he strove and wandered up and down in the singleminded search for enlightenment for a full twelve thousand years; and he attained the *samādhi* called *sarvarūpasaṃdarśana*. After having attained this *samādhi*, he rejoiced a great deal and thought thus:

> I have attained the *samādhi* called *sarvarūpasaṃdarśana* entirely because of the power I attained through hearing the *Lotus Sutra*. I will now pay homage to the Buddha Candrasūryavimalaprabhāsaśrī and the *Lotus Sutra*.

53b "Immediately after he had entered this *samādhi*, *māndārava* and great *māndārava* flowers and finely powdered solid and black sandalwood fell from the sky, filling the air like clouds and raining down upon the earth. It also rained the perfume of sandalwood from the inner seacoast of Mount Sumeru. With this quantity of perfume, six drams of which equal the worth of this *sahā* world, he paid homage to the Buddha. Having paid homage to the Buddha, he emerged from *samādhi* and thought this:

> I have paid homage to the Buddha using my transcendent power. This is, however, by no means equal to the tribute of offering my body.

"For a full one thousand two hundred years, he inhaled the fragrance of sandalwood, olibanum, frankincense, clove, aloeswood, and glue trees and drank the fragrant oil of *campaka* flowers. He then anointed his body with scented ointment. In the presence of the Buddha Candrasūryavimalaprabhāsaśrī he covered his body with a divine jeweled garment and with the fragrant oil. Through his transcendent power and vows he set his body alight, which illuminated worlds equal in number to the sands of eighty *koṭis* of Ganges Rivers. At the same time all the Buddhas in these worlds praised him, saying:

> Splendid, splendid, O son of a virtuous family! This is the true perseverance. This is called the true Dharma offering to the Tathāgata. It stands no comparison, even if one were to pay tribute with flowers, perfumes, necklaces, burning incense, scented powders, ointments, divine silk banners, canopies, perfumes of sandalwood from the inner seacoast of Mount Sumeru, and various other things like this. It stands no comparison, even if one were to offer one's kingdom or wife and children. O son of a virtuous family, this is the supreme offering. This is the highest and best of all offerings, because you offer the Dharma to the Tathāgatas.

"Having spoken these words, all became silent. His body was alight for one thousand two hundred years. After this period passed, his body burned out. Because he had paid tribute to the Dharma like this, Bodhisattva Sarvarūpasaṃdarśana was reborn after his death in the land of the Buddha Candrasūryavimalaprabhāsaśrī. He was born spontaneously, sitting cross-legged in the house of King Vimaladatta.

"Then he immediately spoke these verses for the sake of his father, saying:

> O Great King! You should now know
> That I, in an instant, attained
> The *samādhi* called *sarvarūpasaṃdarśana*
> In the place where I wandered;
> And, practicing with enthusiasm and perseverance,
> I set aside this, my beloved body.
> I have paid homage to the Bhagavat
> In order to attain the utmost wisdom.

"After having spoken these verses, he addressed his father, saying:

> The Buddha Candrasūryavimalaprabhāsaśrī is now in this world. Having previously paid homage to the Buddha, I attained the *dhāraṇī* of understanding the speech of all sentient beings and heard eight hundred thousands of myriads of *koṭi*s of *nayuta*s of verses and tens of billions of verses, hundreds of billions of verses and thousands of billions of verses
> 53c of the *Lotus Sutra*. O Great King, I will now once again pay homage to this Buddha.

"Having spoken this, he sat on the seven-jeweled platform and ascended into the air as high as seven *tāla* trees. Having come before the Buddha, he bowed until his forehead touched the Buddha's feet. He praised the Buddha in verse with his ten fingers pressed together, saying:

> Your countenance is rare and wonderful.
> Your brilliance illuminates the ten directions.
> Once, long ago, I paid you homage.
> I now come to behold you again.

"Thereupon Bodhisattva Sarvarūpasaṃdarśana, having spoken this verse, addressed the Buddha, saying:

> O Bhagavat! The Bhagavat is yet in this world!

"Then the Buddha Candrasūryavimalaprabhāsaśrī said to Bodhisattva Sarvarūpasaṃdarśana:

> O son of a virtuous family! The time of my *parinirvāṇa* has come. The time of extinction has come. I ask you now to prepare my bed. I will enter *parinirvāṇa* tonight.

"The Buddha said again to Bodhisattva Sarvarūpasaṃdarśana:

> O son of a virtuous family! I entrust you with the Buddha-Dharma, and all the bodhisattvas and great *śrāvaka*s as well

> as the Dharma for highest, complete enlightenment. I will also entrust you with the seven-jeweled world, all the jeweled trees, jeweled platforms, and the *deva*s who are my servants in the great manifold cosmos. After my *parinirvāṇa* I will also entrust you with all my relics. You should distribute them far and wide and pay them homage. You should also erect a great many thousands of stupas.

"Having addressed Bodhisattva Sarvarūpasaṃdarśana in this way, the Buddha Candrasūryavimalaprabhāsaśrī entered *parinirvāṇa* in the last watch of that night.

"Thereupon, having seen the Buddha's *parinirvāṇa,* Bodhisattva Sarvarūpasaṃdarśana was grieved and saddened, and longed and yearned for the Buddha. Having prepared a pyre with sandalwood from the inner seacoast of Mount Sumeru, he cremated the Buddha's body in homage. After the fire had gone out, he collected all the relics. He had eighty-four thousand jeweled urns made and erected eighty-four thousand stupas as high as three worlds. They were adorned with poles from which hung all kinds of banners and canopies and various kinds of jeweled bells.

"Then Bodhisattva Sarvarūpasaṃdarśana thought this:

> Although I have paid tribute in this way, I am not yet satisfied. I will now further pay homage to the relics.

"Then he spoke to all the great assemblies of bodhisattvas, great *śrāvaka*s, *deva*s, *nāga*s, and *yakṣa*s, saying:

> You should pay full attention: I will now pay homage to the relics of the Buddha Candrasūryavimalaprabhāsaśrī.

"Having said these words, he made an offering before the eighty-four thousand stupas by burning his arms adorned with hundreds of merits for seventy-two thousand years. He thus made innumerable *śrāvaka*s and immeasurable, incalculable people set forth toward highest, complete enlightenment. All of them were made to dwell in the *samādhi* called *sarvarūpasaṃdarśana.* 54a

"At that time all the bodhisattvas, *deva*s, humans, and *asura*s saw that his arms were missing and became grieved and distressed. They said:

> This Bodhisattva Sarvarūpasaṃdarśana is our teacher. He has led and inspired us. He has now burned his arms, and his body is deformed.

"Then Bodhisattva Sarvarūpasaṃdarśana made a vow and said to the great assembly:

> I have abandoned both my arms, and I shall definitely attain the golden body of the Buddha. If this is true and not false, then may both arms be restored as before.

"Because this bodhisattva was endowed with profound merit and wisdom, after he had made this vow his arms recovered spontaneously. At that very time the great manifold cosmos quaked in six ways. It rained jeweled flowers from the heavens and all the *deva*s and humans experienced an unprecedented marvel."

The Buddha addressed Bodhisattva Nakṣatrarājasaṃkusumitābhijña, saying: "What do you think about this? Is Bodhisattva Sarvarūpasaṃdarśana someone unknown to you? He is none other than this Bodhisattva Bhaiṣajyarāja. He undertook the practice of giving by abandoning his body immeasurable hundreds of thousands of myriads of *koṭi*s of *nayuta*s of times in this way. O Nakṣatrarājasaṃkusumitābhijña! If there is anyone who sets forth and wishes to attain highest, complete enlightenment, he should pay homage to the stupas of the Buddha by burning either a finger or a toe. He is superior to those who pay homage by giving their countries and cities, their wives and children, or the mountains, forests, rivers, ponds, and many other rare treasures.

"If there is anyone who pays homage to all the Buddhas, great bodhisattvas, *pratyekabuddha*s, and arhats by filling the great manifold cosmos with the seven precious treasures, the merit of this person will not be equal to the surpassing merit of one who receives and holds to even a single verse consisting of four lines of the *Lotus Sutra*.

"O Nakṣatrarājasaṃkusumitābhijña! Just as the ocean is the greatest of streams and rivers and of all waters, this *Lotus Sutra* is the most profound of the sutras taught by the Tathāgatas. Just as Mount Sumeru is the greatest of mountains—greater than Earth Mountain, Black Mountain, Mount Cakravāḍa, Mount Mahācakravāḍa, and the ten jeweled mountains—this *Lotus Sutra* is the greatest of the sutras. Just as the moon is the greatest among all the stars, this *Lotus Sutra* is the most illuminating of the thousands of *koṭi*s of sutras. Just as the sun destroys darkness, in the same way this sutra destroys the darkness of erring thought. Just as the noble emperor is the best of all the kings, this sutra is the noblest of all the sutras. Just as Śakra is the king of the thirty-three *deva*s, 54b
this sutra is the King of Sutras. Just as Great Brahma is the father of all the sentient beings, in the same way this sutra is the father of all the wise, the noble, those who have more to learn and those who do not, and those in whom the thought of enlightenment has awakened. Just as those who have entered the stream of the teaching (*srota-āpanna*s), those who are to return to this world once again (*sakṛdāgāmin*s), those who are never to return (*anāgāmin*s), arhats, and *pratyekabuddha*s are the best of all the common people, in the same way this is the best of all the sutras taught by all the Tathāgatas, bodhisattvas, or *śrāvaka*s.

"Those who hold to this sutra are the best of all sentient beings. The bodhisattvas are the best of all *śrāvaka*s and *pratyekabuddha*s. In the same way, this sutra is the best of all sutras. Just as the Buddha is the King of the Dharma, this sutra is the King of Sutras.

"O Nakṣatrarājasaṃkusumitābhijña! This sutra saves all sentient beings. This sutra makes all sentient beings free from suffering. This sutra greatly benefits all sentient beings and brings their aspirations to fulfillment, just as a clear, cool pond satisfies the thirsty, as a fire satisfies those suffering from cold, as clothes for the naked, as a caravan leader for merchants, as a mother for her children, as a boat for the traveler, as a physician for the sick, as a lamp for the gloom, as a treasure for the poor, as a king for the people, as the sea for traders, and a torch for those in darkness. In the same way, this *Lotus Sutra* frees sentient beings from every suffering, all the pains and bonds of sickness and of birth and death. If there is anyone who hears this *Lotus Sutra,* copies it, or moves others to copy it, their merit will be limitless even if it is measured through the Buddha's wisdom. If there is anyone who copies it and pays it tribute with flowers, perfumes, necklaces, burning incense, scented powders, fragrant ointments, banners, canopies, clothes, various kinds of ghee lamps, oil lamps, fragrant oil lamps, lamps of oil made from *campaka, sumanas, pāṭala, vārṣika,* and *navamālikā* trees, that person's merit will also be immeasurable.

"O Nakṣatrarājasaṃkusumitābhijña! If there is anyone who hears this chapter 'Ancient Accounts of Bodhisattva Bhaiṣajyarāja,' they will attain immeasurable and limitless merit. If there is any woman who hears and holds to this chapter 'Ancient Accounts of Bodhisattva Bhaiṣajyarāja,' she will never be reborn with a female body. If there is any woman five hundred years after the *pari-*
54c *nirvāṇa* of the Tathāgata who hears this sutra and practices according to the teaching, she will immediately reach the dwelling of the Buddha Amitāyus in the Sukhāvatī world, surrounded by great bodhisattvas, and will be born on a jeweled seat in a lotus flower. Never again troubled by the [three poisons] of greed, anger, or ignorance, by arrogance or jealousy, he will attain the bodhisattva's transcendent powers and the acceptance of the nonorigination of all *dharma*s. After attaining this acceptance, his faculty of sight will be pure; and with this pure eye faculty, he will see all the Buddha Tathāgatas, equal in number to the sands of seventy-two million *koṭi*s of *nayuta*s of Ganges Rivers. At that time all the Buddhas will praise him from afar, saying:

> Splendid! Splendid! Son of a virtuous family! You have preserved, recited, and contemplated this sutra from the teachings of the Buddha Śākyamuni and taught it to others. The merit you have obtained is immeasurable and limitless. Even fire cannot burn it. Even water cannot wash it away. Even thousands of Buddhas cannot give a complete description of your merit. You have already destroyed the *māra*s. You have

> already conquered the armies of birth and death. You have defeated all enemies. O son of a virtuous family! Hundreds of thousands of Buddhas together protect you with their transcendent powers. There is no one equal to you among the *deva*s and humans of the entire world. With the exception of the Tathāgata, the wisdom and meditation of all *śrāvaka*s, *pratyekabuddha*s, and bodhisattvas can never equal yours.

"O Nakṣatrarājasaṃkusumitābhijña! Such is the power of the merit and wisdom that this bodhisattva has perfected. If there is anyone who hears this chapter 'Ancient Accounts of Bodhisattva Bhaiṣajyarāja,' rejoices in it, and praises it well, in his present life he will always exhale the fragrance of blue lotus flowers from his mouth and will always emit the fragrance of the sandalwood on Mount Oxhead from his pores. The benefits of the qualities he has obtained are just as mentioned above. For this reason, O Nakṣatrarājasaṃkusumitābhijña, I will entrust you with this chapter 'Ancient Accounts of Bodhisattva Bhaiṣajyarāja.' During the period of five hundred years after my *parinirvāṇa* you must spread it far and wide in Jambudvīpa and not allow it to be destroyed. You must not give Māra and his men, or the *deva*s, *nāga*s, *yakṣa*s, and *kumbhāṇḍa* demons any chance of destroying it. O Nakṣatrarājasaṃkusumitābhijña! You should protect this sutra with your transcendent power. Why is this? Because this sutra is good medicine for the ills of the people of Jambudvīpa. If there is any sick person who hears this sutra, his illness will disappear, and he will neither die nor grow old. O Nakṣatrarājasaṃkusumitābhijña! If you see anyone who holds to this sutra, you should scatter blue lotus flowers full of scented powder on him. After scattering them, you should think like this:

> This man will before long destroy the army of Māra, sitting
> on the grass-covered terrace of enlightenment. He will blow 55a
> the conch of the Dharma, beat the drum of the great Dharma, and ferry all sentient beings across the ocean of old age, illness, and death.

"Therefore, if those seeking the Buddha path see those who hold to this sutra, the thought of respect should awaken in them."

When this chapter, "Ancient Accounts of Bodhisattva Bhaiṣajyarāja," was being taught, eighty-four thousand bodhisattvas attained the *dhāraṇī* of understanding the speech of all sentient beings. The Tathāgata Prabhūtaratna in the jeweled stupa praised Bodhisattva Nakṣatrarājasaṃkusumitābhijña, saying: "Splendid! Splendid! O Nakṣatrarājasaṃkusumitābhijña! You have attained marvelous merit, for you have questioned the Buddha Śākyamuni about these things and benefited all of the immeasurable numbers of sentient beings."

Chapter XXIV

Bodhisattva Gadgadasvara

Thereupon, the Buddha Śākyamuni emitted a ray of light from his topknot (*uṣṇīṣa*), the mark of a great person, and also from the tuft of white hair between his eyebrows (*ūrṇā*), thus illuminating all the Buddha worlds in the east equal to the sands of one hundred and eight myriads of *koṭi*s of *nayuta*s of Ganges Rivers. Beyond this number of worlds was the Buddha world called Vairocanaraśmipratimaṇḍitā. In that world was the Buddha named Kamaladalavimalanakṣatrarājasaṃkusumitābhijña, a Tathāgata, Arhat, Completely Enlightened, Perfect in Knowledge and Conduct, Well-Departed, Knower of the World, Unsurpassed, Tamer of Humans, Teacher of Devas and Humans, Buddha, Bhagavat. He was respectfully surrounded by a great assembly of countless, innumerable bodhisattvas, and he expounded his teaching for them. The ray of light emitted from the tuft of white hair between the eyebrows of Śākyamuni Buddha illuminated that entire world.

At that time, in the Buddha world of Vairocanaraśmipratimaṇḍitā there was a bodhisattva whose name was Gadgadasvara (Wonderful Voice). Having planted many roots of good merit over a long period, he paid homage to and closely attended immeasurable hundreds of thousands of myriads of *koṭi*s of Buddhas, and accomplished complete and profound wisdom. He attained the *samādhi*s called *dhvajāgrakeyūra, saddharmapuṇḍarīka, vimaladatta, nakṣatrarājavikrīḍita, anilambha, jñānamudrā, sarvarutakauśalya, sarvapuṇyasamuccaya, prasādavatī, ṛddhivikrīḍita,* 55b
jñānolkā, vyūharāja, vimalaprabhāsa, vimalagarbha, apkṛtsna, and *sūryāvarta*. He thus attained great *samādhi*s equal in number to the sands of hundreds of thousands of myriads of *koṭi*s of Ganges Rivers. As the light of the Buddha Śākyamuni illuminated

his body, he addressed the Buddha Kamaladalavimalanakṣatrarājasaṃkusumitābhijña, saying: "O Bhagavat! I shall go to the *sahā* world, approach the Buddha Śākyamuni in homage and reverence, and see Bodhisattva Mañjuśrī, the Prince of the Dharma, as well as Bodhisattva Bhaiṣajyarāja, Bodhisattva Pradānaśūra, Bodhisattva Nakṣatrarājasaṃkusumitābhijña, Bodhisattva Viśiṣṭacāritra, Bodhisattva Vyūharāja, and Bodhisattva Bhaiṣajyasamudgata."

Then the Buddha Kamaladalavimalanakṣatrarājasaṃkusumitābhijña addressed Bodhisattva Gadgadasvara, saying: "You must not despise that world nor think it inferior. O son of a virtuous family! The land of that *sahā* world is uneven and irregular and is filled with mud, stones, mountains, and filth. The Buddha is short of body, as are the bodhisattvas. By contrast, your body is forty-two thousand *yojanas* tall, and my body is six million eight hundred thousand *yojanas* tall. Your body is perfect in its bearing and illuminated most beautifully with hundreds of millions of merits. Yet, when you go there you must not despise that country nor think the Buddha, bodhisattvas, or the world itself inferior."

The Bodhisattva Gadgadasvara addressed the Buddha, saying: "O Bhagavat! I am now going to the *sahā* world through the power of the Tathāgata, the carefree play of the transcendent powers of the Tathāgata, and the adornment of the qualities and wisdom of the Tathāgata."

At that time Bodhisattva Gadgadasvara, without rising from his seat or moving his body, entered *samādhi*. Through the power of the *samādhi* he caused eighty-four thousand jeweled lotus flowers to appear on Mount Gṛdhrakūṭa, not far from the seat of the Dharma. The stems were made of Jambūnāda gold, the leaves of silver, the pistils of diamond, and the calyces of ruby.

On seeing these lotus flowers, Bodhisattva Mañjuśrī, the Prince of the Dharma, addressed the Buddha, saying: "O Bhagavat! Why has this marvel appeared? There are a great many millions of lotus flowers, whose stems are made of Jambūnāda gold, leaves of silver, pistils of diamond, and calyces of ruby."

The Buddha Śākyamuni answered Mañjuśrī, saying: "The Bodhisattva Gadgadasvara wishes to come to this *sahā* world from the Buddha world called Kamaladalavimalanakṣatrarājasaṃkusumitābhijña, together with eighty-four thousand bodhisattvas as his retinue. He approaches me in homage and reverence, wishing to make offerings and to hear the *Lotus Sutra.*"

Mañjuśrī asked the Buddha, saying: "O Bhagavat! What roots of good merit has he planted, and what merits has he practiced to attain his great transcendent powers? What kind of *samādhi* has 55c
he practiced? I entreat you to tell us the name of this *samādhi*. We wish to practice it with diligence. By practicing this *samādhi* we wish to see the shape, appearance, size, and manner of this bodhisattva. I entreat you, O Bhagavat, to use your transcendent powers and let us see the appearance of that bodhisattva."

Then, the Buddha Śākyamuni spoke to Mañjuśrī, saying: "The Tathāgata Prabhūtaratna, who long ago entered *parinirvāṇa,* will manifest the signs for you."

At that time the Buddha Prabhūtaratna addressed that bodhisattva, saying: "Come, O son of a virtuous family! Mañjuśrī, the Prince of the Dharma, wishes to see you."

Thereupon Bodhisattva Gadgadasvara disappeared from his world and arrived together with eighty-four thousand bodhisattvas. In the worlds through which he passed, the land quaked in six ways, seven-jeweled lotus flowers rained everywhere, and hundreds of thousands of heavenly musical instruments sounded spontaneously without being played. The eyes of this bodhisattva were as large as blue lotus leaves. Even if hundreds of thousands of myriads of moons were gathered together they would not exceed the beauty of his countenance. His body was pure gold in color, adorned with immeasurable hundreds of thousands of merits, radiant with virtuous dignity, and brilliantly illuminated like the adamantine body of the god Nārāyaṇa. Having entered the seven-jeweled platform and ascended into the air, he flew above the earth at a height of seven *tāla* trees. Surrounded by respectful bodhisattvas, he arrived at Mount Gṛdhrakūṭa in this *sahā* world and descended from the seven-jeweled terrace. He came before the Buddha Śākyamuni with a necklace worth hundreds of thousands in his hand and bowed until his forehead reached the Buddha's feet. He presented the necklace to the Buddha, saying: "O Bhagavat! The Buddha Kamaladalavimalanakṣatrarājasaṃkusumitābhijña inquires of the Bhagavat:

> Are you without illness or pain? Is your daily life pleasant? Are you at ease in practice? Is the world around you harmonious? Are your worldly affairs bearable? Is it easy to save sentient beings? Are they not filled with greed, anger, foolishness, avarice, and pride? Are they mindful of their parents? Do they respect *śrāmaṇa*s? Do they not have false views or erring thoughts? Do they control the desires of their five senses? O Bhagavat! Do the sentient beings conquer *māra*s? Has the Tathāgata Prabhūtaratna sitting in the seven-jeweled stupa long after his *parinirvāṇa* come here to hear the Dharma?

Furthermore, he inquired of the Tathāgata Prabhūtaratna, saying: "Are you at ease and without pain? O Bhagavat! Will your life be long and endured with patience? I now wish to see the body of the Buddha Prabhūtaratna. I entreat you, O Bhagavat, to manifest and show it to me."

At that time the Buddha Śākyamuni said to the Buddha Prabhūtaratna: "This Bodhisattva Gadgadasvara wants to see you."

Then, the Buddha Prabhūtaratna addressed Gadgadasvara, saying: "Splendid! Splendid! You have paid homage to the Buddha
56a Śākyamuni and heard the *Lotus Sutra,* and have come here in order to see Mañjuśrī and others."

Thereupon Bodhisattva Padmaśrī addressed the Buddha, saying: "O Bhagavat! What roots of good merit has this Bodhisattva Gadgadasvara planted, and what merits has he practiced to attain these transcendent powers?"

The Buddha answered Bodhisattva Padmaśrī, saying: "In the past there was the Buddha called Meghadundubhisvararāja, a

Tathāgata, Arhat, Completely Enlightened. His world was called Sarvarūpasaṃdarśana and the *kalpa* was called Priyadarśana. For a period of twelve thousand years Bodhisattva Gadgadasvara paid homage to the Buddha Meghadundubhisvararāja with a hundred thousand kinds of music and eighty-four thousand seven-jeweled bowls. As a result of his deeds he was born in the world of the Buddha Kamaladalavimalanakṣatrarājasaṃkusumitābhijña and has attained his transcendent powers. O Padmaśrī! What do you think about this? Is Bodhisattva Gadgadasvara, who paid homage to the Buddha Meghadundubhisvararāja with music and jeweled vessels, someone unknown? Bodhisattva Mahāsattva Gadgadasvara here present is one and the same. O Padmaśrī! Having closely and respectfully attended innumerable Buddhas and planted roots of good merit over a long time, this Bodhisattva Gadgadasvara met hundreds of thousands of myriads of *koṭi*s of *nayuta*s of Buddhas equal in number to the sands of the Ganges River. O Padmaśrī! You think that the body of Bodhisattva Gadgadasvara exists only here; however, this bodhisattva manifests himself in various bodies. He has thus taught this sutra in many places for the sake of the sentient beings. Sometimes he has appeared in the form of Brahma. Sometimes he has appeared in the form of Śakra. Sometimes he has appeared in the form of Īśvara. Sometimes he has appeared in the form of Maheśvara. Sometimes he has appeared in the form of the great commander of the *deva*s. Sometimes he has appeared in the form of Vaiśravaṇa. Sometimes he has appeared in the form of a noble emperor. Sometimes he has appeared in the form of a minor king. Sometimes he has appeared in the form of a wealthy man. Sometimes he has appeared in the form of a householder. Sometimes he has appeared in the form of a state official. Sometimes he has appeared in the form of a brahman. Sometimes he has appeared in the form of a monk, nun, layman, or laywoman. Sometimes he has appeared in the form of the wife of a wealthy man or a householder. Sometimes he has appeared in the form of the wife of a state official. Sometimes he has appeared in the form of the wife of a brahman. Sometimes he has appeared in the form of a boy or a girl. Sometimes he has appeared in the form of a human, or a nonhuman such as a *deva, nāga, yakṣa, gandharva, asura, garuḍa, kiṃnara,* or *mahoraga.*

"In this way he has expounded this sutra and saved those in the states of being of hell-dwellers, hungry ghosts, animals, and those in difficult circumstances. Sometimes he has transformed himself into a female in royal harems and taught this sutra. O Padmaśrī! This Bodhisattva Gadgadasvara saves all sentient beings in the *sahā* world. This Bodhisattva Gadgadasvara has transformed himself into various forms and taught this sutra for the sake of all sentient beings. Nevertheless, his transcendent power
56b has never decreased, nor his power of transformation or his wisdom. This bodhisattva illuminates the *sahā* world with his great wisdom and causes every sentient being to attain what should be known. He does exactly the same in all the worlds of the ten directions, which are equal in number to the sands of the Ganges River. If he is able to save them in the form of a *śrāvaka,* he teaches the Dharma by changing himself into the form of a *śrāvaka.* If he is able to save them in the form of a *pratyekabuddha,* he teaches the Dharma by changing himself into the form of a *pratyekabuddha.* If he is able to save them in the form of a bodhisattva, he teaches the Dharma by changing himself into the form of a bodhisattva. If he is able to save them in the form of a Buddha, he teaches the Dharma by changing himself into the form of a Buddha. Thus he transforms himself in various ways according to the capacities of those who are to be saved. If he is able to save them by means of *parinirvāṇa,* he manifests *parinirvāṇa* to them. O Padmaśrī! Bodhisattva Mahāsattva Gadgadasvara has achieved his transcendent powers and the power of wisdom in just such a manner."

Thereupon, Bodhisattva Padmaśrī addressed the Buddha, saying: "O Bhagavat! Deep are the roots of good merit that this Bodhisattva Gadgadasvara has planted! O Bhagavat! In what *samādhi* did this bodhisattva dwell, such that he was able to appear in various places in this way, and bring sentient beings to the path?"

The Buddha answered Bodhisattva Padmaśrī, saying: "O son of a virtuous family! That *samādhi* was called *sarvarūpasaṃdarśana*. Dwelling in this *samādhi*, Bodhisattva Gadgadasvara has benefited innumerable sentient beings in this way."

When this chapter "Bodhisattva Gadgadasvara," was being taught, those eighty-four thousand people who had come with Bodhisattva Gadgadasvara attained the *samādhi* called *sarvarūpasaṃdarśana*. Innumerable bodhisattvas in this *sahā* world also attained this *samādhi* and *dhāraṇī*. Then Bodhisattva Mahāsattva Gadgadasvara paid homage to the Buddha Śākyamuni and the stupa of the Buddha Prabhūtaratna and returned to his own world.

Those worlds through which he traveled quaked in six ways and it rained jeweled lotus flowers. Hundreds of thousands of myriads of *koṭi*s of variegated music was heard. Having returned to his own world, he approached the Buddha Kamaladalavimalanakṣatrarājasaṃkusumitābhijña, surrounded by eighty-four thousand bodhisattvas, and said to him: "O Bhagavat! I have been to the *sahā* world and benefited the sentient beings. Having seen the Buddha Śākyamuni and the stupa of the Buddha Prabhūtaratna, I paid homage to them and made them offerings. Having seen Bodhisattva Mañjuśrī, the Prince of the Dharma, Bodhisattva Bhaiṣajyarāja, Bodhisattva Vīryabalavegaprāpta, and Bodhisattva Pradānaśūra, I caused these eighty-four thousand bodhisattvas to attain the *samādhi* called *sarvarūpasaṃdarśana*."

When this chapter, "The Coming and Going of Bodhisattva Gadgadasvara," was taught, forty-two thousand sons of the *deva*s attained the acceptance of the nonorigination of all *dharma*s; and
Bodhisattva Padmaśrī attained the *saddharmapuṇḍarīka samādhi*. 56c

Chapter XXV

The Gateway to Every Direction [Manifested by Bodhisattva Avalokiteśvara]

Thereupon arising from his seat with his right shoulder bared, Bodhisattva Akṣayamati faced the Buddha with his palms pressed together, and spoke thus to him: "O Bhagavat! For what reason is Bodhisattva Avalokiteśvara (Hearer of the Sounds of the World) called Avalokiteśvara?"

The Buddha answered Bodhisattva Akṣayamati, saying: "O son of a virtuous family! If innumerable hundreds of thousands of myriads of *koṭi*s of sentient beings who experience suffering hear of Bodhisattva Avalokiteśvara and wholeheartedly chant his name, Bodhisattva Avalokiteśvara will immediately perceive their voices and free them from their suffering. Even if those who hold to the name of Bodhisattva Avalokiteśvara were to enter a great fire, because of this bodhisattva's transcendent power, the fire would not be able to burn them. If they were adrift on the great waters, by chanting his name they would reach the shallows. There are hundreds of thousands of myriads of *koṭi*s of sentient beings who enter the great ocean to seek such treasures as gold, silver, lapis lazuli, mother-of-pearl, agate, coral, amber, and pearl. Even if a cyclone were to blow the ship of one of these toward the land of *rākṣasa* demons, they would all become free from the danger of those *rākṣasa* demons if there were even a single person among them who chanted the name of Bodhisattva Avalokiteśvara. For this reason he is called Avalokiteśvara.

"If anyone who is about to be beaten chants the name of Bodhisattva Avalokiteśvara, the sticks and swords will immediately be broken into pieces and he will be delivered. If the *yakṣa*s and *rākṣasas* filling the great manifold cosmos come with the intent to afflict the people but hear them chanting, those demons' evil eyes will be unable to see them, so how could they possibly hurt them?

"If anyone, whether guilty or innocent, is bound with fetters or chains, such bonds will be broken into pieces; and those who have been bound will become free by chanting the name of Bodhisattva Avalokiteśvara. When a caravan leader travels on a dangerous road together with his fellow merchants, carrying precious treasures in a great manifold cosmos filled with evil robbers, if there be a single person who says:

> O sons of a virtuous family! Do not fear! You should wholeheartedly chant the name of Bodhisattva Avalokiteśvara. This bodhisattva bestows fearlessness upon sentient beings. If you chant his name, you will be free from these evil robbers.

"Now, if those merchants chant loudly in unison, saying:

> Homage to Bodhisattva Avalokiteśvara!

"Then, by chanting his name, the caravan will immediately gain
57a deliverance. O Akṣayamati! The transcendent power of Bodhisattva Mahāsattva Avalokiteśvara is as great and mighty as this.

"If there are any sentient beings who are greatly subject to sensual desires, if they contemplate Bodhisattva Avalokiteśvara with respect, they will become free from these desires. If there are any sentient beings who often become angry, if they contemplate Bodhisattva Avalokiteśvara with respect, they will become free from anger. If there are any sentient beings who are greatly confused, if they contemplate Bodhisattva Avalokiteśvara with respect, they will become free from their confusion. O Akṣayamati! Thus Bodhisattva Avalokiteśvara greatly benefits sentient beings through his transcendent power. For this reason sentient beings should always turn their thoughts to him.

"If any woman wanting to have a baby boy pays homage and makes offerings to Bodhisattva Avalokiteśvara, she will bear a baby boy endowed with good merit and wisdom. If she wants to have a baby girl, she will bear a beautiful and handsome baby girl who has planted roots of good merit and will have the love of sentient beings. O Akṣayamati! Such are the transcendent powers of Bodhisattva Avalokiteśvara that if any sentient being reverently respects him, the merit they achieve will never be in vain. For this reason sentient beings should hold to the name of Bodhisattva Avalokiteśvara. O Akṣayamati! What do you think of someone who holds to the names of the bodhisattvas equal in number to the sands of sixty-two *koṭis* of Ganges Rivers and pays homage to them with drink and food, clothes, bedding, and medicine. Is the merit of this son or daughter of a virtuous family great or not?"

Akṣayamati answered, saying: "O Bhagavat! It is great."

The Buddha said: "If there is anyone who holds to the name of Bodhisattva Avalokiteśvara and anyone who pays homage to him and makes offerings even for a moment, the merit of these two people will be equal and the same; it will never be extinguished after hundreds of thousands of myriads of *koṭis* of *kalpas*. O Akṣayamati! Those who hold to the name of Bodhisattva Avalokiteśvara will attain such benefits of immeasurable and limitless merit."

The Bodhisattva Akṣayamati addressed the Buddha, saying: "O Bhagavat! How does Bodhisattva Avalokiteśvara wander through this *sahā* world? How does he teach the Dharma for the sake of sentient beings? What of his power of skillful means?"

The Buddha said to Bodhisattva Akṣayamati: "O son of a virtuous family! If there is any land where sentient beings are to be saved by the form of a Buddha, Bodhisattva Avalokiteśvara teaches the Dharma by changing himself into the form of a Buddha. To those who are to be saved by the form of a *pratyekabuddha,* he teaches the Dharma by changing himself into the form of a *pratyekabuddha.* To those who are to be saved by the form of a *śrāvaka,* he teaches the Dharma by changing himself into the form of a *śrāvaka.* To those who are to be saved by the form of Brahma, he teaches the Dharma by changing himself into the form of Brahma. To those who are to be saved by the form of Śakra, he teaches the Dharma by changing himself into the form of Śakra.

57b To those who are to be saved by the form of Īśvara, he teaches the Dharma by changing himself into the form of Īśvara. To those who are to be saved in the form of Maheśvara, he teaches the Dharma by changing himself into the form of Maheśvara. To those who are to be saved by the form of the great commander of the *devas*, he teaches the Dharma by changing himself into the form of the great commander of the *devas*. To those who are to be saved by the form of Vaiśravaṇa, he teaches the Dharma by changing himself into the form of Vaiśravaṇa. To those who are to be saved by the form of a minor king, he teaches the Dharma by changing himself into the form of a minor king. To those who are to be saved by the form of a wealthy man, he teaches the Dharma by changing himself into the form of a wealthy man. To those who are to be saved by the form of a householder, he teaches the Dharma by changing himself into the form of a householder. To those who are to be saved by the form of a state official, he teaches the Dharma by changing himself into the form of a state official. To those who are to be saved by the form of a brahman, he teaches the Dharma by changing himself into the form of a brahman. To those who are to be saved by the form of a monk, nun, layman, or laywoman, he teaches the Dharma by changing himself into the form of a monk, nun, layman, or laywoman. To those who are to be saved by the form of a wife of either a wealthy man, a householder, a state official, or a brahman, he teaches the Dharma by changing himself into the form of such a wife. To those who are to be saved by the form of a boy or a girl, he teaches the Dharma by changing himself into the form of a boy or a girl. To those who are to be saved by the form of a human or of a nonhuman such as a *deva, nāga, yakṣa, gandharva, asura, garuḍa, kiṃnara,* or *mahoraga,* he teaches the Dharma by changing himself into any of these forms. To those who are to be saved by the form of Vajrapāṇi, he teaches the Dharma by changing himself into the form of Vajrapāṇi.

"O Akṣayamati! This Bodhisattva Avalokiteśvara displays such qualities, wanders through many lands in various forms, and saves sentient beings. For this reason you should wholeheartedly pay homage to Bodhisattva Avalokiteśvara. This Bodhisattva Avalokiteśvara bestows fearlessness in times of fearful calamity. For this reason everybody in this *sahā* world calls him Abhayaṃdada (Giver of Fearlessness).

The Bodhisattva Akṣayamati addressed the Buddha, saying: "O Bhagavat! I shall now pay homage to Bodhisattva Avalokiteśvara."

He then took from his neck a many-jeweled necklace worth hundreds of thousands of gold coins, gave it to him, and said: "I entreat you to accept this rare-jeweled necklace for the Dharma."

At that time Bodhisattva Avalokiteśvara did not dare to receive it. Akṣayamati addressed Bodhisattva Avalokiteśvara, saying: "I entreat you to accept this necklace out of pity for us."

Then the Buddha said to Bodhisattva Avalokiteśvara: "You 57c
should accept this necklace out of pity for such humans and nonhumans as this Bodhisattva Akṣayamati, the fourfold assembly, *devas*, *nāgas*, *yakṣas*, *gandharvas*, *asuras*, *garuḍas*, *kiṃnaras*, and *mahoragas*."

The Bodhisattva Avalokiteśvara accepted the necklace out of pity for the fourfold assembly, *devas*, *nāgas*, humans, nonhumans, and the rest. He then divided it into two parts and gave one part to the Buddha Śākyamuni and the other part to the stupa of the Buddha Prabhūtaratna.

"O Akṣayamati! With such inherent transcendent powers Bodhisattva Avalokiteśvara wanders throughout the *sahā* world."

Thereupon, Bodhisattva Akṣayamati asked a question in verse, saying:

> O Bhagavat, endowed with excellent marks!
> I now wish to ask you about him once again:
> For what reason is the heir of the Buddha
> Named Avalokiteśvara?

The Bhagavat, endowed with excellent marks, answered Akṣayamati in verse:

Listen to the practices of Avalokiteśvara,
Which have their application to all!
His vow is deep like the ocean
And his *kalpa* is of inconceivable length.
After having attended
Many thousands of *koṭi*s of Buddhas,
He made a great, pure vow.
I will now explain it to you in brief:
If you hear his name and see his body,
And contemplate him in thought,
Your life will not be in vain;
And you will extinguish all suffering.
If anyone wants to hurt you
And pushes you into a great firepit,
If you contemplate the power of Avalokiteśvara,
The firepit will change into a pond.
If you drift upon the great ocean and meet danger
From dragons, fish, and demons,
If you contemplate the power of Avalokiteśvara,
You will not be swallowed by the waves.
If you are on the peak of Sumeru
And are pushed by somebody,
If you contemplate the power of Avalokiteśvara,
You will stay suspended in the air like the sun.
If any evil one chases you
And pushes you from Mount Diamond,
If you contemplate the power of Avalokiteśvara,
Not even a single hair will be hurt.
If evil robbers surround you
Each with a sword and the intent to harm,
If you contemplate the power of Avalokiteśvara,
The thought of mercy will awaken in them.
If you suffer under the punishment of a king
And your life is to be ended by execution,
If you contemplate the power of Avalokiteśvara,

The sword will be immediately broken into pieces.
If you are imprisoned with a neck chain,
Your hands and feet fettered,
If you contemplate the power of Avalokiteśvara, 58a
They will disappear and you will be released.
If anyone wants to hurt your body
With a curse or poison,
If you contemplate the power of Avalokiteśvara,
These ills will return and afflict their authors.
If you meet evil *rākṣasa*s,
Poisonous dragons, or demons,
If you contemplate the power of Avalokiteśvara,
They will not dare to hurt you.
If you are surrounded by evil animals
Whose teeth and claws are fearfully sharp,
If you contemplate the power of Avalokiteśvara,
They will run away swiftly
And to an immeasurable distance.
If there are lizards, snakes, vipers, or scorpions,
Whose breath is poisonous like a flaming smoke,
If you contemplate the power of Avalokiteśvara,
They will turn away swiftly at the sound of your voice.
If thunder resounds, lightning flashes,
Hail falls, and a great rain pours out of the clouds,
If you contemplate the power of Avalokiteśvara,
They will disappear immediately.
If sentient beings are in great adversity,
And immeasurable pain afflicts them,
The wonderful power of the wisdom of Avalokiteśvara
Can relieve the suffering of the world.
Endowed with transcendent powers
And having fully mastered wisdom and skillful means,
In all the worlds of the ten directions,
There is no place where he will not manifest himself.
The suffering of those in the troubled states of being:

Hell-dwellers, hungry ghosts, and animals;
And the suffering of birth, old age, illness, and death
Will gradually be extinguished.
He who perceives the world with truth, purity,
And vast knowledge,
And with benevolence and compassion,
Should be ever longed for and looked up to.
He is a spotless pure ray of light,
A sun of wisdom that destroys the darkness,
A flame that withstands the winds of calamity.
He brilliantly illuminates the entire world.
His will, the essence of which is compassion,
Shakes like thunder;
And the mind of mercy
Is like a beautiful overspreading cloud,
Which pours the Dharma rain of immortality
And extinguishes the flame of desires.
In a dispute before judges,
Or fearful in the midst of battle,
If you contemplate the power of Avalokiteśvara,
All enemies will flee away.
He has a wondrous voice,
The voice of one who perceives the world,
A voice like Brahma's, a voice like the rolling tide,
A voice unsurpassed in this world;
For this reason you should always contemplate him.
You should have no doubt, even for a moment.
The pure seer Avalokiteśvara will be a refuge
When suffering distress or the misery of death.
58b He is endowed with every quality,
Sees the sentient beings with his benevolent eyes,
And his ocean of merit is immeasurable;
For this reason you should pay him homage.

At that time Bodhisattva Dharaṇiṃdhara arose from his seat, went before the Buddha and said to him: "O Bhagavat! If there are any sentient beings who hear of this chapter, 'Bodhisattva Avalokiteśvara,' and these effortless deeds, the manifestation of the gateway to all directions, and the transcendent powers, know that their merit will not be little!"

When the Buddha taught the chapter, "The Gateway to Every Direction," the thought of incomparable highest, complete enlightenment awoke in eighty-four thousand sentient beings in the assembly.

Chapter XXVI

Dhāraṇī

Thereupon, rising from his seat with his right shoulder bared, Bodhisattva Bhaiṣajyarāja faced the Buddha with his palms pressed together, and spoke to him, saying: "O Bhagavat! If there is any son or daughter of a virtuous family who preserves the *Lotus Sutra* and recites it, is versed in it, and copies it, how much merit will he or she attain?"

Then the Buddha addressed Bhaiṣajyarāja, saying: "If there is any son or daughter of a virtuous family who pays homage to Buddhas numbering as many as the sands of eight hundred myriads of *koṭi*s of *nayuta*s of Ganges Rivers, what do you think? Will the merit he or she attains be great or not?"

He answered: "It will be great, O Bhagavat!"

The Buddha said: "If any son or daughter of a virtuous family preserves a verse of four lines of this sutra, recites it, understands the meaning, or practices what it teaches, his or her merit will be very great."

Thereupon, Bodhisattva Bhaiṣajyarāja addressed the Buddha, saying: "O Bhagavat! I will now give the *dhāraṇī*s to the expounders of the Dharma and protect them."

He then recited a *dhāraṇī:*

> *Anye manye mane mamane citte carite same samitā viśānte*
> *mukte muktatame same avisame samasame jaye kṣaye akṣaye*
> *akṣiṇe śānte samite dhāraṇi ālokabhāṣe pratyavekṣaṇi ni-*
> *dhiru abhyantaranirviṣte abhyantarapāriśuddhi mutkule*
> *araḍe paraḍe sukāṇkṣi asamasame buddhavilokite dharma-*
> *parikśite saṃgha-nirghoṣanirghoṇi bhayābhayaviśodhani*
> *mantre mantrākṣayate rute rutakauśalye akṣaye akṣaya-* 58c
> *vanatāye vakkule valoḍa amanyanatāye.*

"O Bhagavat! This mantra-*dhāraṇī* was spoken by Buddhas equal in number to the sands of sixty-two *koṭi*s of Ganges Rivers. Anyone who attacks or slanders an expounder of the Dharma also attacks or slanders these Buddhas."

Thereupon, the Buddha Śākyamuni praised Bodhisattva Bhaiṣajyarāja, saying: "Splendid! Splendid! O Bhaiṣajyarāja! Out of compassion you have taught this *dhāraṇī* in order to protect the expounders of the Dharma. It will greatly benefit all sentient beings."

Then Bodhisattva Pradānaśūra addressed the Buddha, saying: "O Bhagavat! I also will teach a *dhāraṇī* in order to protect anyone who recites and preserves the *Lotus Sutra.* If expounders of the Dharma attain this *dhāraṇī,* no *yakṣa, rākṣasa, pūtana, kṛtya, kumbhāṇḍa,* or hungry ghost will ever have a chance to strike at their weaknesses even if they try to do so."

59a In the presence of the Buddha he taught a *dhāraṇī,* saying:

Jvale mahājvale ukke mukke aḍe aḍāvati nṛtye nṛtyāvati iṭṭini viṭṭini ciṭṭini nṛtyani nṛtyāvati.

"O Bhagavat! This mantra-*dhāraṇī* has been spoken by Buddhas equal in number to the sands of the Ganges River and everyone has rejoiced in it. Anyone who attacks or slanders an expounder of the Dharma also attacks or slanders these Buddhas."

Thereupon, the Devarāja Vaiśravaṇa, a world-protector, addressed the Buddha, saying: "O Bhagavat! I will also teach a *dhāraṇī* out of pity for sentient beings and in order to protect expounders of the Dharma."

He then recited a *dhāraṇī,* saying:

Aṭṭe naṭṭe vanaṭṭe anaḍe nāḍi kunaḍi.

"O Bhagavat! With this mantra-*dhāraṇī* I protect the expounders of the Dharma; I will also protect those who hold to this sutra. All heavy cares shall be banished for a hundred *yojana*s around."

At that time the Devarāja Dhṛtarāṣṭra was present in the assembly, respectfully surrounded by thousands of myriads of *koṭi*s of *nayutas* of *gandharvas*. He came before the Buddha together with them and addressed the Buddha with his palms pressed together, saying: "O Bhagavat! With a mantra-*dhāraṇī* I will also protect those who hold to the *Lotus Sutra*."

He then recited the *dhāraṇī*, saying:

> *Agaṇe gaṇe gauri gandhāri caṇḍāli mātaṅgi jaṅguli vrūsaṇi agasti.*

"O Bhagavat! This mantra-*dhāraṇī* was spoken by forty-two *koṭis* of Buddhas. Anyone who attacks or slanders an expounder of the Dharma also attacks or slanders these Buddhas.

"At that time there were ten *rākṣasīs*. Their names were Lambā, Vilambā, Kūṭadantī, Puṣpadantī, Makuṭadantī, Keśinī, Acalā, Mālādhāri, Kuntī, and Sarvasattvojohārī. These ten *rākṣasīs*, together with Hārītī and their children and retinues, came before the Buddha and addressed him in unison, saying: "O Bhagavat! We also want to protect those who recite and preserve the *Lotus Sutra* and rid them of their heavy cares. Those who try to strike at the expounders of the Dharma through their weaknesses shall never be able to do so."

They then recited a *dhāraṇī* in the presence of the Buddha, 59b
saying:

> *Iti me iti me iti me iti me iti me nime nime nime nime nime ruhe ruhe ruhe ruhe stuhe stuhe stuhe stuhe stuhe.*

"Let troubles come upon our heads rather than distress the expounders of the Dharma. No *yakṣa*, no *rākṣasa*, no hungry ghost, no *pūtana*, no *kṛtya*, no *vetāla*, no *skanda*, no *omāraka*, no *apasmāraka*, no *yakṣakṛtya*, no *manuṣyakṛtya*, no fever; no fever for one day, for two days, for three days, for four days or even up to seven days or at any time; no one in the form of a man, no one in the form of a woman, no one in the form of a boy, no one in the form of a maiden, no one who may appear even in a dream, in any of these forms shall cause them distress."

They then spoke to the Buddha in verse, saying:

If anyone does not accept my *dhāraṇī*,
And troubles one who expounds the Dharma,
His head will be split into seven pieces
Just like a branch of the *arjaka* tree.
Consider the transgression of parricide,
Of pressing sesame mixed with impurities,
Of cheating people with scales;
Consider the transgression committed by Devadatta
Who divided the sangha.
Those who slander this expounder of the Dharma
Shall suffer consequences such as these.

After having spoken these verses the *rākṣasī*s addressed the Buddha, saying: "O Bhagavat! We also want to protect those who preserve, recite, and practice this sutra, and cause them to live at ease, rid them of their weighty cares, and drive out various poisons."

The Buddha said to the *rākṣasī*s: "Splendid! Splendid! You protect those who preserve the name of the *Lotus Sutra*. Your merit is immeasurable. How much more merit is there in protecting those who perfectly preserve and revere the sutra in various ways; such as by offering flowers, perfumes, necklaces, fragrant ointments, scented powders, burning incense, banners, canopies, and music, or by lighting ghee lamps, oil lamps, fragrant oil lamps, lamps of oil made from *sumanas, campaka, vārṣika,* and *utpala* flowers! How much more merit is there in offering such things in hundreds to thousands of ways! O Kuntī! You and your retinues should protect the expounders of the Dharma in this way."

When this chapter, *"Dhāraṇī,"* was taught, sixty-eight thousand people attained the acceptance of the nonorigination of all *dharma*s.

Chapter XXVII

Ancient Accounts of King Śubhavyūha

Thereupon, the Buddha addressed the great assembly, saying: "Once upon a time, immeasurable, limitless, inconceivable, and incalculable *kalpas* ago, there was a Buddha named Jaladhara- 59c
garjitaghoṣasusvaranakṣatrarājasaṃkusumitābhijña, a Tathāgata, Arhat, Completely Enlightened. His land was called Vairocanaraśmipratimaṇḍitā and the *kalpa* was named Priyadarśana. There was a king practicing the teaching of the Buddha. He was called Śubhavyūha, and his consort was named Vimaladatta. They had two sons. One was named Vimalagarbha, and the other Vimalanetra. These two sons were endowed with great transcendent power, merit, and wisdom, and practiced the bodhisattva path for a long time. They were versed in the perfections of giving (*dāna*), good conduct (*śīla*), perseverance (*kṣānti*), effort (*vīrya*), meditation (*dhyāna*), wisdom (*prajñā*), and skillful means and compassion, benevolence, joy, and generosity; as well as the thirty-seven helpful ways to attain the Dharma. Furthermore, they were also versed in the bodhisattva *samādhis* of *vimala, nakṣatrarājāditya, vimalanirbhāsa, vimalarūpa, vimalabhāsa, alaṃkāraśubha,* and *mahātejogarbha.*

"Then the Buddha, wanting to guide King Śubhavyūha, and out of compassion for sentient beings, taught this *Lotus Sutra.* At that time Prince Vimalagarbha and Prince Vimalanetra approached their mother and addressed her with their palms and ten fingers pressed together, saying:

> We entreat you, O mother, to go before the Buddha Jaladharagarjitaghoṣasusvaranakṣatrarājasaṃkusumitābhijña. We shall also go before him together with you, attend him, make

> offerings to him, and pay him homage. Why is this? Because this Buddha teaches the *Lotus Sutra* amid the assembly of all the *deva*s and humans. Thus we should all listen to him.

"Their mother answered the sons, saying:

> Your father follows heresies and is deeply attached to the
> 60a teachings of the brahmans. You should go to your father to ask him to come with us.

"Vimalagarbha and Vimalanetra said to their mother with their palms and ten fingers pressed together:

> We are the children of the King of the Dharma, although we were born in this house of wrong views.

"The mother replied to her sons, saying:

> You should have compassion for your father and show him great miracles. If he sees them, his mind will certainly be purified. He will then allow us to go before the Buddha.

"Thereafter the two sons jumped up into the air as high as seven *tāla* trees and, out of their love for their father, showed him various miracles. They walked, stood, sat, and slept in the air, causing water to flow from their upper bodies and blowing fire out of their lower bodies, causing water to flow from their lower bodies, and blowing fire out of their upper bodies; enlarging their bodies so that they filled the air, making them small and then enlarging them again; disappearing in midair and instantly reappearing on the earth; entering the earth as if it were water and walking on the water as though on the earth. By showing various marvels like these, they purified their father's mind and caused him to believe them. When their father saw the transcendent powers of his sons, he rejoiced a great deal at his unprecedented experience and addressed his sons with his palms pressed together, saying:

> Who is your teacher? Whose pupils are you?

"The two sons said:

> O great king! The Buddha Jaladharagarjitaghoṣasusvarana-kṣatrarājasaṃkusumitābhijña is now sitting on the seat of the Dharma under the seven-jeweled *bodhi* tree and teaching the *Lotus Sutra* extensively to the assembly of all the *deva*s and humans in this world. He is our teacher. We are his pupils.

"The father said to his sons:

> I now also wish to see your teacher. Let me go with you!

"Thereupon, the two sons descended from the air, approached their mother, and addressed her with their palms pressed together, saying:

> Our father believed us and the thought of highest, complete enlightenment can now awaken in him. We have done the Buddha's work for the sake of our father. We entreat you, O mother, to allow us to renounce household life and practice the bodhisattva path under the guidance of that Buddha.

"At that time the two sons addressed the mother in verse, wanting to elaborate on this meaning further, saying:

> We entreat you, O mother, to allow us
> To renounce household life
> And to become *śrāmaṇa*s!
> It is extremely difficult to meet Buddhas.
> We will learn by following this Buddha.
> It is more difficult to meet a Buddha
> Than to see *uḍumbara* flowers.
> It is also difficult to escape from adversity.
> We entreat you to allow us
> To renounce household life.

"Their mother addressed them immediately, saying:

> I give my consent for you to renounce household life. What is the reason for this? It is because it is difficult to meet a Buddha.

"Then the two sons addressed their parents, saying:

> Splendid! O father and mother! We entreat you now to
> approach and meet the Buddha Jaladharagarjitaghoṣasu-
> svaranakṣatrarājasaṃkusumitābhijña and pay homage to
> him. Why is this? Because it is difficult to meet a Buddha,
> 60b just as it is to see *uḍumbara* flowers or for a one-eyed turtle
> to find the hole in a floating piece of wood. Because of our
> profound merits accumulated in the past, we were born to
> meet the Buddha-Dharma. For this reason our father and
> mother should allow us to renounce household life. Why is
> this? Because it is difficult to meet Buddhas and it is also
> difficult to obtain an opportunity for meeting them.

"At that time eighty-four thousand women in the palace of King Śubhavyūha all became capable of preserving this *Lotus Sutra*. Bodhisattva Vimalanetra had already been versed in the *saddharmapuṇḍarīka samādhi* for a long time and Bodhisattva Vimalagarbha had also been versed in the *sarvasattvapāpajahana samādhi* for immeasurable hundreds of thousands of myriads of *koṭi*s of *kalpa*s, for he wanted all sentient beings to be separated from evil states of being. The consort of that king attained the *sarvabuddhasaṃgīti samādhi* and the secret treasure house of the Buddhas was revealed to her. In this way the two sons inspired their father through the power of their skillful means and caused him to have faith and pleasure in the Buddha-Dharma.

"Then King Śubhavyūha together with his subjects and retinue, Queen Vimaladatta together with her servants and retinue, and the two princes together with forty-two thousand people came before the Buddha at the same time. Having approached the Buddha, they bowed until their foreheads touched his feet, then circled around him three times and sat to one side.

"At that time the Buddha expounded and taught the Buddha-Dharma for the king's sake, greatly benefiting and rejoicing him. Then King Śubhavyūha and his queen took off their pearl necklaces worth hundreds of thousands and scattered them over the

Buddha. In the air they transformed into a four-pillared jeweled platform. On the platform was a great jeweled bed, spread with hundreds of thousands of myriads of heavenly clothes. The Buddha sat cross-legged upon it, emitting great rays of light. Then King Śubhavyūha thought:

> The Buddha's form is marvelous, most superior in dignity, and given perfection by the most delicate countenance.

"Thereupon the Buddha Jaladharagarjitaghoṣasusvaranakṣatrarājasaṃkusumitābhijña addressed the fourfold assembly, saying:

> Do you see King Śubhavyūha standing with his palms pressed together in my presence? This king has become a monk in my Dharma. He will diligently practice the Dharma that aids those on the Buddha path, and will become a Buddha. He will be called Śālendrarāja. His land will be called Vistīrṇavatī and the *kalpa* Abhyudgatarāja. With this Buddha Śālendrarāja will be innumerable bodhisattvas and *śrāvaka*s. His land will be level. Such will be his merits.

"That king immediately gave his kingdom to his younger brother. He renounced household life and practiced the Buddha-Dharma together with his queen, two sons, and their retinue. For a period of eighty-four thousand years after their renunciation the king continued to make diligent efforts and practiced the *Lotus Sutra*. After this he attained the *sarvaguṇālaṃkāravyūha samādhi*. He ascended instantly into the air to a height of seven *tāla* 60c
trees and addressed the Buddha, saying:

> O Bhagavat! My two sons have done the Buddha's work. Through their miracles they have reformed my erring mind so that I dwell in the Buddha-Dharma. These two sons are my good friends; they enabled me to see the Bhagavat. It was because they wanted to nurture the roots of good merit accumulated in my past and benefit me that they were born in my house.

"Then the Buddha Jaladharagarjitaghoṣasusvaranakṣatrarājasaṃkusumitābhijña addressed King Śubhavyūha, saying:

> Exactly! Exactly! It is exactly as you have said. If the sons and daughters of a virtuous family make good friends throughout many lives, after having planted roots of good merit, those good friends will perform the Buddha's work, illuminating, teaching, benefiting, and gladdening them, and will cause them to enter highest, complete enlightenment. O great king! You should know that a good friend is indeed the great spur that brings inspiration to others, causing them to meet a Buddha and the thought of highest, complete enlightenment to awaken in them. O great king! Do you see these two sons? These two sons have already paid homage to Buddhas equal in number to the sands of sixty-five hundred thousands of myriads of *koṭi*s of *nayuta*s of Ganges Rivers, closely attended the Buddhas with respect, accepted the *Lotus Sutra* in their presence, and, in their compassion, caused sentient beings with false views to dwell in right views.

"Immediately after that, King Śubhavyūha descended from the air and addressed the Buddha, saying:

> O Bhagavat! The Tathāgata is extraordinary. Because he is endowed with merits and wisdom, his topknot is brilliantly illuminated, his deep blue eyes are long and wide, the tuft of hair between his eyebrows is white like the bright moon, his white teeth are even and always shining, and his scarlet lips are like the *bimba* fruit in their beauty.

"At that time King Śubhavyūha praised immeasurable hundreds of thousands of myriads of *koṭi*s of qualities of the Buddha like these and, again, wholeheartedly addressed the Buddha with his palms pressed together, in the presence of the Tathāgata, saying:

> O Bhagavat! This is unprecedented. The Tathāgata's Dharma is endowed and perfected with inconceivable subtle qualities.

> His teaching, integrity, and deeds are serene and comfortable. From today on we shall never act selfishly and the wrongful thoughts of false views, pride and anger shall never awaken in us.

"Having spoken these words he bowed to the Buddha and went away."

The Buddha addressed the great assembly, saying: "What do you think about this? Is King Śubhavyūha someone unknown? He is none other than this Bodhisattva Padmaśrī. His Queen Vimaladatta is none other than this Vairocanaraśmipratimaṇḍitādhvajarāja now in the presence of the Buddha. Because she had compassion for King Śubhavyūha and his retinue, she was born here. These two sons are none other than Bodhisattva Bhaiṣajyarāja and Bodhisattva Bhaiṣajyasamudgata. These bodhisattvas Bhaiṣajyarāja and Bhaiṣajyasamudgata perfected great qualities such as these and, having planted many roots of good merit under the guidance of innumerable hundreds of thousands of myriads of *koṭi*s of Buddhas, perfected inconceivable good merit. If anyone holds 61a
the names of these two bodhisattvas in memory, the *deva*s and humans in this entire world will certainly pay homage to those bodhisattvas."

When the Buddha taught this chapter, "Ancient Accounts of King Śubhavyūha," eighty-four thousand people removed themselves from impurity, rid themselves of defilement, and attained pure Dharma-eyes with which to see the teachings.

Chapter XXVIII

Encouragement of Bodhisattva Samantabhadra

Thereupon Bodhisattva Samantabhadra, through his effortless transcendent power, dignity, and fame, arrived from the east together with innumerable, limitless, and incalculable numbers of great bodhisattvas. All the lands quaked universally wherever he passed. Jeweled lotus flowers rained down and immeasurable hundreds of thousands of myriads of *koṭi*s of kinds of music were heard. He was surrounded by a great assembly of innumerable beings: humans and such nonhumans as *deva*s, *nāga*s, *yakṣa*s, *gandharva*s, *asura*s, *garuḍa*s, *kiṃnara*s, and *mahoraga*s, each manifesting dignity and transcendent powers. He then arrived at Mount Gṛdhrakūṭa in the *sahā* world. He prostrated himself before Śākyamuni Buddha and circled around him to the right. He then addressed him, saying: "O Bhagavat! Afar in the land of the Buddha Ratnatejo'bhyudgatarāja I heard you expound the *Lotus Sutra* in this *sahā* world. I have come here to listen to you, together with the assembly of immeasurable and limitless hundreds of thousands of myriads of *koṭi*s of bodhisattvas. I entreat you, O Bhagavat, to teach us how the sons and daughters of a virtuous family may attain the *Lotus Sutra* after the *parinirvāṇa* of the Tathāgata."

The Buddha said to Bodhisattva Samantabhadra: "After the *parinirvāṇa* of the Tathāgata the sons and daughters of a virtuous family will attain the *Lotus Sutra* if they achieve the four necessary accomplishments: the first is to be protected by the Buddhas; the second is to plant roots of good merit; the third is to enter a group of those who are rightly resolute; and the fourth is to awaken the thought of saving all sentient beings. Those sons and daughters of a virtuous family will definitely attain this sutra after the *parinirvāṇa* of the Tathāgata if they perfect these four accomplishments."

Then Bodhisattva Samantabhadra addressed the Buddha, saying: "O Bhagavat! If there are those who preserve this sutra in the troubled world of five hundred years after, I will protect them and rid them of their heavy cares, cause them to attain happiness, and allow no one to strike at them through their weaknesses. I will not give Māra any chance to afflict them, nor the sons of Māra, daughters of Māra, minions of Māra, those possessed by Māra, *yakṣas*, *rākṣasas*, *kumbhāṇḍas*, *piśācas*, *kṛtyas*, *pūtanas*, or *vetālas*. If they recite this sutra, whether walking or standing, I will then come before
61b them on a white elephant king with six tusks, together with the assembly of great bodhisattvas, manifest myself, pay homage and protect them, and console their minds for the sake of revering the *Lotus Sutra*. If they sit contemplating upon this sutra, I will then manifest myself before them on a white elephant king. If they forget a single line or a verse in the *Lotus Sutra,* I will teach and recite it with them and cause them to become proficient in it. At that time those who accept and recite the *Lotus Sutra* will be able to see me and, greatly rejoicing, will thus make further efforts. As a result of seeing me they will attain the *samādhi* and *dhāraṇīs* named *āvartā dhāraṇī, koṭiśatasahasrāvartā dhāraṇī,* and *sarvarutakauśalyāvartā dhāraṇī*. They will attain *dhāraṇīs* like these. O Bhagavat! In the troubled world of five hundred years after those monks, nuns, laymen, and laywomen who seek, preserve, recite, copy, and wish to practice this *Lotus Sutra* should persevere singlemindedly for twenty-one days. After a full twenty-one days I will appear on a white elephant with six tusks, accompanied by innumerable bodhisattvas who themselves will also be surrounded by their retinues, and manifest myself before sentient beings in whatever form they wish to see. Then I will expound and teach the Dharma to them and gladden them. I will also give them a *dhāraṇī*-spell. When they attain this *dhāraṇī,* nonhumans will have no power to destroy them and women no power to trouble them. I myself will also protect these people. I entreat you, O Bhagavat, to allow me to teach this *dhāraṇī.*"

Thus he taught the spell in the presence of the Buddha, saying:

Adaṇḍe daṇḍapati daṇḍāvartani daṇḍakuśale daṇḍasudhāri sudhāri sudhārapati buddhapaśyane sarvadhāraṇī āvartani sarvabhāṣyāvartane su-āvartane saṃghaparīkṣani saṃgha-nirghātani asaṃge saṃgāpa-gate tṛ-adhvasaṃgatulyaprāpte sarvasaṃgasamatikrānte sarvadharmasuparīkṣite sarva-sattvarutakauśalyānugate siṃhavikrīḍite.

"O Bhagavat! If there is any bodhisattva who hears this *dhāraṇī,* he should know it is because of the transcendent power of Samantabhadra. If there is anyone who accepts the *Lotus Sutra* 61c
practiced in Jambudvīpa, he should think: 'This is nothing but Samantabhadra's virtuous power.' If there is anyone who preserves, recites, correctly remembers, understands this meaning, and practices in accordance with the teaching, know that they are practicing the practice of Samantabhadra. They plant deep roots of good merit in the presence of innumerable and limitless Buddhas. The Tathāgatas will caress their heads. If they copy this sutra, after their death they will be born in the Trāyastriṃśa Heaven. At that time eighty-four thousand heavenly maidens will welcome them, performing various kinds of music. They will wear seven-jeweled coronets and be happy among their female servants. How much more for those who preserve, recite, remember correctly, understand the meaning, and practice in accordance with the teaching! If there is anyone who preserves, recites, and understands this meaning, at the end of their life a thousand Buddhas will offer their hands, so that they will neither be afraid nor fall into the troubled states of being. They will thus arrive in the Tuṣita Heaven of Bodhisattva Maitreya, who is endowed with the thirty-two marks and surrounded by an assembly of great bodhisattvas and a retinue of hundreds of thousands of myriads of *koṭi*s of heavenly maidens. There they will be born and such will be their merit and benefits. For this reason the wise should wholeheartedly copy, move others to copy, preserve, recite, and remember it correctly and practice in accordance with the teaching. O Bhagavat! Through

my transcendent powers I will now protect, extensively distribute and keep this sutra from extermination in Jambudvīpa after the *parinirvāṇa* of the Tathāgata."

Thereupon the Buddha Śākyamuni praised him, saying: "Splendid! Splendid! O Samantabhadra! You will protect this sutra and bring benefit and happiness to sentient beings in many places. You have already accomplished inconceivable merits and profound compassion. Long, long ago the thought of highest, complete enlightenment awakened in you, and you made this vow of transcendent power: 'I will protect this sutra. Through my transcendent powers I will protect the one who holds to the name of Bodhisattva Samantabhadra.' O Samantabhadra! If there is anyone who preserves, recites, correctly remembers, practices, and copies this *Lotus Sutra,* they should know that they will meet the Buddha Śākyamuni and hear this sutra from the mouth of the Buddha.
62a By this they should know that they are paying homage to the Buddha Śākyamuni. They should know that they will be praised by the Śākyamuni Buddha with the word 'Splendid!' They should know that the hand of the Buddha Śākyamuni will caress their heads. They should know that they will be clad in the robe of the Buddha Śākyamuni. Such people are not attached to worldly pleasures. They dislike heretical scriptures and writings. They are not pleased to consort with heretics, wicked people, butchers, those who keep boars, sheep, chickens, or dogs, hunters, or those who make a living by pandering. They will be honest in mind, and will have correct recollection and the power of merit. They will not be troubled by the three kinds of poison. Nor will they be confused by jealousy, selfishness, false pride, or arrogance. Having little desire they can know satisfaction and practice the practice of Samantabhadra. O Samantabhadra! If you meet anyone who preserves and recites the *Lotus Sutra* five hundred years after the *parinirvāṇa* of the Tathāgata, you should think like this:

> This man will before long approach the terrace of enlightenment, destroy the hosts of Māra, attain highest, complete

enlightenment, turn the wheel of the Dharma, beat the drum of the Dharma, blow the conch of the Dharma, pour down the rain of the Dharma, and will sit on the lion seat of the Dharma in the great assembly of *deva*s and humans.

"O Samantabhadra! Those who preserve and recite this sutra in the future world will not be greedy for clothes, bedding, food and drink, and the necessities of life. Their aspirations will not be unrewarded, and their happy reward will be attained in this world. If there is anyone who despises them, saying: 'You are mad. This practice of yours is in vain and will attain nothing at the end,' they will have no eyes lifetime after lifetime as a retribution for this wrongdoing. If there is anyone who pays them homage and praises them, he will attain tangible rewards in this world. If anyone sees those who preserve this sutra and speaks maliciously about their faults, whether true or not, such a person will suffer from leprosy in this life. If anyone scorns them, that person's teeth will be either loose or missing; their lips will be ugly, their nose will be flat, their limbs will be crooked; they will squint; their body will stink and be dirty, suffering from evil tumors, oozing pus; their belly will swell with water; and they will have tuberculosis and other evil and serious illnesses. For this reason, O Samantabhadra, if you see anyone who holds to this sutra, you should stand up and show your respect even from afar, just as you would pay homage to the Buddha."

When this chapter, "Encouragement of Bodhisattva Samantabhadra," was being taught, innumerable and limitless bodhisattvas equal in number to the sands of Ganges Rivers attained hundreds of thousands of myriads of *koṭi*s of *dhāraṇī*s named *āvartā,* and bodhisattvas equal to the number of atoms in the manifold cosmos mastered the path of Samantabhadra.

When the Buddha had taught this sutra, the entire great assembly of bodhisattvas including Samantabhadra, the *śrāvaka*s including Śāriputra, *deva*s, *nāga*s, humans, and nonhumans rejoiced greatly, accepted the Buddha's word, bowed to him and departed.

Glossary

anuttarā samyaksaṃbodhi: Complete, perfect enlightenment.

apasmāraka: A class of demonic beings.

arhat ("one who is worthy"): A saint who has completely eradicated the passions and attained liberation from the cycle of birth and death (samsara); arhatship is the highest of the four stages of spiritual attainment in the Hinayana. Capitalized, the term is an epithet for a Buddha. *See also* birth and death; Hinayana.

asura: A class of supernatural beings that are in constant conflict with the gods (*deva*s). *See also deva.*

Avalokiteśvara: The name of a great bodhisattva who represents great compassion.

Bhagavat ("Blessed One"): A venerable teacher; an epithet of a Buddha.

birth and death (samsara): The cycle of existence, the continuous round of birth and death through which beings transmigrate; the world of suffering, contrasted with the bliss of nirvana. *See also* nirvana; *sahā* world; triple world.

bodhisattva ("enlightenment being"): The spiritual ideal of the Mahayana, a selfless being with universal compassion who has generated the profound aspiration to achieve enlightenment in order to benefit sentient beings. In the course of their spiritual careers, bodhisattvas engage in the practice of the six perfections and pass through stages of increasingly higher levels of spiritual accomplishment. *See also* Mahayana; six perfections.

bodhi tree: The tree under which a Buddha attains enlightenment.

Buddhahood: The state of becoming or being a Buddha; the goal of the bodhisattva path.

Buddha land: A cosmic world or realm in which a particular Buddha dwells.

Brahma: Lord of the *sahā* world. *See also sahā* world.

brahman: The priestly caste in the Indian caste system; in the *Lotus Sutra* the term also applies to a class of heavenly beings.

Decadent Dharma: The last of the three ages of the Dharma, following the age of the Semblance Dharma, in which only the teaching of the Buddha exists but correct practice is no longer possible. *See also* Semblance Dharma; True Dharma.

dependent origination (*pratītyasamutpāda*): The Buddhist doctrine which holds that all phenomena (*dharmas*) arise in relation to causes and conditions and in turn are the causes and conditions for the arising of other phenomena. Nothing exists independently of its causes and conditions. *See also dharma.*

deva: A class of supernatural beings; a god or divine being.

Devadatta ("God-given"): A cousin of the Buddha who became his disciple but later tried to murder him and assume leadership of the sangha.

dhāraṇī: A powerful verbal incantation or mantra.

dharma: Any phenomenon, thing, or element; the elements that make up the perceived phenomenal world.

Dharma: The truth, law; the teachings of the Buddha. *See also* Decadent Dharma; Semblance Dharma; True Dharma.

Dharma body (*dharmakāya*): The manifestation of the Buddha as ultimate reality.

emptiness (*śūnyatā*): The absence of substantiality or inherent existence of the self and all phenomena (*dharmas*); all *dharmas* arise only through the dependent origination of causes and conditions (*pratītyasamutpāda*). Direct insight into emptiness is the attainment of *prajñā* (transcendental wisdom). *See also* dependent origination; *dharma; prajñā.*

five *skandhas*: The five elements of form, feeling, conception, mental process, and consciousness which comprise the personality and give rise to the mistaken view of a permanent, inherent self.

four modes of birth: According to Buddhism, the four possible ways that a being may be born, i.e., 1) from a womb, 2) from an egg, 3) from moisture, or 4) through metamorphosis or spontaneous generation.

Four Noble Truths: The basic doctrine of Buddhism: 1) the truth of suffering,

2) the truth regarding the cause of suffering, 3) the truth regarding the extinction of suffering, and 4) the truth regarding the path to nirvana.

gandharva: A heavenly musician.

garuḍa: A mythological being in the form of a giant bird.

Hinayana ("Lesser Vehicle"): A derogatory term applied by Mahayana Buddhists to early schools of Buddhism whose primary soteriological aim is individual salvation. Hinayana followers are grouped into the two categories of *śrāvaka*s and *pratyekabuddha*s and there are four stages of spiritual attainment, culminating in arhatship. *See also* arhat; Mahayana; non-returner; once-returner; *pratyekabuddha; śrāvaka;* stream-enterer.

Jambudvīpa: A mythological continent, one of the four continents that surround Mount Sumeru; the world of human beings. *See also* Mount Sumeru.

kalpa: An eon, an immensely long period of time.

karma ("action"): Any action of body, speech, or mind (thought), which may be either morally good, bad, or neutral. The concept of karma is connected with the Buddhist theory of transmigration in the cycle of birth and death. *See also* birth and death.

kiṃnara: A class of mythological beings, half bird and half human, that make celestial music.

koṭi: A large unit of measurement, said to equal ten million.

kṛtya: A class of evil beings, sorcerers.

kṣatriya: The warrior caste in the Indian caste system; the politically governing or military.

kumbhāṇḍa: A class of demonic beings.

lion's roar: A metaphor for great eloquence in teaching the Dharma.

Mahayana: ("Great Vehicle"): A form of Buddhism that developed in India around 100 B.C.E. and which exalts as its religious ideal the bodhisattva, great beings who aspire to enlightenment on behalf of all sentient beings. *See also* bodhisattva.

mahoraga: A class of snake-like mythical beings.

Maitreya: The future Buddha, currently still a bodhisattva. *See also* bodhisattva.

Mañjuśrī: The bodhisattva who represents great wisdom. *See also* bodhisattva.

manuṣyakṛtya: A class of human sorcerers. *See also kṛtya; yakṣakṛtya.*

Māra: The Evil One, the personification of death. The lower-case term *māra* refers to the afflictions that hinder progress on the path to Buddhahood.

Mount Sumeru: In Buddhist cosmology, the highest mountain rising from the center of the world, surrounded by an ocean in which the four continents that comprise the world of human beings are situated.

nayuta: A large unit of numerical measurement, said to be equal to ten million or one hundred billion.

nirvana: Liberation from the cycle of birth and death, a state in which all passions are extinguished and the highest wisdom (*prajñā*) attained; *bodhi,* enlightenment. *See also* birth and death; *prajñā.*

non-returner (*anāgāmin*): The third of the four stages of spiritual attainment in the Hinayana; one who has attained this stage is no longer subject to rebirth in the realm of desire. *See also* Hinayana; triple world.

once-returner (*sakṛdāgāmin*): The second of the four stages of spiritual attainment in the Hinayana; one who has attained this state is subject to rebirth only once in each of the three realms of the triple world before attaining nirvana. *See also* Hinayana; nirvana; triple world.

parinirvāṇa: Complete nirvana *See also* nirvana.

prajñā: Transcendental, liberative wisdom; one of the six perfections. *See also* six perfections.

pratyekabuddha ("solitary enlightened one"): One of the two kinds of Hinayana followers, along with *śrāvaka*s, who seek to reach the stage of arhat and attain nirvana. A *pratyekabuddha* attains liberation through direct observation and understanding of the principle of dependent origination without the guidance of a teacher, and does not teach others. *See also* arhat; dependent origination; Hinayana; nirvana; *śrāvaka.*

piśāca: A class of demonic beings.

pūtana: A class of demonic beings that cause disease in children.

rākṣasa: A type of demon. The female form is *rākṣasī.*

sahā world: The world of endurance, suffering.

Śakra: Lord of the *devas*. *See also deva*.

Śākyamuni ("Sage of the Śākyas"): The historical Buddha, who lived in India in the fifth century B.C.E. and whose life and teachings form the basis for Buddhism.

Śākyas: The name of the historical Buddha Śākyamuni's family clan.

samādhi: Mental concentration; a meditative state.

sangha: The Buddhist order, the community of Buddhist followers.

Semblance Dharma: The second of the three ages of the Buddhist Dharma, following the age of the True Dharma, in which the Buddha's teaching is practiced but enlightenment is no longer possible. *See also* Decadent Dharma; True Dharma.

sense faculties: The sense perceptions that correspond to the six sense organs (eyes, ears, nose, tongue, body, and mind)—visual, auditory, olfactory, gustatory, tactile, and mental perceptions.

single vehicle (*ekayāna*): The one Buddha vehicle, the Mahayana teaching espoused in the *Lotus Sutra* that leads to complete enlightenment and attainment of Buddhahood, contrasted with the teachings of the two Hinayana vehicles. The single vehicle includes and transcends all three vehicles of the *śrāvaka, pratyekabuddha,* and bodhisattva paths. *See also* three vehicles; two vehicles.

six perfections (*parāmitās*): Six qualities perfected by bodhisattvas—1) giving (*dāna*), 2) integrity or good conduct (*śīla*), 3) perseverance (*kṣānti*), 4) diligence or effort (*vīrya*), 5) meditation (*dhyāna*), and 6) wisdom (*prajñā*). *See also* bodhisattva; *prajñā*.

skillful means (*upāya*): The various methods and means used by Buddhas and bodhisattvas to guide and teach sentient beings, adapted to their different capacities.

śramaṇa: Mendicant, monk; a Buddhist monk, originally applied to those who maintained an ascetic practice.

śrāmaṇera: A novice in the Buddhist sangha.

śrāvaka ("auditor"): Originally, a disciple of the Buddha, one of those who heard him expound the teachings directly; later, the term came to refer to one of the two kinds of Hinayana followers, along with *pratyekabuddhas*, to distinguish them from followers of the Mahayana. *See also* Hinayana; Mahayana; *pratyekabuddha*.

stream-enterer (*srota-āpanna*): The first of the four stages of spiritual attainment in the Hinayana; one who has entered the stream of the Dharma by destroying various wrong views. *See also* Hinayana.

stupa: A tope; a structure in which the relics of a Buddha are placed.

Sugata ("Well-gone"): An epithet for a Buddha; one who has attained bliss.

sutra: A Buddhist scripture, a discourse of the Buddha.

Tathāgata: An epithet for a Buddha. It means "one who has gone to (*gata*) and come from (*āgata*) the truth of suchness (*tathā*)," i.e., "one who embodies the truth of suchness."

three vehicles: The paths of the *śrāvaka*s, *pratyekabuddha*s, and bodhisattvas, respectively. *See also* bodhisattva; *pratyekabuddha; śrāvaka.*

triple world: The three realms of samsaric existence in which living beings transmigrate as a result of their karma: 1) the realm of desire (*kāmadhātu*), i.e., the world of ordinary consciousness accompanied by desires; the realm of form (*rūpadhātu*), in which desires have been eliminated but the physical body remains; and the formless realm (*ārūpyadhātu*), in which the physical body no longer exists.

True Dharma: The first of the three ages of the Buddhist Dharma, in which the Buddhist teaching is properly practiced and enlightenment can be attained. *See also* Decadent Dharma; Semblance Dharma.

two vehicles: The two Hinayana paths of *śrāvaka*s and *pratyekabuddha*s. *See also* Hinayana; *pratyekabuddha; śrāvaka.*

universal monarch (*cakravartin*): The ideal king, as conceived of in Indian philosophy.

yakṣa: A class of demonic beings.

yakṣakṛtya: A class of demonic sorcerers. *See also kṛtya.*

yojana: An Indian unit of distance, roughly equivalent to seven to nine miles, based on the distance the royal army could march in one day.

Bibliography

Burnouf, Eugène. *Le Lotus de la Bonne Loi. Traduit du sanscrit, accompagné d'une commentaire et de vingt et une mémoires relatifs au Buddhisme.* Paris: Imprimerie Nationale, 1852.

Ehara, Ryozui. "The Lotus of the Wonderful Truth" (Chapters 2, 3, 10, 11, 16). *Manual of Nichiren Buddhism.* Edited by R. Ehara. Honolulu & Tokyo: Young East Association, 1953, pp. 5–32.

Heng Yen, et al. *The Dharma Flower Sutra.* Volumes 1–10. San Francisco: Buddhist Text Translation Society, 1977–82.

Hurvitz, Leon. *Scripture of the Lotus Blossom of the Fine Dharma (The Lotus Sutra).* New York: Columbia University Press, 1976.

Karashima, Seishi. *A Glossary of Kumārajīva's Translation of the Lotus sutra (Miao fa lian hua jing ci dian).* Tokyo: International Research Institute for Advanced Buddhology, Soka University, 2001.

Katō, Bunnō, et al. *Myōhō-renge-kyō: The Sutra of the Lotus Flower of the Wonderful Law.* Tokyo: Rissho Kosei-kai, 1971. Revised by William E. Soothill and Wilhelm Schiffer.

Katō, Bunnō, et al. *The Threefold Lotus Sutra.* New York and Tokyo: Weatherhill and Kosei, 1975.

Kern, Jan Hendrik. *Saddharmapuṇḍarīka, or The Lotus of the True Law.* Oxford: Clarendon, 1884.

Murano, Senchū. *The Sutra of the Lotus Flower of the Wonderful Law.* Tokyo: Nichiren Shu Headquarters, 1974.

Nakamura, Hajime. *Indian Buddhism: A Survey with Bibliographical Notes.* Hirakata: Kansai University of Foreign Studies Publication, 1980.

Shen, Haiyan. *The Profound Meaning of the Lotus Sutra: T'ien-tai Philosophy of Buddhism.* New Delhi: Distributed by D.K. Publishers Dostributors, 2005.

Soothill, William E. *The Lotus of the Wonderful Law, or The Lotus Gospel.* Oxford: Clarendon, 1930. Reprint, San Francisco: Chinese Materials Center, 1977.

Wang, Eugene Y. *Shaping the Lotus Sutra: Buddhist Visual Culture in Medieval China.* Seattle, WA: University of Washington Press, 2005.

Yuyama, Akira. *A Bibliography of the Sanskrit Texts of the Saddharmapuṇḍarīkasūtra.* Canberra: Australian National University Press, 1970.

—. *Eugène Burnouf: The Background to His Research into the Lotus Sutra.* Tokyo, International Research Institute for Advanced Buddhology, Soka University, 2000.

Index

C

D

K

Kabutogi, Shōkō xiii–xiv
kalaviṅka birds 127, 261
Kālodāyin 153
kalpa(s) 19, 25, 32, 37, 44, 73, 74, 77, 80, 81, 98, 119, 120, 121, 127, 129, 135, 136, 140, 142, 143, 154, 160, 163, 166, 168, 184, 188, 208, 216, 222, 226, 231, 232, 234, 238, 241, 245, 246, 247, 257, 275, 276, 278, 280, 281, 291, 311, 314, 326
  Abhyudgatarāja 327
  auspicious 148
  decadent 32
  immeasurable 55, 79, 98, 101, 117, 119, 120, 122, 132, 133, 148, 149, 173, 180, 187, 189, 190, 191, 196, 236, 246, 247, 249, 251, 275, 286, 291, 323
  incalculable 13, 16, 153, 181, 196, 232, 236, 238, 275, 285, 289, 323
  inconceivable 53, 275, 323
  innumerable 16, 24, 25, 38, 46, 77, 110, 225, 227, 237, 238
  intermediate 15, 16, 19, 20, 54, 55, 56, 109, 111, 112, 113, 114, 115, 116, 117, 121, 122, 140, 189, 218, 229
  Mahāratnapratimaṇḍita 54
  Mahārūpa 119
  Mahāvyūha 109
  Manojñaśabdābhigarjita 160
  Prabhūratna 55
  Priyadarśana 305, 323
  Ratiprapūrṇa 116
  Ratnāvabhāsa 112, 149, 151
  Vinirbhoga 275
Kamaladalavimalanakṣatrarājasaṃkusumitābhijña 301–7
Kapphiṇa 3, 153
karma 17, 34, 166
Kāśyapa (*see also* Mahākāśyapa) 101, 103, 104, 108, 110, 154
Kauṇḍinya (*see also* Ājñātakauṇḍinya) 153
Kawabata, S. xv
Keśinī 321
Kharaskandha 4
Khotan xiv
kiṃnara(s) 5, 14, 17, 56, 124, 127, 129, 131, 165, 175, 260, 268, 283, 284, 291, 306, 312, 313, 331
  four kings of 4
King(s) of the Dharma (*see also* Dharma King) 9, 20, 29, 46, 89, 98, 103, 111, 211, 297, 324
King of Sutras (*see also Lotus Sutra*) 172, 297
kovidāra trees 263
kṛtya 320, 321, 332
kṣānti (*see also* perfections; perseverance) 18, 38, 245, 249, 252, 323
kṣatriya(s) 85, 88, 94
Kucha xiii
Kumārajīva xiii, xiv
kumbhāṇḍa(s) 67, 68, 69, 299, 320, 332
Kuntī 321, 322
Kūṭadantī 321

L

Lambā 321
lay Buddhist(s), laypeople 198, 210, 212
layman, laymen 4, 5, 6, 14, 26, 30, 33, 56, 165, 171, 173, 202, 206, 208, 210, 253, 268, 275, 276, 277, 278, 280, 283, 285, 305, 312, 332
laywoman, laywomen 4, 5, 6, 14, 26, 30, 33, 56, 165, 171, 173, 202, 203,

M

N

O

P

Q

X

Y

A List of the Volumes of the BDK English Tripiṭaka (First Series)

Abbreviations

Ch.: Chinese
Skt.: Sanskrit
Jp.: Japanese
Eng.: Published title
T.: Taishō Tripiṭaka

Vol. No.		Title	*T.* No.
1, 2	*Ch.*	Ch‘ang-a-han-ching (長阿含經)	1
	Skt.	Dīrghāgama	
3–8	*Ch.*	Chung-a-han-ching (中阿含經)	26
	Skt.	Madhyamāgama	
9-I	*Ch.*	Ta-ch‘eng-pên-shêng-hsin-ti-kuan-ching (大乘本生心地觀經)	159
9-II	*Ch.*	Fo-so-hsing-tsan (佛所行讃)	192
	Skt.	Buddhacarita	
10-I	*Ch.*	Tsa-pao-ts‘ang-ching (雜寶藏經)	203
	Eng.	The Storehouse of Sundry Valuables	
10-II	*Ch.*	Fa-chü-p‘i-yü-ching (法句譬喩經)	211
	Eng.	The Scriptural Text: Verses of the Doctrine, with Parables	
11-I	*Ch.*	Hsiao-p‘in-pan-jo-po-lo-mi-ching (小品般若波羅蜜經)	227
	Skt.	Aṣṭasāhasrikā-prajñāpāramitā-sūtra	

Vol. No.		Title	*T.* No.
11-II	*Ch.*	Chin-kang-pan-jo-po-lo-mi-ching (金剛般若波羅蜜經)	235
	Skt.	Vajracchedikā-prajñāpāramitā-sūtra	
11-III	*Ch.*	Jên-wang-pan-jo-po-lo-mi-ching (仁王般若波羅蜜經)	245
	Skt.	Kāruṇikārājā-prajñāpāramitā-sūtra (?)	
11-IV	*Ch.*	Pan-jo-po-lo-mi-to-hsing-ching (般若波羅蜜多心經)	251
	Skt.	Prajñāpāramitāhṛdaya-sūtra	
12-I	*Ch.*	Ta-lo-chin-kang-pu-k'ung-chên-shih-san-mo-yeh-ching (大樂金剛不空眞實三麼耶經)	243
	Skt.	Adhyardhaśatikā-prajñāpāramitā-sūtra	
12-II	*Ch.*	Wu-liang-shou-ching (無量壽經)	360
	Skt.	Sukhāvatīvyūha	
	Eng.	The Larger Sutra on Amitāyus (In The Three Pure Land Sutras)	
12-III	*Ch.*	Kuan-wu-liang-shou-fo-ching (觀無量壽佛經)	365
	Skt.	Amitāyurdhyāna-sūtra	
	Eng.	The Sutra on Contemplation of Amitāyus (In The Three Pure Land Sutras)	
12-IV	*Ch.*	A-mi-t'o-ching (阿彌陀經)	366
	Skt.	Sukhāvatīvyūha	
	Eng.	The Smaller Sutra on Amitāyus (In The Three Pure Land Sutras)	
12-V	*Ch.*	Ti-ts'ang-p'u-sa-pên-yüan-ching (地藏菩薩本願經)	412
	Skt.	Kṣitigarbhapraṇidhāna-sūtra (?)	
12-VI	*Ch.*	Yao-shih-liu-li-kuang-ju-lai-pên-yüan-kung-tê-ching (藥師琉璃光如來本願功徳經)	450
	Skt.	Bhaiṣajyaguruvaiḍūryaprabhāsapūrva-praṇidhānaviśeṣavistara	
12-VII	*Ch.*	Mi-lê-hsia-shêng-ch'êng-fo-ching (彌勒下生成佛經)	454
	Skt.	Maitreyavyākaraṇa (?)	
12-VIII	*Ch.*	Wên-shu-shih-li-wên-ching (文殊師利問經)	468
	Skt.	Mañjuśrīparipṛcchā (?)	

Vol. No.		Title	T. No.
13-I	*Ch.*	Miao-fa-lien-hua-ching (妙法蓮華經)	262
	Skt.	Saddharmapuṇḍarīka-sūtra	
	Eng.	The Lotus Sutra	
13-II	*Ch.*	Wu-liang-i-ching (無量義經)	276
13-III	*Ch.*	Kuan-p'u-hsien-p'u-sa-hsing-fa-ching (觀普賢菩薩行法經)	277
14–19	*Ch.*	Ta-fang-kuang-fo-hua-yen-ching (大方廣佛華嚴經)	278
	Skt.	Avataṃsaka-sūtra	
20-I	*Ch.*	Shêng-man-shih-tzŭ-hou-i-ch'eng-ta-fang-pien-fang-kuang-ching (勝鬘師子吼一乘大方便方廣經)	353
	Skt.	Śrīmālādevīsiṃhanāda-sūtra	
	Eng.	The Sutra of Queen Śrīmālā of the Lion's Roar	
20-II	*Ch.*	Chin-kuang-ming-tsui-shêng-wang-ching (金光明最勝王經)	665
	Skt.	Suvarṇaprabhāsa-sūtra	
21–24	*Ch.*	Ta-pan-nieh-p'an-ching (大般涅槃經)	374
	Skt.	Mahāparinirvāṇa-sūtra	
25-I	*Ch.*	Fo-ch'ui-pan-nieh-p'an-liao-shuo-chiao-chieh-ching (佛垂般涅槃略説教誡經)	389
	Eng.	The Bequeathed Teaching Sutra (In Apocryphal Scriptures)	
25-II	*Ch.*	Pan-chou-san-mei-ching (般舟三昧經)	418
	Skt.	Pratyutpannabuddhasammukhāvasthitasamādhi-sūtra	
	Eng.	The Pratyutpanna Samādhi Sutra	
25-III	*Ch.*	Shou-lêng-yen-san-mei-ching (首楞嚴三昧經)	642
	Skt.	Śūraṅgamasamādhi-sūtra	
	Eng.	The Śūraṅgama Samādhi Sutra	
25-IV	*Ch.*	Chieh-shên-mi-ching (解深密經)	676
	Skt.	Saṃdhinirmocana-sūtra	
	Eng.	The Scripture on the Explication of Underlying Meaning	

Vol. No.		Title	T. No.
25-V	*Ch.*	Yü-lan-p'ên-ching (盂蘭盆經)	685
	Skt.	Ullambana-sūtra (?)	
	Eng.	The Ullambana Sutra (In Apocryphal Scriptures)	
25-VI	*Ch.*	Ssŭ-shih-êrh-chang-ching (四十二章經)	784
	Eng.	The Sutra of Forty-two Sections (In Apocryphal Scriptures)	
26-I	*Ch.*	Wei-mo-chieh-so-shuo-ching (維摩詰所説經)	475
	Skt.	Vimalakīrtinirdeśa-sūtra	
	Eng.	The Vimalakīrti Sutra	
26-II	*Ch.*	Yüeh-shang-nü-ching (月上女經)	480
	Skt.	Candrottarādārikāparipṛcchā	
26-III	*Ch.*	Tso-ch'an-san-mei-ching (坐禪三昧經)	614
26-IV	*Ch.*	Ta-mo-to-lo-ch'an-ching (達磨多羅禪經)	618
	Skt.	Yogācārabhūmi-sūtra (?)	
27	*Ch.*	Yüeh-têng-san-mei-ching (月燈三昧經)	639
	Skt.	Samādhirājacandrapradīpa-sūtra	
28	*Ch.*	Ju-lêng-ch'ieh-ching (入楞伽經)	671
	Skt.	Laṅkāvatāra-sūtra	
29-I	*Ch.*	Ta-fang-kuang-yüan-chio-hsiu-to-lo-liao-i-ching (大方廣圓覺修多羅了義經)	842
	Eng.	The Sutra of Perfect Enlightenment (In Apocryphal Scriptures)	
29-II	*Ch.*	Su-hsi-ti-chieh-lo-ching (蘇悉地羯囉經)	893
	Skt.	Susiddhikaramahātantrasādhanopāyika-paṭala	
	Eng.	The Susiddhikara Sutra (In Two Esoteric Sutras)	
29-III	*Ch.*	Mo-têng-ch'ieh-ching (摩登伽經)	1300
	Skt.	Mātaṅgī-sūtra (?)	
30-I	*Ch.*	Ta-p'i-lu-chê-na-chêng-fo-shên-pien-chia-ch'ih-ching (大毘盧遮那成佛神變加持經)	848
	Skt.	Mahāvairocanābhisambodhivikurvitādhiṣṭhāna-vaipulyasūtrendrarāja-nāma-dharmaparyāya	
	Eng.	The Vairocanābhisaṃbodhi Sutra	

Vol. No.		Title	*T.* No.
30-II	*Ch.*	Ching-kang-ting-i-ch'ieh-ju-lai-chên-shih-shê-ta-ch'eng-hsien-chêng-ta-chiao-wang-ching (金剛頂一切如來眞實攝大乘現證大教王經)	865
	Skt.	Sarvatathāgatatattvasaṃgrahamahāyānābhisamayamahākalparāja	
	Eng.	The Adamantine Pinnacle Sutra (In Two Esoteric Sutras)	
31–35	*Ch.*	Mo-ho-sêng-ch'i-lü (摩訶僧祇律)	1425
	Skt.	Mahāsāṃghika-vinaya (?)	
36–42	*Ch.*	Ssŭ-fên-lü (四分律)	1428
	Skt.	Dharmaguptaka-vinaya (?)	
43, 44	*Ch.*	Shan-chien-lü-p'i-p'o-sha (善見律毘婆沙)	1462
	Pāli	Samantapāsādikā	
45-I	*Ch.*	Fan-wang-ching (梵網經)	1484
	Skt.	Brahmajāla-sūtra (?)	
45-II	*Ch.*	Yu-p'o-sai-chieh-ching (優婆塞戒經)	1488
	Skt.	Upāsakaśīla-sūtra (?)	
	Eng.	The Sutra on Upāsaka Precepts	
46-I	*Ch.*	Miao-fa-lien-hua-ching-yu-po-t'i-shê (妙法蓮華經憂波提舍)	1519
	Skt.	Saddharmapuṇḍarīka-upadeśa	
46-II	*Ch.*	Fo-ti-ching-lun (佛地經論)	1530
	Skt.	Buddhabhūmisūtra-śāstra (?)	
	Eng.	The Interpretation of the Buddha Land	
46-III	*Ch.*	Shê-ta-ch'eng-lun (攝大乘論)	1593
	Skt.	Mahāyānasaṃgraha	
	Eng.	The Summary of the Great Vehicle	
47	*Ch.*	Shih-chu-p'i-p'o-sha-lun (十住毘婆沙論)	1521
	Skt.	Daśabhūmika-vibhāṣā (?)	
48, 49	*Ch.*	A-p'i-ta-mo-chü-shê-lun (阿毘達磨俱舍論)	1558
	Skt.	Abhidharmakośa-bhāṣya	
50–59	*Ch.*	Yü-ch'ieh-shih-ti-lun (瑜伽師地論)	1579
	Skt.	Yogācārabhūmi	

Vol. No.		Title	T. No.
60-I	*Ch.*	Ch'êng-wei-shih-lun (成唯識論)	1585
	Eng.	Demonstration of Consciousness Only (In Three Texts on Consciousness Only)	
60-II	*Ch.*	Wei-shih-san-shih-lun-sung (唯識三十論頌)	1586
	Skt.	Triṃśikā	
	Eng.	The Thirty Verses on Consciousness Only (In Three Texts on Consciousness Only)	
60-III	*Ch.*	Wei-shih-êrh-shih-lun (唯識二十論)	1590
	Skt.	Viṃśatikā	
	Eng.	The Treatise in Twenty Verses on Consciousness Only (In Three Texts on Consciousness Only)	
61-I	*Ch.*	Chung-lun (中論)	1564
	Skt.	Madhyamaka-śāstra	
61-II	*Ch.*	Pien-chung-pien-lun (辯中邊論)	1600
	Skt.	Madhyāntavibhāga	
61-III	*Ch.*	Ta-ch'eng-ch'êng-yeh-lun (大乘成業論)	1609
	Skt.	Karmasiddhiprakaraṇa	
61-IV	*Ch.*	Yin-ming-ju-chêng-li-lun (因明入正理論)	1630
	Skt.	Nyāyapraveśa	
61-V	*Ch.*	Chin-kang-chên-lun (金剛針論)	1642
	Skt.	Vajrasūcī	
61-VI	*Ch.*	Chang-so-chih-lun (彰所知論)	1645
	Eng.	The Treatise on the Elucidation of the Knowable	
62	*Ch.*	Ta-ch'eng-chuang-yen-ching-lun (大乘莊嚴經論)	1604
	Skt.	Mahāyānasūtrālaṃkāra	
63-I	*Ch.*	Chiu-ching-i-ch'eng-pao-hsing-lun (究竟一乘寶性論)	1611
	Skt.	Ratnagotravibhāgamahāyānottaratantra-śāstra	
63-II	*Ch.*	P'u-t'i-hsing-ching (菩提行經)	1662
	Skt.	Bodhicaryāvatāra	
63-III	*Ch.*	Chin-kang-ting-yü-ch'ieh-chung-fa-a-nou-to-lo-san-miao-san-p'u-t'i-hsin-lun (金剛頂瑜伽中發阿耨多羅三藐三菩提心論)	1665

Vol. No.		Title	T. No.
63-IV	*Ch.*	Ta-ch'eng-ch'i-hsin-lun (大乘起信論)	1666
	Skt.	Mahāyānaśraddhotpāda-śāstra (?)	
	Eng.	The Awakening of Faith	
63-V	*Ch.*	Na-hsien-pi-ch'iu-ching (那先比丘經)	1670
	Pāli	Milindapañhā	
64	*Ch.*	Ta-ch'eng-chi-p'u-sa-hsüeh-lun (大乘集菩薩學論)	1636
	Skt.	Śikṣāsamuccaya	
65	*Ch.*	Shih-mo-ho-yen-lun (釋摩訶衍論)	1688
66-I	*Ch.*	Pan-jo-po-lo-mi-to-hsin-ching-yu-tsan (般若波羅蜜多心經幽賛)	1710
	Eng.	A Comprehensive Commentary on the Heart Sutra (Prajñāpāramitā-hṛdaya-sūtra)	
66-II	*Ch.*	Kuan-wu-liang-shou-fo-ching-shu (觀無量壽佛經疏)	1753
66-III	*Ch.*	San-lun-hsüan-i (三論玄義)	1852
66-IV	*Ch.*	Chao-lun (肇論)	1858
67, 68	*Ch.*	Miao-fa-lien-hua-ching-hsüan-i (妙法蓮華經玄義)	1716
69	*Ch.*	Ta-ch'eng-hsüan-lun (大乘玄論)	1853
70-I	*Ch.*	Hua-yen-i-ch'eng-chiao-i-fên-ch'i-chang (華嚴一乘教義分齊章)	1866
70-II	*Ch.*	Yüan-jên-lun (原人論)	1886
70-III	*Ch.*	Hsiu-hsi-chih-kuan-tso-ch'an-fa-yao (修習止觀坐禪法要)	1915
70-IV	*Ch.*	T'ien-t'ai-ssŭ-chiao-i (天台四教儀)	1931
71, 72	*Ch.*	Mo-ho-chih-kuan (摩訶止觀)	1911
73-I	*Ch.*	Kuo-ch'ing-pai-lu (國清百録)	1934
73-II	*Ch.*	Liu-tsu-ta-shih-fa-pao-t'an-ching (六祖大師法寶壇經)	2008
	Eng.	The Platform Sutra of the Sixth Patriarch	

Vol. No.		Title	*T.* No.
73-III	*Ch.*	Huang-po-shan-tuan-chi-ch'an-shih-ch'uan-hsin-fa-yao (黄檗山斷際禪師傳心法要)	2012A
	Eng.	Essentials of the Transmission of Mind (In Zen Texts)	
73-IV	*Ch.*	Yung-chia-chêng-tao-ko (永嘉證道歌)	2014
74-I	*Ch.*	Chên-chou-lin-chi-hui-chao-ch'an-shih-wu-lu (鎭州臨濟慧照禪師語録)	1985
	Eng.	The Recorded Sayings of Linji (In Three Chan Classics)	
74-II	*Ch.*	Wu-mên-kuan (無門關)	2005
	Eng.	Wumen's Gate (In Three Chan Classics)	
74-III	*Ch.*	Hsin-hsin-ming (信心銘)	2010
	Eng.	The Faith-Mind Maxim (In Three Chan Classics)	
74-IV	*Ch.*	Ch'ih-hsiu-pai-chang-ch'ing-kuei (勅修百丈清規)	2025
	Eng.	The Baizhang Zen Monastic Regulations	
75	*Ch.*	Fo-kuo-yüan-wu-ch'an-shih-pi-yen-lu (佛果圜悟禪師碧巖録)	2003
	Eng.	The Blue Cliff Record	
76-I	*Ch.*	I-pu-tsung-lun-lun (異部宗輪論)	2031
	Skt.	Samayabhedoparacanacakra	
	Eng.	The Cycle of the Formation of the Schismatic Doctrines	
76-II	*Ch.*	A-yü-wang-ching (阿育王經)	2043
	Skt.	Aśokarāja-sūtra (?)	
	Eng.	The Biographical Scripture of King Aśoka	
76-III	*Ch.*	Ma-ming-p'u-sa-ch'uan (馬鳴菩薩傳)	2046
	Eng.	The Life of Aśvaghoṣa Bodhisattva (In Lives of Great Monks and Nuns)	
76-IV	*Ch.*	Lung-shu-p'u-sa-ch'uan (龍樹菩薩傳)	2047
	Eng.	The Life of Nāgārjuna Bodhisattva (In Lives of Great Monks and Nuns)	

Vol. No.		Title	T. No.
76-V	*Ch.*	P'o-sou-p'an-tou-fa-shih-ch'uan (婆藪槃豆法師傳)	2049
	Eng.	Biography of Dharma Master Vasubandhu (In Lives of Great Monks and Nuns)	
76-VI	*Ch.*	Pi-ch'iu-ni-ch'uan (比丘尼傳)	2063
	Eng.	Biographies of Buddhist Nuns (In Lives of Great Monks and Nuns)	
76-VII	*Ch.*	Kao-sêng-fa-hsien-ch'uan (高僧法顯傳)	2085
	Eng.	The Journey of the Eminent Monk Faxian (In Lives of Great Monks and Nuns)	
76-VIII	*Ch.*	Yu-fang-chi-ch'ao: T'ang-ta-ho-shang-tung chêng-ch'uan (遊方記抄: 唐大和上東征傳)	2089-(7)
77	*Ch.*	Ta-t'ang-ta-tz'ŭ-ên-ssŭ-san-ts'ang-fa-shih-ch'uan (大唐大慈恩寺三藏法師傳)	2053
	Eng.	A Biography of the Tripiṭaka Master of the Great Ci'en Monastery of the Great Tang Dynasty	
78	*Ch.*	Kao-sêng-ch'uan (高僧傳)	2059
79	*Ch.*	Ta-t'ang-hsi-yü-chi (大唐西域記)	2087
	Eng.	The Great Tang Dynasty Record of the Western Regions	
80	*Ch.*	Hung-ming-chi (弘明集)	2102
81–92	*Ch.*	Fa-yüan-chu-lin (法苑珠林)	2122
93-I	*Ch.*	Nan-hai-chi-kuei-nei-fa-ch'uan (南海寄歸内法傳)	2125
	Eng.	Buddhist Monastic Traditions of Southern Asia	
93-II	*Ch.*	Fan-yü-tsa-ming (梵語雑名)	2135
94-I	*Jp.*	Shō-man-gyō-gi-sho (勝鬘經義疏)	2185
94-II	*Jp.*	Yui-ma-kyō-gi-sho (維摩經義疏)	2186
95	*Jp.*	Hok-ke-gi-sho (法華義疏)	2187
96-I	*Jp.*	Han-nya-shin-gyō-hi-ken (般若心經秘鍵)	2203

Vol. No.		Title	T. No.
96-II	*Jp.*	Dai-jō-hos-sō-ken-jin-shō (大乘法相研神章)	2309
96-III	*Jp.*	Kan-jin-kaku-mu-shō (觀心覺夢鈔)	2312
97-I	*Jp.*	Ris-shū-kō-yō (律宗綱要)	2348
	Eng.	The Essentials of the Vinaya Tradition	
97-II	*Jp.*	Ten-dai-hok-ke-shū-gi-shū (天台法華宗義集)	2366
	Eng.	The Collected Teachings of the Tendai Lotus School	
97-III	*Jp.*	Ken-kai-ron (顯戒論)	2376
97-IV	*Jp.*	San-ge-gaku-shō-shiki (山家學生式)	2377
98-I	*Jp.*	Hi-zō-hō-yaku (秘藏寶鑰)	2426
	Eng.	The Precious Key to the Secret Treasury (In Shingon Texts)	
98-II	*Jp.*	Ben-ken-mitsu-ni-kyō-ron (辨顯密二教論)	2427
	Eng.	On the Differences between the Exoteric and Esoteric Teachings (In Shingon Texts)	
98-III	*Jp.*	Soku-shin-jō-butsu-gi (即身成佛義)	2428
	Eng.	The Meaning of Becoming a Buddha in This Very Body (In Shingon Texts)	
98-IV	*Jp.*	Shō-ji-jis-sō-gi (聲字實相義)	2429
	Eng.	The Meanings of Sound, Sign, and Reality (In Shingon Texts)	
98-V	*Jp.*	Un-ji-gi (吽字義)	2430
	Eng.	The Meanings of the Word Hūṃ (In Shingon Texts)	
98-VI	*Jp.*	Go-rin-ku-ji-myō-hi-mitsu-shaku (五輪九字明秘密釋)	2514
	Eng.	The Illuminating Secret Commentary on the Five Cakras and the Nine Syllables (In Shingon Texts)	
98-VII	*Jp.*	Mitsu-gon-in-hotsu-ro-san-ge-mon (密嚴院發露懺悔文)	2527
	Eng.	The Mitsugonin Confession (In Shingon Texts)	

Vol. No.		Title	T. No.
98-VIII	*Jp.*	Kō-zen-go-koku-ron (興禪護國論)	2543
	Eng.	A Treatise on Letting Zen Flourish to Protect the State (In Zen Texts)	
98-IX	*Jp.*	Fu-kan-za-zen-gi (普勧坐禪儀)	2580
	Eng.	A Universal Recommendation for True Zazen (In Zen Texts)	
99–103	*Jp.*	Shō-bō-gen-zō (正法眼藏)	2582
104-I	*Jp.*	Za-zen-yō-jin-ki (坐禪用心記)	2586
	Eng.	Advice on the Practice of Zazen (In Zen Texts)	
104-II	*Jp.*	Sen-chaku-hon-gan-nen-butsu-shū (選擇本願念佛集)	2608
	Eng.	Senchaku Hongan Nembutsu Shū	
104-III	*Jp.*	Ris-shō-an-koku-ron (立正安國論)	2688
	Eng.	Risshōankokuron or The Treatise on the Establishment of the Orthodox Teaching and the Peace of the Nation (In Two Nichiren Texts)	
104-IV	*Jp.*	Kai-moku-shō (開目抄)	2689
	Eng.	Kaimokushō or Liberation from Blindness	
104-V	*Jp.*	Kan-jin-hon-zon-shō (觀心本尊抄)	2692
	Eng.	Kanjinhonzonsho or The Most Venerable One Revealed by Introspecting Our Minds for the First Time at the Beginning of the Fifth of the Five Five Hundred-year Ages (In Two Nichiren Texts)	
104-VI	*Ch.*	Fu-mu-ên-chung-ching (父母恩重經)	2887
	Eng.	The Sutra on the Profundity of Filial Love (In Apocryphal Scriptures)	
105-I	*Jp.*	Ken-jō-do-shin-jitsu-kyō-gyō-shō-mon-rui (顯淨土眞實教行証文類)	2646
	Eng.	Kyōgyōshinshō: On Teaching, Practice, Faith, and Enlightenment	
105-II	*Jp.*	Tan-ni-shō (歎異抄)	2661
	Eng.	Tannishō: Passages Deploring Deviations of Faith	

Vol. No.		Title	*T*. No.
106-I	*Jp.*	Ren-nyo-shō-nin-o-fumi (蓮如上人御文)	2668
	Eng.	Rennyo Shōnin Ofumi: The Letters of Rennyo	
106-II	*Jp.*	Ō-jō-yō-shū (往生要集)	2682
107-I	*Jp.*	Has-shū-kō-yō (八宗綱要)	蔵外
	Eng.	The Essentials of the Eight Traditions	
107-II	*Jp.*	San-gō-shī-ki (三教指帰)	蔵外
107-III	*Jp.*	Map-pō-tō-myō-ki (末法燈明記)	蔵外
	Eng.	The Candle of the Latter Dharma	
107-IV	*Jp.*	Jū-shichi-jō-ken-pō (十七條憲法)	蔵外